PREFACE TO THE SECOND EDITION

When I was writing the first edition of this book, the climate for purposive contractual interpretation was positively balmy. In a series of cases, the House of Lords, led by Lord Hoffmann, had stressed the contextual nature of the interpretative process, warned that words do not have a natural meaning except in context, and sanctioned the use of background facts to mould the meaning of the words of the contract. We were basking in the warmth of the prevailing sou'westerlies and anticipating a barbeque summer.

Four years on, the weather patterns have changed. There is a distinct chill in the air. An east wind is blowing off the North Sea of the kind you get during the Boxing Day swim in Aldeburgh. The Supreme Court, under the influence of Lord Neuberger, has stressed that the main focus should be on the natural meaning of the words the parties have used, and that twisting the meaning of those words to reflect commercial common sense should be a minority sport.

This change in approach should come as no surprise. Trends in contractual interpretation go in cycles. It is an art—not a science—and it is very much dependent on the approach of the interpreter. If you ask three lawyers the answer to a question of property law, or of tort law, you are likely to get three similar answers if they have the time to do their research. But if you ask the same three lawyers to interpret some words in a contract, you will be lucky to get away with fewer than three answers. That is the nature of contractual interpretation.

And who would be prepared to forecast where we will be in five—or fifteen—years' time? It takes courage to emulate Michael Fish. Who knows what hurricanes are around the corner?

The second edition takes account of the important new cases and articles that have appeared over the last four years. The most important cases have been the decisions of the Supreme Court in *Arnold v Britton* and *Marks and Spencer v BNP Paribas* in 2015. They both go to the root of how contracts are interpreted in practice and they have required substantial changes to Chapters 7 and 8.

The other seminal case is the decision of the Supreme Court in *Cavendish v Makdessi*, also in 2015, which has rewritten the penalty doctrine. Interpreting contracts is concerned with giving effect to what the parties have agreed. Anything which impinges on freedom of contract is relevant to that process, and the penalty doctrine is the main practical limitation on freedom of contract in commercial cases. The way in which the law has changed is discussed in Chapter 1.

There has been little important case law on rectification, but there has been an explosion of articles on the subject—many of them by judges—which must affect the way in which we think about rectification. These developments have been reflected in Chapter 9, but the law is still in a state of flux.

The other area of uncertainty is the extent to which background facts must be taken into account when interpreting contracts. There has been some new case law in this area, and it has been taken into account in Chapter 4. But the law is far from being settled and, if there is one area of the law in which we need guidance from the Supreme Court, it is here. There is no doubt that interpretation is contextual and that the document must be read against its background facts. But we still do not really know what is meant by 'background facts' in this context. It needs to be defined—and limited—in order to balance the need for contextual interpretation against the requirement for certainty and the interests of third parties.

I would like to thank two people in particular. One is David McLauchlan, Professor of Law at Victoria University of Wellington in New Zealand, who has been a constant source of inspiration and encouragement. I can do no better than to echo what Justice Thomas said of David in the Supreme Court of New Zealand in *Gibbons v Wholesale Distributors* [2008] 1 NZLR 277 at [113]: 'His work to bring some logic and cohesion into the task of contractual interpretation has been as outstanding as it has been tireless.' The other is my secretary Jan Ball, who has kept my nose to the grindstone and turned my thoughts into prose.

Richard Calnan
September 2016

PRINCIPLES OF CONTRACTUAL
INTERPRETATION

PRINCIPLES OF CONTRACTUAL INTERPRETATION

SECOND EDITION

RICHARD CALNAN
Partner, Norton Rose Fulbright LLP

OXFORD
UNIVERSITY PRESS

OXFORD
UNIVERSITY PRESS

Great Clarendon Street, Oxford, OX2 6DP,
United Kingdom

Oxford University Press is a department of the University of Oxford.
It furthers the University's objective of excellence in research, scholarship,
and education by publishing worldwide. Oxford is a registered trade mark of
Oxford University Press in the UK and in certain other countries

© Richard Calnan 2017

The moral rights of the author have been asserted

First Edition published in 2013
Second Edition published in 2017

Impression: 1

Published in the United States of America by Oxford University Press
198 Madison Avenue, New York, NY 10016, United States of America

British Library Cataloguing in Publication Data
Data available

Library of Congress Control Number: 2016960619

ISBN 978–0–19–879230–7 (hbk)
ISBN 978–0–19–879231–4 (pbk)

Printed and bound by
CPI Group (UK) Ltd, Croydon, CR0 4YY

For James and Robert

PREFACE TO THE FIRST EDITION

Commercial lawyers spend much of their time reading and writing contracts. Understanding how the courts interpret contracts is therefore a key part of the job of any commercial lawyer. When reading a contract, it is important to understand how a judge will perform the same task. When drafting a contract, the draftsman should always have in mind how what he or she has written will be interpreted by a court.

The purpose of this book is to explain the principles of contractual interpretation. Interpretation is particularly suited to a principles-based approach. Unlike the substantive law—for instance, the law of tort, or the law of property—interpretation is ultimately intuitive. There are no rules. There are basic principles which guide the interpreter, and it is these which this book explores. And, because the principles often pull in different directions, each principle does need to be read in the context of the others. For that reason, I have kept the book as brief as I can in the hope that it will be read as a whole.

The Prologue discusses the nature of the interpretation process and why it is important. The law of contractual interpretation is then discussed by reference to ten Principles. And the book ends with an Epilogue, which discusses how the Principles should affect how documents are drafted.

Amongst all the people who have helped me to write this book, I should mention two in particular. As ever, it simply would not have appeared without my secretary, Sandra Pratt; and I am also grateful to Nicola Liu for her helpful comments on the manuscript.

Richard Calnan
April 2013

PRINCIPLES OF CONTRACTUAL INTERPRETATION

Principle 1: The purpose of contractual interpretation is to establish the intention of the parties to the contract. This is done objectively: what would a reasonable person understand their common intention to be from what they have written, said, and done?

Principle 2: Where the contract is in writing, it is the writing which is the primary source of the parties' objective intention.

Principle 3: Contracts are read as a whole.

Principle 4: Contracts are read in the context of their background facts. These are the facts reasonably available to the parties which are relevant to establishing how a reasonable person would understand what the parties intended by the contract when it was entered into.

Principle 5: Words are nearly always given their ordinary meaning in their context.

Principle 6: If words are ambiguous in their context, they are given the meaning the parties are most likely objectively to have intended.

Principle 7: Very occasionally, it is clear that the parties cannot objectively have intended words they have used to have their ordinary meaning. If so, they are given the meaning which the parties must objectively have intended. The more unreasonable the result, the more unlikely it is that the parties can have intended it.

Principle 8: Words are implied into a contract if the parties must objectively have intended them. This will be the case either if they are so obvious that there was no need to express them, or if they are necessary to make the contract work in a business context.

Principle 9: If a written contract does not record the parties' common intention at the time it was entered into, it will be amended to reflect that intention.

Principle 10: If the parties to a contract have dealt with each other on the basis of a common understanding about the meaning or effect of the contract, that interpretation will bind them if it would be unjust to go back on it.

TABLE OF CONTENTS

III UNDERSTANDING WORDS

IV ADDING WORDS

8. Principle 8: Implied Terms

V CHANGING WORDS

9. Principle 9: Rectification

TABLE OF CASES

TABLE OF LEGISLATION

LIST OF ABBREVIATIONS

This book attempts to provide an explanation of the principles of contractual interpretation within a brief compass, not least because the way contracts are interpreted can only really be understood if the process is seen as a whole.

There are a number of longer books on contractual interpretation, to which anyone who studies this topic is indebted; and I have referred to them in the footnotes in order to assist further research. In addition to the two established textbooks by Sir Kim Lewison and Gerard McMeel, there are now two major Australian textbooks—one by John Carter, the other an Australian edition of Sir Kim Lewison's book by Sir Kim and David Hughes. And there are also important monographs by Catherine Mitchell and Steven Burton.

The following abbreviations of these textbooks are used in this book:

Burton   Steven J. Burton, *Elements of Contract Interpretation* (Oxford University Press, 2009)

Carter   J.W. Carter, *The Construction of Commercial Contracts* (Hart, 2013)

Lewison   Sir Kim Lewison, *The Interpretation of Contracts* (6th edn, Sweet & Maxwell, 2015)[1]

McMeel   Gerard McMeel, *The Construction of Contracts* (2nd edn, Oxford University Press, 2011)

Mitchell Catherine Mitchell, *Interpretation of Contracts* (Routledge Cavendish, 2007).

---

[1] The Australian edition of this book is Lewison and Hughes, *The Interpretation of Contracts in Australia* (Thomson Reuters, 2012).

PROLOGUE

A. The Nature of the Interpretative Process

'How difficult can it be, Boss?' An expression used by one of my colleagues when we **Pr.01** were about to embark upon a transaction seems particularly apposite to the question of contractual interpretation. We may hesitate to offer an opinion on a point of law, but we are all prepared to express a view on what a document means. Surely we can all read English. So what is the problem?

The problem is that interpretation of contracts is an art, not a science. So said **Pr.02** Johan Steyn in the John Lehane Memorial Lecture 2002.[1] It is his fourth general proposition of interpretation. Robert Walker LJ made the same point in *John v PricewaterhouseCoopers*:[2]

> The process of construction often ... involves the assessment of disparate (and therefore incommensurable) factors to reach what is ultimately an intuitive (but not irrational) conclusion.

The reason why it is an art, not a science, is because we are ultimately trying to work **Pr.03** out what the parties wanted to achieve from what they have said and done. The interpreter puts himself or herself in the position of a reasonable person with all the relevant background information available to the parties at the time the contract was entered into with a view to establishing what the contract means. And that is ultimately a matter of judgement on which two perfectly reasonable people can have quite different views. In the words of Lord Steyn: '[interpretation] is an exercise involving the making of choices between feasible interpretations'.[3] And as Lord Hoffmann said in *Chartbrook v Persimmon Homes*:[4]

---

[1] Steyn, 'The Intractable Problem of the Interpretation of Legal Texts' (2003) 25(1) Sydney Law Review 5, reproduced in Worthington (ed.), *Commercial Law and Commercial Practice* (Hart, 2003) 123 at 126. And see also Lord Steyn's comment in *Deutsche Genossenschaftsbank v Burnhope* [1995] 1 WLR 1580 at 1587 that interpretation is often a matter of first impression.

[2] [2002] EWCA Civ 899 at [94]. And see Lewison, *The Interpretation of Contracts* (6th edn, Sweet & Maxwell, 2015) at 2.12.

[3] Steyn, 'The Intractable Problem of the Interpretation of Legal Texts', 123 at 126.

[4] [2009] 1 AC 1101 at [15].

It is, I am afraid, not unusual that an interpretation which does not strike one person as sufficiently irrational to justify a conclusion that there has been a linguistic mistake will seem commercially absurd to another ...

Pr.04 The result is that, however far we try to create a body of law which explains how to interpret contracts, the interpretation of any particular contract will ultimately involve a question of judgement. You can get a long way with principled reasoning, but the final step is a leap of faith. It is important to understand the limits of logic, and where intuition takes over.

Pr.05 We therefore have to recognize that books on interpretation can only carry the putative interpreter so far. Ultimately, we are on our own.

B. The Purpose of This Book

Pr.06 The purpose of this book is, therefore, to try to state the principles which guide anyone who has to interpret contracts.[5]

Pr.07 They are principles, rather than rules, both because they need to be stated at a relatively high level of generality and also because they are by their nature general approaches to the problem, rather than specific answers to it.

Pr.08 There are also related concepts, such as implied terms, rectification, and estoppel by convention, which play a part in the overall question of how contracts are read; and these also need explanation.

Pr.09 And finally, the Epilogue contains a brief discussion of the effect of all this on the way in which contracts should be drafted. This is, after all, the other side of the coin.

C. Why is it Important?

Pr.10 The law of contract is about the voluntary assumption of obligations. Although there are plenty of rules concerned with matters such as the formation and discharge of contracts, in practice much of contract law is about the interpretation of the promises which the parties have made to each other, rather than about particular rules of law.

Pr.11 This point was made by Professor Patrick Atiyah in his *Essays on Contract*[6] when he said:

---

[5] The process is sometimes called construction, and sometimes interpretation. In this context, interpretation and construction are synonyms.

[6] Atiyah, *Essays on Contract* (Oxford University Press, 1986).

[i]t hardly seems open to doubt that construction has become by far the most popular technique for the solution of practically all problems in the law of contract which do not depend on unyielding rules of positive law, such as incapacity, illegality and the requirements of consideration.

The reason for this is straightforward. Because contractual obligations are assumed **Pr.12** voluntarily, rather than imposed by law, the extent of one person's contractual claim against another depends on what the contract says, rather than on what the law says. Issues do arise in relation to whether or not a contract has been created (for instance, whether the promisee has provided consideration) or whether it is affected by illegality or mistake, but the vast majority of questions in relation to contracts are concerned with what they mean.[7]

In practice, courts are also often able to avoid dealing with difficult legal issues by **Pr.13** interpreting the contract in a particular way. Two examples can illustrate how this is done—*The Didymi*[8] and *Associated Japanese Bank v Credit du Nord*.[9]

The Didymi[10] concerned a time charterparty. The contract provided for the char- **Pr.14** terer to pay a particular daily rate of hire, and there was also provision for that rate of hire to be increased if the vessel out-performed certain criteria, and to be reduced if it under-performed. The contract provided for the hire to be 'equitably [increased/decreased] by an amount to be mutually agreed between owners and charterers'. The owners claimed an increase in hire under this provision, and the charterers denied liability on the basis that it was an agreement to agree, and therefore not binding.

If it had been an agreement to agree, it would not have been binding.[11] But the **Pr.15** Court of Appeal managed to avoid the conclusion that this provision had no effect by interpreting it in such a way that it did not amount to an agreement to agree. The court decided that there was a binding obligation to adjust the charter hire 'equitably', and that the required agreement of the parties was simply a mechanism to give effect to that essential term. If the mechanism did not work, because the parties did not agree, then the court could establish what was equitable.

The interesting thing about this case (and, indeed, many others) is that the court **Pr.16** gets round a difficult legal issue (in this case, that an agreement to agree is not binding) by interpreting the contract in such a way that the difficult issue does not arise on the facts (in this case, by deciding that the agreement was not an agreement to

---

[7] See the comments of Sir Christopher Staughton in: 'How Do the Courts Interpret Commercial Contracts?' (1999) 58 CLJ 303 at 303.
[8] *Didymi Corporation v Atlantic Lines* [1988] 2 Lloyd's Rep 108.
[9] [1989] 1 WLR 255.
[10] *Didymi Corporation v Atlantic Lines* [1988] 2 Lloyd's Rep 108.
[11] *Walford v Miles* [1992] 2 AC 128.

agree). A clause which appears to require the parties to reach an agreement is interpreted as being an agreement to do something objective, with the agreement of the parties being merely a mechanism to give effect to it.

Pr.17 Whether that was an appropriate thing to do in the circumstances is beside the point in this context. What is important is that the court was able to avoid having to deal with a difficult legal issue concerning agreements to agree by interpreting the contract in a particular way. This is not uncommon. A few years earlier, the House of Lords had done the same thing in a dispute concerning a lease.[12]

Pr.18 The other example is *Associated Japanese Bank v Credit du Nord*.[13] A bank purchased some machines and then leased them back. The lessee's obligations under the lease were guaranteed by another bank. It subsequently transpired that the machines did not exist and that a fraud had been committed on both banks. The lessor bank sued the guarantor bank under the guarantee.

Pr.19 Steyn J decided that the guarantor was not liable to the lessor. He gave three reasons. The first was that, under the terms of the guarantee, the existence of the machines was an express condition precedent to the guarantor's liability. The second was that, even if there was no express condition precedent, the existence of the machines was an implied condition precedent to the guarantor's obligations. A reasonable man, faced with the suggested term, would, without hesitation, have said that it must be implied: it was so obvious that it went without saying.[14] The third reason was that, if the first two reasons were wrong, the contract was void for mistake in any event.

Pr.20 Steyn J did in fact deal with the difficult question of whether the contract was void for mistake. But he did not strictly need to do so because of the way in which he interpreted the contract—by deciding that the existence of the machines was a condition precedent to the guarantor's liability. Questions of mistake are frequently really about the express or implied allocation of risk between the parties to the contract. What is important is not so much abstract rules of law but the express or implied intention of the parties.

Pr.21 These cases are illustrations of a broad tendency for common law courts to deal with problems that arise in a contractual case by looking more to questions of interpretation than to matters of law. Since contracts involve the voluntary assumption of liability, this is hardly surprising.

---

[12] *Sudbrook Trading Estate v Eggleton* [1983] AC 444.
[13] [1989] 1 WLR 255.
[14] See Principle 8: Implied Terms.

D. The Principles

Most of this book consists of the elucidation of ten Principles which, it is suggested, **Pr.22** underlie all aspects of contractual interpretation. Like any writing, the Principles need to be read as a whole, and that is why this book is relatively brief.

The Principles are divided into five Parts. Part I describes the Guiding Principle— **Pr.23** that interpretation is concerned with the objective common intention of the parties to the contract. Part II is concerned with the materials available to the person interpreting the contract. Parts III to V are concerned with the words used: Part III with what the words mean, Part IV with adding words, and Part V with changing words.

The book is primarily concerned with commercial transactions, rather than con- **Pr.24** sumer ones and, generally, with written contracts, because these are ubiquitous in commercial transactions. But the principles are relevant to the interpretation of all contracts and also to unilateral documents, such as wills, subject to any statutory provisions to the contrary.[15]

E. Principles, Rules, and Precedent

One of the reasons for stating the law concerning contractual interpretation by ref- **Pr.25** erence to principles, rather than rules, is that it is necessary to state the law at a level of generality sufficient to take account of the fact that interpretation is an art, rather than a science. As Sir Anthony Clarke MR has said:[16] 'It is to my mind possible to over-elaborate the relevant principles [of contractual interpretation]. Indeed there was a tendency to do so during the argument in this appeal.'

Case law can be authority for the general approach to interpretation, but it cannot **Pr.26** lay down what particular words mean, except in the most general way. Words take their meaning from the contract in which they appear and the background facts at the time the contract was entered into. What particular words mean in one contract at one time in one context cannot bind a judge deciding what the same words mean in a different contract at a different time and in a different context.[17] Cases should be cited for their guidance on matters of principle, not for what they actually decided.[18]

---

[15] *Marley v Rawlings* [2015] AC 129 at [23].

[16] In *Pratt v Aigaion Insurance Co* [2009] 1 Lloyd's Rep 225 at [9]. The need for simple and clear principles is also true of other areas of the law of contract—for instance, what constitutes a repudiation. See *Eminence Property Developments v Heaney* [2010] 2 All ER (Comm) 223.

[17] See the comments of Lord Hoffmann in *Bank of Credit & Commerce International v Ali* [2002] 1 AC 251 at [51] and those of Moore-Bick LJ in *Transocean Drilling v Providence Resources* [2016] EWCA Civ 372 at [15]; and see Carter at 13.09.

[18] See Lord Morris's comments in *Schuler v Wickman Machine Tool Sales* [1974] AC 235 at 256. This issue is discussed further under Principle 5.

Pr.27 Although the interpretation of an oral contract is a question of fact, the interpretation of a written contract is a question of law.[19] The reason is purely historical—it comes from a time when civil cases were tried by a judge with a (frequently illiterate) jury, and it was therefore necessary for the interpretation of the writing to be left to the judge.

Pr.28 An important practical effect of this rule is that cases concerning interpretation frequently end up in the Court of Appeal and, quite often, in the Supreme Court.[20] Paul Davies has argued[21] that the person best equipped to interpret the words of a contract in light of the documents as a whole and in the context of the surrounding facts is the judge who tries the case. An appeal court may take a different view of interpretation (and very frequently does) but, on a cost-benefit analysis, it is not at all clear that having so many appeals on questions of interpretation is of any real commercial benefit. 'It would be preferable for the meaning of the contract to be resolved quickly and more efficiently by a first instance judge applying clear principles.'[22]

Pr.29 This point was recognized by the Supreme Court of Canada in *Sattva Capital v Creston Moly*.[23] They decided that, in Canada, the interpretation of a written contract should no longer be regarded as a question of law, but as a mixed question of law and fact. The reason why it is a question of law is purely historical; and, because interpretation is now seen as being contextual, deference should be given to the first instance judge on points of contractual interpretation. There is much to be said for this approach, and it remains to be seen whether other common law jurisdictions will follow suit.

F. Recent Developments

Pr.30 Over the past twenty years, there has been an unprecedentedly large number of cases at the highest level concerned with the principles of the interpretation of contracts. Much of the credit for this must go to Lord Hoffmann who, in a series of cases, has elaborated what have been described as modern principles for the interpretation of contracts.[24] Some commentators see these cases as having changed the landscape of

---

[19] *The Nema, Pioneer Shipping v BTP Tioxide* [1982] AC 724 at 736 (Lord Diplock).

[20] For instance, the Supreme Court recently gave judgment in *Tael One Partners v Morgan Stanley* [2015] UKSC 12, in a case where the amounts involved were substantial but there was no question of principle involved.

[21] Davies, 'Rectification Versus Interpretation' (2016) 75 CLJ 62 at 71–2.

[22] (2016) 75 CLJ 62 at 72.

[23] [2014] 2 RCS 633 at [42]–[55].

[24] Lord Hoffmann's contribution to the law in this area is analysed by Paul Davies in 'The Meaning of Commercial Contracts' in Davies and Pila (eds), *The Jurisprudence of Lord Hoffmann* (Hart, 2015) at 215.

contractual interpretation; others see them more as changing the emphasis. Some accept it with enthusiasm; others approach it with caution, sometimes bordering on hostility.

In *Investors Compensation Scheme v West Bromwich Building Society*,[25] Lord Hoffmann **Pr.31** set out five principles of contractual interpretation, which have generally been followed in subsequent cases. He prefaced these principles with a comment that the process of interpreting legal documents has largely been assimilated with 'the common sense principles by which any serious utterance would be interpreted in ordinary life'.[26] Much of the 'old intellectual baggage of "legal" interpretation has been discarded'.[27] The formalistic 'canons of construction' now have a much smaller part to play in what is recognized as being essentially an intuitive exercise.

This is a welcome development. Lawyers should not be allowed to make up their **Pr.32** own rules of interpretation which preclude others. It should be possible for any intelligent business person to have a reasonable stab at understanding what a contract means. Lord Hoffmann put this point very clearly in an article written shortly before the *Investors Compensation Scheme* case.[28] He referred to:

> something which laymen find puzzling, and even slightly repellent, about lawyers, namely their claim to use language in a special way which only other lawyers can understand. Contracts are made by businessmen ... Why, therefore, should any special techniques be required for their interpretation? ... It is these rules which give rise to public unease about what lawyers are up to.

But the analogy between legal documents and other utterances cannot be carried **Pr.33** too far.[29] The process of creating a commercial contract is far removed from everyday utterances—even serious ones. We have different expectations of the former than the latter. Novelists aspire to ambiguity;[30] lawyers eschew it. This creates a tension in the interpretation process, as can be seen when the Principles are discussed.

There is a temptation to see what Lord Hoffmann said in *Investors Compensation* **Pr.34** *Scheme v West Bromwich Building Society*[31] almost as if it were a statutory provision, to be followed to the letter without question. This would be a mistake. As Munby J said, in this context, in *Beazer Homes v Stroude*:[32] 'Utterances, even of the demigods, are not to be approached as if they were speaking the language of statute.'

---

[25] [1998] 1 WLR 896 at 912–13.

[26] [1998] 1 WLR 896 at 912.

[27] [1998] 1 WLR 896 at 912.

[28] Hoffmann, 'The Intolerable Wrestle with Words and Meanings' (1997) 114 South African Law Journal 656.

[29] See the penetrating observations on this point in Carter at [5.05]–[5.17].

[30] Even to the extent of the titles of their novels, as Ian McEwan's *Enduring Love* (Vintage, 1998) attests.

[31] [1998] 1 WLR 896 at 912–13.

[32] [2005] EWCA Civ 265 at [28], quoted in Mitchell, 61.

Lord Hoffmann would be the first to recognize that what he said has to be read in context—against the background of the cases which preceded it, and in the light of the facts of the case in question.[33]

Pr.35 Indeed, there is a tendency in the more recent decisions of the Supreme Court to temper the approach in the *Investors Compensation Scheme* case with an acceptance of the fact that parties enter into legal documents because they want a clear record of the terms of their contractual relationship and that a great deal of effort will have gone into the creation of a text which is intended to do just that.[34]

G. The Two Opposing Views

Pr.36 For practically every statement about how to interpret contracts, you will find a contradictory one. There is authority for just about every approach to interpretation.

Pr.37 The law of the interpretation of contracts can be seen, in large part, as an eternal conflict between two different approaches, which are sometimes described as the literal approach and the purposive approach. The way in which contracts are in fact interpreted cannot be understood without an understanding of this conflict.

Pr.38 A book on substantive legal topics can tell you what the answers are, or at least have a good stab at it. That cannot be done with interpretation. It is ultimately a matter of judgement, which will depend on the approach of the judge concerned.

Pr.39 It should therefore come as no surprise that, as David McLauchlan has pointed out,[35] the outcome of cases concerning interpretation of contracts is difficult to predict. Decisions on interpretation by one tribunal are frequently overruled on appeal; and there are very often dissenting judgments within the tribunals themselves. *The Laura Prima*[36] is a good example. Here there were two possible interpretations of a contract. The umpire said that the contract meant A. The judge at first instance said that it meant B. The Court of Appeal reversed the judge, and said that it meant A. And the House of Lords reversed the Court of Appeal and said that it meant B.

Pr.40 Another example is the *Mannai* case.[37] There, in an interpretation dispute between a landlord and a tenant, the tenant won by three to two in the House of Lords, but only by four to five overall.

---

[33] It should also be read in the light of the article which preceded it, and on which it is based: Hoffmann, 'The Intolerable Wrestle with Words and Meanings'.

[34] See, for instance, *Arnold v Britton* [2015] AC 1619 and *Marks and Spencer v BNP Paribas* [2016] AC 743.

[35] McLauchlan, 'Contract Interpretation: What Is It About?' (2009) 31(1) Sydney Law Review 5.

[36] *Nereide v Bulk Oil* [1982] 1 Lloyd's Rep 1.

[37] *Mannai Investment Co v Eagle Star Life Assurance Co* [1997] AC 749.

It is sometimes said that the history of the law of contractual interpretation is the **Pr.41** history of a movement from formalism to rationalism, from the literal to the purposive.[38] But that is not true. As Joanna McCunn has recently demonstrated[39] purposive interpretation was all the rage in the mid-sixteenth century, and then gave way to a more textual approach in succeeding generations.

The truth is that trends in interpretation go in cycles. There is no doubt that the **Pr.42** *Investors Compensation Scheme* case did herald a more purposive approach than had been common in the preceding decades. But there is now a considerable amount of evidence that the courts are moving back to a more textual approach and are much less comfortable to twist the meaning of the words to suit the desired commercial outcome. One only has to compare the approach of Lord Hoffmann in the *Investors Compensation Scheme* case with that Lord Neuberger in *Arnold v Britton*[40] to see the difference.

It is therefore important to understand the reasons why different judges take dif- **Pr.43** ferent approaches. There are two main areas of dispute in relation to contractual interpretation:

- how much background information should be available in interpreting a written contract; and
- how much leeway a court should have in twisting the words of the contract to reach what it regards as a 'commercial' result.[41]

At one end of the spectrum are those who would severely limit the background **Pr.44** information available and who would frown upon too much word-twisting. If the parties have written their contract, they expect it to be interpreted, not rewritten. At the other end of the spectrum are those who believe that words can only really be understood in the context of the entirety of the background facts, and that the court should do its best to resolve a case in a fair and commercial way.

It is rather like the conflict described by Sellar and Yeatman in *1066 and All That*[42] **Pr.45** between the Cavaliers (Wrong but Wromantic) and the Roundheads (Right but Repulsive). In this context, the Cavaliers are those who would twist the words to

---

[38] Wigmore, *A Treatise on the Anglo-American System of Evidence*, vol 9 (3rd edn, Little, Brown and Company, 1940).

[39] McCunn, 'Revolutions in Contractual Interpretation: A Historical Perspective', available on the Social Science Research Network (https://www.ssrn.com).

[40] [2015] AC 1619.

[41] The Scottish Law Commission's Discussion Paper on Interpretation of Contracts (Discussion Paper No. 147, February 2011) contains a useful review of the issues. Earlier discussions of the issues by the Scottish Law Commission are contained in Interpretation in Private Law (Discussion Paper No. 101, August 1996) and Report on Interpretation in Private Law (Scot Law Com No. 160, October 1997).

[42] Methuen, 1930.

reach the 'right result', the Roundheads those who would apply the words used without mercy.

Pr.46 Very few lawyers fall into either of these extreme camps. Most fall somewhere between. But where the line is drawn on this spectrum will vary depending on the background and nature of the person concerned.

Pr.47 There will always be a tension between accepting what the words say and trying to bend them. It is only by recognizing that fact that it is possible to understand how interpretation disputes are resolved in practice.

Pr.48 It is possible to give guidance as to the principles to be adopted but, ultimately, interpretation is a matter of intuition and judgement and defies logical analysis. It is as important to understand what principles of interpretation cannot do, as to understand what they can.

Part I

THE GUIDING PRINCIPLE

Principle 1: The purpose of contractual interpretation is to establish the intention of the parties to the contract. This is done objectively: what would a reasonable person understand their common intention to be from what they have written, said, and done?

1

PRINCIPLE 1: OBJECTIVE COMMON INTENTION

Principle 1: The purpose of contractual interpretation is to establish the intention of the parties to the contract. This is done objectively: what would a reasonable person understand their common intention to be from what they have written, said, and done?

A. Intention

The ultimate purpose of contractual interpretation is to find out what the parties intended. **1.01**

This follows from the basic concept that the law of contract is about the voluntary assumption of liability. In the words of Professor Brian Coote:[1] 'The one characteristic essential to a contract is that it should be a means by which legal contractual liability can effectively be assumed by the party or parties to it.' The law of contract gives effect to promises made for consideration or by deed, and the extent of those promises ultimately depends on what the parties agreed. In practice, most contractual disputes are concerned with establishing the precise scope of the promise. **1.02**

Sir Christopher Staughton, writing extra-judicially,[2] has said, in relation to contractual interpretation, that: 'Rule One is that the task of the judge when interpreting a written contract is to find the intention of the parties. In so far as one can be sure of anything these days, that proposition is unchallenged.' And in *The Starsin*,[3] Lord Bingham said: 'When construing a commercial document in the ordinary way the **1.03**

---

[1] Coote, *Contract as Assumption* (Hart, 2010).
[2] Staughton, 'How Do the Courts Interpret Commercial Contracts?' (1999) 58 CLJ 303 at 304.
[3] *Homburg Houtimport v Agrosin* [2004] 1 AC 715 at [9].

task of the court is to ascertain and give effect to the intentions of the contracting parties.'[4]

B. Objectivity

1.04 In common law jurisdictions (unlike many civil law ones), the intention of the parties is established objectively. We are not concerned with the parties' actual, subjective intentions, but with the outward manifestation of those intentions. The question is how a reasonable person would interpret their intentions from what they have said, written, and done.[5]

1.05 This is a very important qualification. Although the law is striving to find the intention of the parties, it will not look into their minds. It will only look at what has passed between them. And in doing so, it is not concerned with their actual intention, but with how a reasonable person would understand their common intention from its objective manifestation.

1.06 The principle was expressed by Lord Wilberforce in *Reardon Smith Line v Yngvar Hansen-Tangen*:[6]

> When one speaks of the intention of the parties to the contract, one is speaking objectively—the parties cannot themselves give direct evidence of what their intention was—and what must be ascertained is what is to be taken as the intention which reasonable people would have had if placed in the situation of the parties.

1.07 Lord Steyn expressed it this way in *Deutsche Genossenschaftsbank v Burnhope*:[7]

> It is true the objective of the construction of a contract is to give effect to the intention of the parties. But our law of construction is based on an objective theory. The methodology is not to probe the real intentions of the parties, but to ascertain the contextual meaning of the relevant contractual language. Intention is determined by reference to expressed rather than actual intention.

1.08 It is this emphasis on objectivity which enabled Lord Hoffmann, in *Investors Compensation Scheme v West Bromwich Building Society*,[8] to express the principle rather differently:

> Interpretation is the ascertainment of the meaning which the document would convey to a reasonable person having all the background knowledge which would reasonably have been available to the parties in the situation in which they were at the time of the contract.

---

[4] See Carter, *The Construction of Commercial Contracts* (Hart, 2013), Chapter 2.
[5] See Lewison, *The Interpretation of Contracts* (6th edn, Sweet & Maxwell, 2015) at 2.02, 2.03, and 2.05; McMeel, *The Construction of Contracts* (2nd edn, Oxford University Press, 2011), Chapter 3.
[6] [1976] 1 WLR 989 at 996.
[7] [1995] 1 WLR 1580 at 1587.
[8] [1998] 1 WLR 896 at 912.

Here, there is no reference at all to the intention of the parties—just to the mean- **1.09**
ing of the document. What is important is not what the parties thought, but what
they wrote.

C. Is Intention Still Relevant?

This might suggest that intention is really a chimera. Although we purport to strive **1.10**
for it, we do not really do so.[9] What we really do is look at the document.[10]

Sir George Leggatt has asked:[11] 'If actual intentions are irrelevant, what purpose, if **1.11**
any, is served by using the language of "intention" at all?' It is a good question. But
to say that subjective intention is irrelevant is not to deny the importance of the
objective manifestation of intention. It is important to know what we are ultimately
trying to achieve, even if we do not carry it out completely. Even though we adopt
an objective test, what we are ultimately trying to elicit is what the parties meant.
The common law has this at least in common with the civil law tradition—which
tends to adopt a more subjective approach.

The common law does not carry this to its logical conclusion and try to establish the **1.12**
subjective intention of the parties. But anyone interpreting a contract is still trying
to work out what the parties really meant from what they have done.

Of course, the establishment of intention is sometimes fictional. In some cases, the **1.13**
parties may simply not have considered the matter in hand. David McLauchlan
has said that: '*the great majority* of interpretation disputes that come before the
courts have the common feature that the parties did not, at the time of formation,
contemplate the situation that has arisen'.[12] But, even here, it is surely true to say
that what we are trying to do is to establish what the parties would have intended
if they had set their minds to it. We do this by extrapolation from what they have
agreed (and have not agreed) and in the light of the background facts at the time
the contract was entered into. It is a difficult matter of judgement, but what the
parties would have intended must be what is guiding the person interpreting the
contract.

It is therefore suggested that it is still important to recognize that what underlies **1.14**
the principles of interpretation is a desire to establish the common intention of the

---

9   Stevens, 'Contract Interpretation: what it says on the tin' (available on the Inner Temple website).
10   See the comments of Lord Hoffmann in *Attorney General of Belize v Belize Telecom* [2009] 1
WLR 1988 at [16].
11   Leggatt, 'Making Sense of Contracts: The Rational Choice Theory' (2015) 131 LQR 454 at
456.
12   McLauchlan, 'Contract Interpretation: What Is It About?' (2009) 31(1) Sydney Law Review 5,
part 2. Emphasis in the original.

parties, albeit objectively. Lord Bingham made the point clearly in *Bank of Credit and Commerce International v Ali*:[13]

> In construing [a] ... contractual provision, the object of the court is to give effect to what the contracting parties intended ... To ascertain the parties' intentions the court does not of course inquire into the parties' subjective states of mind but makes an objective judgment ...

D. Why an Objective Approach?

1.15 The objective theory of the common law tradition is frequently distinguished from the more subjective approach of the civil law tradition.[14] One example of the civil law approach that is easily accessible by common lawyers is Article 4.1 of the *Unidroit Principles of International Commercial Contracts* (2010 edition),[15] which says:

(1) A contract shall be interpreted according to the common intention of the parties.
(2) If such an intention cannot be established, the contract shall be interpreted according to the meaning that reasonable persons of the same kind as the parties would give to it in the same circumstances.

1.16 Here, the objective approach is a fallback mechanism if it is not possible to establish the subjective common intention of the parties. Why does the common law not adopt the same approach? If the law of contract is concerned with the voluntary assumption of liability, why not carry it to its logical conclusion and say that what matters is what the parties actually intended?

1.17 One reason is that the objective approach to interpretation sits well with the objective theory of the common law of contract. Whether there is a contract and, if so, what are its terms, is broadly determined objectively.[16]

1.18 The requirement for objectivity in relation both to the formation of contracts and to their interpretation has been stressed recently by Heydon and Crennan JJ in the High Court of Australia in *Byrnes v Kendle*.[17] After discussing the principle that the

---

[13] [2002] 1 AC 251 at [8].

[14] In practice, the divide may be narrower than is sometimes assumed. See Vogenauer, 'Interpretation of Contracts: Concluding Comparative Observations', Chapter 7, in Burrows and Peel (eds), *Contract Terms* (Oxford University Press, 2007).

[15] See Lord Hoffmann's comments on this in *Chartbrook v Persimmon Homes* [2009] 1 AC 1101 at [39].

[16] *Chitty on Contracts* (32nd edn, Thomson Reuters, 2015), 2-002. The classic case is *Smith v Hughes* (1871) LR 6 QB 597. For a more recent illustration, see *Shogun Finance v Hudson* [2004] 1 AC 919.

[17] (2011) 243 CLR 253 at [98]–[101] following similar statements by the High Court of Australia in *Pacific Carriers v BNP Paribas* (2004) 218 CLR 451 at [22] and *Toll (FGCT) v Alphapharm* (2004) 219 CLR 165 at [35]–[41].

purpose of contractual interpretation is to discover the objective intention of the parties, rather than their subjective intentions, their Honours continued:[18]

> These conclusions flow from the objective theory of contractual obligation. Contractual obligation does not depend on actual mental agreement. Mr Justice Holmes said:[19]
>
> > [P]arties may be bound by a contract to things which neither of them intended, and when one does not know the other's assent ...
> >
> > [T]he making of a contract depends not on the agreement of two minds in one intention, but on the agreement of two sets of external signs,—not on the parties' having *meant* the same thing but on their having *said* the same thing.

This approach to contract formation has been criticized by David McLauchlan. **1.19** There is a continuing debate about whether the creation of a contract is a purely objective exercise—based on how a reasonable person would view the actions of the parties—or whether the court is more concerned with how a reasonable person in the position of the *promisee* would view what the *promisor* has said and done.[20] But, whatever the outcome of this debate about how a contract is created,[21] it is clear that, when it comes to interpreting the contract, this is done objectively—by reference to a reasonable person having the background knowledge which would reasonably have been available to the parties.[22]

Why does the law treat the interpretation of contracts in this objective fashion? **1.20** There are four main reasons.

In the first place, establishing the subjective common intention of parties to a com- **1.21** plex contract can be difficult, if not impossible, to achieve. Even if we can establish the subjective intentions of each of the parties, it is difficult to know which parts of their (frequently opposing) individual intentions were held in common. Indeed, if each party separately intends to contract on a particular basis, but the parties do not communicate with each other, they have not reached an agreement and they do not have a common intention.[23] Establishing subjective common intention can only be achieved by objective methods.

---

[18] (2011) 243 CLR 253 at [100].

[19] Oliver Wendell Holmes, Jr, 'The Path of the Law' (1897) 10 Harvard Law Review 457, 463–4. Emphasis in the original.

[20] See, for instance, *Chitty on Contracts* (31st edn, Thomson Reuters, 2012) at 5.067 and 5.117; McLauchlan, 'The "Drastic" Remedy of Rectification for Unilateral Mistake' (2008) 124 LQR 608 at 611; and see McMeel, Chapter 3 and Carter at [2.18]–[2.22].

[21] The problem with the latter approach in practice is knowing which of the parties is the promisor and which the promisee.

[22] *Investors Compensation Scheme v West Bromwich Building Society* [1998] 1 WLR 896 at 912 (Lord Hoffmann's first principle). The distinction between the approach to formation and interpretation is clearly drawn in McMeel, Chapter 3.

[23] Leggatt, 'Making Sense of Contracts: The Rational Choice Theory' (2015) 131 LQR 454 at 460–2.

1.22   Secondly, many of the issues from which disputes arise will simply not have been considered by the parties when they were drafting the contract.[24] And, in order to get the deal done, the parties may have agreed on the words to be used without necessarily agreeing what they mean. One practical way round these problems is to ask what a reasonable person would have understood the parties to have intended from what they have said and done.

1.23   Lord Wilberforce put the point this way in *Prenn v Simmonds*:[25]

> The words used may, and often do, represent a formula which means different things to each side, yet may be accepted because that is the only way to get 'agreement' and in the hope that disputes will not arise. The only course then can be to try to ascertain the 'natural' meaning. Far more, and indeed totally, dangerous is to admit evidence of one party's objective—even if this is known to the other party. For however strongly pursued this may be, the other party may only be willing to give it partial recognition, and in a world of give and take, men often have to be satisfied with less than they want.

> So, again, it will be a matter of speculation how far the common intention was that the particular objective should be realised.

1.24   Thirdly, and particularly importantly, the objective process is considered to promote certainty[26] and to save time and costs. This is an important theme of contractual interpretation, and appears throughout this book. If the meaning of a contract can only be established by examining the subjective intentions of the parties, the outcome is difficult to predict; and to establish it will involve considerable delay and expense. But if its meaning can be established from its external manifestation— normally the written agreement—it is easier to predict the outcome, and the time and cost of establishing it should be reduced.

1.25   A fourth reason is that the objective approach protects third parties, such as assignees. They are not parties to the discussions between the parties and could be prejudiced by interpreting a provision differently from how it appears in the document.[27] Again, this is a theme which recurs throughout this book.

1.26   Not everyone is happy with this approach. There are those who consider that it carries the search for objectivity too far. Lord Nicholls is one of those. In 'My Kingdom for a Horse: The Meaning of Words', an article in the Law Quarterly Review in 2005,[28] he asked:

---

[24] See *Dumbrell v Regional Group* (2007) 279 DLR (4th) 201 at [50].

[25] [1971] 1 WLR 1381 at 1385.

[26] See Lord Goff's comments in *President of India v Jebsens* [1991] 1 Lloyd's Rep 1 at 9.

[27] See the comments of Briggs J at first instance in *Chartbrook v Persimmon Homes* [2007] 2 P&CR 9 at [34]–[38]. The decision was overruled, but not on this point.

[28] (2005) 121 LQR 577 at 581.

Why should it be thought [that] evidence of the parties' actual intentions ... can never assist in determining the objective purpose of a contractual provision or the objective meaning of the words the parties have used?

The point was taken further by David McLauchlan in 'Contract Interpretation: What **1.27** Is It About?', an article in the Sydney Law Review in 2009:[29]

[it] would [be] perverse to exclude evidence that potentially could have allowed [one party to the contract] to get away with repudiating the parties' actual common understanding at the time of the contract ...

Even more tellingly, Lord Nicholls has asked: 'Why should the judge have to guess **1.28** when he can know?'[30]

These are powerful arguments.[31] They mirror what Lord Bingham said in a dif- **1.29** ferent context:[32] 'You need not gaze into the crystal ball when you can read the book.' But the problem with this argument is that it proves too much. Taken to its logical conclusion it would destroy the objective principle altogether. In relation to any contract, it may be the case that evidence of the parties' subjective intentions would enable the court to get a better understanding of what the parties actually intended. But that would simply replace objectivity with subjectivity. The dangers of this approach are those which have already been discussed: uncertainty, cost, and delay; and potential prejudice to third parties. As is so often the case in English law, pragmatism wins out over theory. Absolute justice gives way to a practical method of enforcing people's bargains more quickly and with a greater degree of certainty than would otherwise be possible.

E. Freedom of Contract and its Limits

One reason why the interpretation of contracts is of such importance in practice **1.30** is that English law generally recognizes the principle of freedom of contract, and therefore that what the parties have agreed is of paramount importance.

This was particularly apparent in the nineteenth century, when Sir George Jessel **1.31** MR said, in *Printing and Numerical Registering Company v Sampson*:[33]

It must not be forgotten that you are not to extend arbitrarily those rules which say that a given contract is void as being against public policy, because if there is one

---

[29] (2009) 31(1) Sydney Law Review 5; and see McLauchlan, 'The Contract That Neither Party Intends' (2012) 29 JCL 26.
[30] (2005) 121 LQR 577 at 581.
[31] For a discussion on the approach to this issue in the United States, see Burton, *Elements of Contract Interpretation* (Oxford, 2009), Chapter 1.
[32] *The Golden Victory, Golden Strait Corp v Nippon Yusen Kubishika Kaisha* [2007] 2 AC 353 at [12].
[33] (1874–75) LR 19 Eq 462 at 465.

thing which more than another public policy requires it is that men of full age and competent understanding shall have the utmost liberty of contracting, and that their contracts when entered into freely and voluntarily shall be held sacred and shall be enforced by Courts of justice. Therefore, you have this paramount public policy to consider—that you are not lightly to interfere with this freedom of contract.

1.32 Inroads were made into this principle in the twentieth century, to such an extent that Professor Atiyah was able to record what he described as 'The Rise and Fall of Freedom of Contract'.[34]

1.33 But, by the end of the twentieth century, the pendulum had swung back, with the courts being less inclined to override those contractual provisions which they did not like. So, in *Photo Production v Securicor*,[35] Lord Diplock was able to say:

A basic principle of the common law of contract, to which there are no exceptions that are relevant in the instant case, is that parties to a contract are free to determine for themselves what primary obligations they will accept.

1.34 This return to the principle of freedom of contract may have had much to do with the fact that Parliament had by now intervened to protect consumers, thereby leaving the courts free to give effect to freedom of contract where that legislation did not apply. In commercial transactions, the courts are now much more willing to accept that the parties should be the final determinant of what is good for them.

1.35 There are now few general exceptions to this basic principle of freedom of contract in commercial transactions. Perhaps the most important one in practice is the doctrine of penalties.

1.36 In England, the penalty doctrine is restricted to cases where there is a breach of contract.[36] It cannot be used to strike down the primary obligations of the parties under the contract—only the secondary obligations which arise on breach of those primary obligations. The logic of this distinction has sometimes been challenged. Why override the secondary obligations which arise on breach of primary obligations, but not the primary obligations themselves? Or, to put it the other way round, if the parties can agree their primary obligations, what is the logic of preventing them from agreeing the effect of breach of those obligations?

1.37 It is this which led the High Court of Australia in *Andrews v Australia and New Zealand Banking Group*[37] in 2012 to decide that the penalty doctrine could apply even where there was no breach of contract. The penalty doctrine in Australia can therefore strike down primary obligations as well as secondary ones.

---

[34] Atiyah, *The Rise and Fall of Freedom of Contract* (Oxford, 1979).

[35] [1980] AC 827, 848.

[36] *Export Credits Guarantee Department v Universal Oil Products* [1983] 1 WLR 399 at 403 (Lord Roskill).

[37] (2012) 247 CLR 205.

The United Kingdom Supreme Court considered this issue in *Cavendish Square* **1.38**
Holding v Makdessi; ParkingEye v Beavis[38] in 2015 and decided not to extend the
penalty doctrine to primary obligations.[39] In England, the penalty doctrine deals,
and has always dealt, with secondary obligations payable on breach, not with primary obligations; and it would not be appropriate to extend it.

It is therefore important to decide whether a particular provision of a contract is a **1.39**
primary or a secondary obligation. As a general principle, the expression 'primary'
obligation is used to describe the terms of the contract; and a 'secondary' obligation
describes the obligation which a party incurs under the general law for breaching a
primary obligation—normally a liability to pay damages.[40] But, in the context of
penalties, the distinction is drawn between two different types of contractual term.
In this context, a secondary obligation is a contractual provision which provides
what will happen if a party breaches another provision of the contract; and a primary obligation is any other provision of the contract.

Lords Neuberger and Sumption illustrated the difference in the *Makdessi* case:[41] **1.40**

> [Where] a contract contains an obligation on one party to perform an act, and also
> provides that, if he does not perform it, he will pay the other party a specified sum
> of money, the obligation to pay the specified sum is a secondary obligation which
> is capable of being a penalty; but if the contract does not impose (expressly or im-
> pliedly) an obligation to perform the act, but simply provides that, if one party does
> not perform, he will pay the other party a specified sum, the obligation to pay the
> specified sum is a conditional primary obligation and cannot be a penalty.

Whether a provision of a contract is a primary or secondary obligation is a question **1.41**
of categorization.[42] It involves a two-stage process. First, the rights and duties of the
parties under the provision are established. That is a matter of interpretation of the
contract. Once the court has established what the provision means, the second stage
is to determine whether it falls into the category of a primary or secondary obligation according to the legal rules concerned.

Whether a provision is a primary or secondary obligation is a question of substance, **1.42**
not of form. It does not matter how the parties themselves categorize the provision.[43] Once the court has established what the parties intend their rights and duties
to be, the categorization of that provision depends on the application of the legal
rule. However it is described, it will be a secondary obligation if it comes into effect
on breach of the contract.

---

[38] [2015] 3 WLR 1373. It is referred to in this book as the *Makdessi* case.
[39] [2015] 3 WLR 1373 at [40]–[43]
[40] See Lord Diplock's speech in *Photo Production v Securicor* [1980] AC 827 at 848–9.
[41] [2015] 3 WLR 1373 at [14].
[42] Categorization is discussed under Principle 5 (at paras 5.83–5.90).
[43] [2015] 3 WLR 1373 at [15].

1.43 Even if the provision concerned is a secondary obligation, the chance of it being struck down as a penalty has been substantially diminished as a result of the decision in the *Makdessi* case. The Supreme Court heard appeals from two separate Court of Appeal decisions. One case was a consumer transaction, the other a commercial one.

1.44 In the consumer case, a motorist had parked his car in a car park run by a company. The contract provided that the maximum permitted stay was two hours, that parking was free during that period, but that £85 would be charged to those who stayed longer. It was recognized that the amount of the payment was not a genuine pre-estimate of the loss which would have been recoverable by the company for breach of contract. On the basis of the existing law, that payment would therefore have been a penalty, and would not have been recoverable. All the company could have recovered would have been its actual loss.[44] But the Supreme Court decided that the payment was not a penalty because the company had a legitimate interest in charging the amount.[45] There is no longer a simple dichotomy between a provision which is a genuine pre-estimate of loss, and one which is penal.[46] The real question is whether it is penal, not whether it is a genuine pre-estimate of loss.[47] The innocent party may have a legitimate interest in having the contract performed which extends beyond the prospect of pecuniary compensation flowing directly from the breach.[48]

1.45 Lords Neuberger and Sumption expressed the test in this way:[49]

> The true test is whether the impugned provision is a secondary obligation which imposes a detriment on the contract-breaker out of all proportion to any legitimate interest of the innocent party in the enforcement of the primary obligation. The innocent party can have no proper interest in simply punishing the defaulter. His interest is in performance or in some appropriate alternative to performance.

1.46 Lord Hodge described the test as being 'whether the sum or remedy stipulated as a consequence of a breach of contract is exorbitant or unconscionable when regard is had to the innocent party's interest in the performance of the contract'.[50] Lords Mance[51] and Toulson[52] agreed with this formulation, Lord Mance adding 'extravagant' as an alternative. These pejorative adjectives (reminiscent, perhaps, of the time when equity varied by reference to the length of the Chancellor's foot) are not easy to apply in practice, but they do emphasize how difficult it is now to set aside a provision as a penalty.

---

[44] *Dunlop Pneumatic Tyre Co v New Garage and Motor Co* [1915] AC 79.
[45] [2015] 3 WLR 1373 at [98]. Nor did it breach the relevant consumer protection legislation.
[46] [2015] 3 WLR 1373 at [152].
[47] [2015] 3 WLR 1373 at [31].
[48] [2015] 3 WLR 1373 at [28].
[49] [2015] 3 WLR 1373 at [32].
[50] [2015] 3 WLR 1373 at [255].
[51] [2015] 3 WLR 1373 at [152].
[52] [2015] 3 WLR 1373 at [293].

Makdessi has very considerably raised the bar for a penalty claim. As Christopher **1.47**
Clarke LJ said in the Court of Appeal: 'The law of penalties is a blatant interference
with freedom of contract.'[53] The decision of the Supreme Court can be seen as a
clear and deliberate response to that concern.[54]

The extent to which this has fundamentally changed the law can be seen from the **1.48**
decision in the commercial case. In this case, a seller sold a controlling interest in
his business to a buyer and entered into a restrictive covenant. The consideration
for the sale included a large amount for goodwill, and much of it was payable on a
deferred basis after completion. The contract contained a clause by which the seller
would not be entitled to receive that further consideration if he was in breach of
the restrictive covenant. The seller breached the restrictive covenant but claimed
payment of the deferred consideration on the basis that the clause which prevented
it being paid was a penalty. The amount of the deferred consideration was an ex-
tremely large sum—a multiple many times of the amount which would have been
recoverable by the buyer for breach of the restrictive covenant. The Supreme Court
nevertheless decided that the clause was not a penalty because the detriment to the
seller was not out of all proportion to the buyer's legitimate interest in enforcing
the restrictive covenant.[55] The seller's undertaking not to compete with the business
after completion was an important term of the contract and was a key part of the
value of the business being acquired.

One factor which the court considered to be of great importance was that this was **1.49**
a commercial transaction in which both parties were represented by lawyers. In a
commercial transaction in which both parties are legally represented, it is up to the
parties to determine what the contract should say, and the court will not intervene
except in the most egregious of cases.

The test of whether a contractual provision is a penalty was reconsidered by the **1.50**
High Court of Australia in *Paciocco v Australia and New Zealand Banking Group*[56]
in 2016. It has been seen that the penalty doctrine extends more widely in Australia
than in England. But, in this case, High Court of Australia had to consider the
test of whether a provision is a penalty. And here, the approach is very similar to
that in the *Makdessi* case. French CJ and Keifel J[57] adopted the same approach as
Lords Neuberger and Sumption in the *Makdessi* case—is the provision out of all

---

[53] [2013] 2 CLC 968 at [44].
[54] [2015] 3 WLR 1373 at [33].
[55] There are indications in the judgments of two different reasons for this conclusion. One was
that the clause was in substance a primary obligation—a price adjustment clause ([2015] 3 WLR
1373 at [74]). The other was that it was a secondary obligation, but not penal ([2015] 3 WLR 1373
at [270]).
[56] [2016] HCA 28.
[57] [2016] HCA 28 at [2] and [69].

proportion to the innocent party's legitimate interest in enforcing the contract? Keane J[58] adopted the same approach as Lord Hodge in the *Makdessi* case—is the provision exorbitant or unconscionable when regard is had to the innocent party's interest in the performance of the contract? Gageler J[59] considered that the question was whether the stipulation in issue was properly characterized as having no purpose other than to punish—also a theme that comes out very clearly in *Makdessi*. Although the types of provision to which the penalty doctrine can apply is broader in Australia than it is in England, the test of whether or not a provision is a penalty now looks to be the same in both jurisdictions.

1.51 In summary, the penalty doctrine has been curtailed very substantially in England. It only applies if the provision concerned is a secondary obligation and, even then, it will only be struck down if it is out of all proportion to the legitimate interest of the innocent party in the enforcement of the contract. Freedom of contract may have taken a fall in the twentieth century but, in the twenty-first century, it is alive and well and living in Westminster.

F. The Guiding Principle

1.52 The principle that contractual interpretation is about establishing the objective common intention of the parties underlies all aspects of contractual interpretation. The other principles in this book are subsidiary to this basic principle, and need to be understood in the light of it. They are essentially ways of achieving this underlying purpose.

---

[58] [2016] HCA 28 at [270].
[59] [2016] HCA 28 at [166].

Part II

TEXT AND CONTEXT

Principle 2: Where the contract is in writing, it is the writing which is the primary source of the parties' objective intention.

Principle 3: Contracts are read as a whole.

Principle 4: Contracts are read in the context of their background facts. These are the facts reasonably available to the parties which are relevant to establishing how a reasonable person would understand what the parties intended by the contract when it was entered into.

The purpose of Part II is to describe the materials available to a person interpreting a contract. **Pt 2.01**

2

PRINCIPLE 2: THE TEXT

Principle 2: Where the contract is in writing, it is the writing which is the primary source of the parties' objective intention.

A. The Primacy of the Text

When interpreting a written contract, the starting point has to be the text itself. **2.01** Having negotiated and written the contract, the parties are entitled to expect that it will be given effect. Most commercial contracts are in writing for this reason.[1]

This point is made very clearly by two eminent commercial judges, each writing **2.02** extra-judicially. In the words of Lord Steyn:[2] 'The mandated point of departure must be the text itself. The primacy of the text is the first rule of interpretation for the judge considering a point of interpretation.' Sir Christopher Staughton made the same point even more bluntly:[3] 'The first place where you look for the intention of the parties is in the language which they themselves used. And it is very often the last place too.'

This principle has also been expounded in the cases many times. In *River Wear* **2.03** *Commissioners v Adamson*,[4] Lord Blackburn said: 'The object is to see what is the intention expressed by the words used.' Lord Steyn again, in *National Commercial Bank Jamaica v Guyana Refrigerators*,[5] said that: 'the paramount principle to which all other principles of construction are subordinate requires loyalty to the contractual text viewed in its relevant context'. And, in the High Court of Australia, Gibbs J in *Australian Broadcasting Commission v Australasian Performing Rights Association*[6]

---

[1] See Lewison, *The Interpretation of Contracts* (6th edn, Sweet & Maxwell, 2015) at 3.01.
[2] Steyn, 'The Intractable Problem of the Interpretation of Legal Texts' (2003) 25(1) Sydney Law Review 5, reproduced in Worthington (ed.), *Commercial Law and Commercial Practice* (Hart, 2003) 123 at 125.
[3] Staughton, 'How Do the Courts Interpret Commercial Contracts?' (1999) 58 CLJ 303 at 305.
[4] (1877) 2 App Cas 743 at 763.
[5] [1998] 4 LRC 36 at 40.
[6] (1973) 129 CLR 99 at 109.

said: 'It is trite law that the primary duty of a court in construing a written contract is to endeavour to discover the intention of the parties from the words of the instrument in which the contract is embodied.'

2.04 The reason is obvious. Parties put their contracts in writing in order to clarify what they have agreed. Having done so, they expect what they have written to be given effect.[7]

2.05 This point was made by Lord Blackburn in *Inglis v Buttery*, quoting with approval words of Lord Gifford:[8]

> Lord Gifford expresses in extremely clear words exactly what I think myself when he said:
>
>> Now, I think it is quite fixed—and no more wholesome or salutory rule relative to written contracts can be devised—that where parties agree to embody, and do actually embody, their contract in a formal written deed, then in determining what the contract really was and really meant, a court must look to the formal deed and to that deed alone. This is only carrying out the will of the parties. The only meaning of adjusting a formal contract is, that the formal contract shall supersede all loose and preliminary negotiations—that there shall be no room for misunderstandings which may often arise, and which do constantly arise, in the course of long, and it may be desultory conversations, or in the course of correspondence or negotiations during which the parties are often widely at issue as to what they will insist on and what they will concede. The very purpose of a formal contract is to put an end to the disputes which would inevitably arise if the matter were left upon verbal negotiations or upon mixed communings partly consisting of letters and partly of conversations. The written contract is that which is to be appealed to by both parties, however different it may be from their previous demands or stipulations, whether contained in letters or in verbal conversation. There can be no doubt that this is the general rule ...
>
> Now, my Lords, I agree in every word of that.

2.06 This is not the law now—if it ever was. Contracts have to be read in the light of their background facts, as Principle 4 demonstrates. But it does illustrate very clearly the reasons why commercial lawyers are nervous of bringing too much background into the interpretation process.

2.07 Principle 2 is one aspect of the objective theory of interpretation described in Principle 1. The common intention of the parties is established from its outward manifestations—and what could be a more obvious outward manifestation of their intention than what they have jointly written? The benefits of this approach are the

---

[7] See the comments of the High Court of Australia in *Equuscorp v Glengallan Investments* (2004) 218 CLR 471 at [32]–[36].
[8] (1877) 3 App Cas 552 at 577.

same as those discussed under Principle 1—promoting certainty, saving time and expense, and protecting third parties.

B. What is the Contract?

The first question to ask is: 'What is the contract?' Until you know what the contract is, you cannot start to interpret it. **2.08**

Just because the parties have entered into a document, it does not necessarily follow that it is the whole contract. There may be other documents (such as letters or emails or standard terms), or even oral statements, which might form part of the contract.[9] **2.09**

Whether they do form part of the contract depends, as would be expected, on the objective intention of the parties.[10] Would a reasonable person consider that the parties would have intended them to form part of the contractual arrangements between them? If so, they are part of the contract. But even if they are not, they may still amount to representations inducing the contract, and would still have some legal (though extra-contractual) effect in equity or in tort.[11] **2.10**

In *Inntrepreneur Pub Co v East Crown*,[12] Lightman J described the circumstances in which a document or statement which is not part of the written agreement is contractually binding. He set out five principles, the first two of which are particularly important:[13] **2.11**

> The relevant legal principles regarding the recognition of pre-contractual promises or assurances as contractual warranties may be stated as follows:
> (1) a pre-contractual statement will only be treated as having contractual effect if the evidence shows that parties intended this to be the case. Intention is a question of fact to be decided by looking at the totality of the evidence;
> (2) the test is the ordinary objective test for the formation of a contract: what is relevant is not the subjective thought of one party but what a reasonable outside observer would infer from all the circumstances ...

Lightman J went on to say:[14] **2.12**

> The task in all cases is to consider the representation or assurance in the context of the totality of the facts, and the question to be addressed is whether reliance on the inducement afforded by the representation or promise should be understood as intended to continue and extend to the contract subsequently concluded.

---

[9] For a discussion of this issue in an American context, see Burton, Chapter 3.
[10] *Heilbut, Symons & Co v Buckleton* [1913] AC 30.
[11] See, generally, *Chitty on Contracts* (32nd edn, Thomson Reuters, 2015), Chapter 6.
[12] [2000] 2 Lloyd's Rep 611.
[13] [2000] 2 Lloyd's Rep 611 at [10]. The last three principles are simply examples of, and elaborations on, the first two principles.
[14] [2000] 2 Lloyd's Rep 611 at [11].

2.13 This is a basic principle of the law of contract and is not directly concerned with their interpretation. But there are two matters which do need to be mentioned, if only briefly, because they do impinge upon issues of interpretation. These are the parol evidence rule and entire agreement clauses.

C. The Parol Evidence Rule

2.14 The parol evidence rule is one of those ancient principles of the law of contract which is much talked about in theory but hardly ever applied in practice. The idea behind the parol evidence rule is simple. If the parties have gone to the trouble of writing down their agreement, then the courts should give effect to that agreement without being distracted by other things which the parties may have said or done. The contract stands and falls with the document.[15]

2.15 As a basic principle, this has much to commend it. The issue with the parol evidence rule is that it should not be carried too far. It is all very well to exclude extrinsic evidence if that is what the parties intended, but it is clearly inappropriate if the parties did intend their contract to consist of something other than just the one document.

2.16 The parol evidence rule was described by P.O. Lawrence J in *Jacobs v Batavia*[16] as requiring that: 'parol evidence cannot be admitted to add to, vary or contradict a … written instrument'. In the 1970s and 1980s, the Law Commission analysed the parol evidence rule, and the report they produced in 1986[17] contains a very clear discussion of the rule and its effect.

2.17 The Law Commission regarded the 'parol evidence rule' as being:[18]

> a proposition of law which is no more than a circular statement: *when it is proved or admitted that the parties to the contract intended that all the express terms of their agreement should be as recorded in a particular document or documents, evidence will be inadmissible (because irrelevant) if it is tendered only for the purpose of adding to, varying, subtracting from or contradicting the express terms of that contract.*

2.18 In other words, it is all a question of the intention of the parties. The issue is whether the parties intended that the whole of their agreement should be as recorded in a particular document. If they did, other evidence is excluded. If they did not, it is not. And, as usual, that intention is to be judged objectively.[19]

---

[15] See Lewison at 3.11.
[16] [1924] 1 Ch 287 at 296.
[17] Law of Contract: The Parol Evidence Rule (Law Com No. 154).
[18] Law Com No. 154 at 2.7. Emphasis in the original.
[19] Law Com No. 154 at 2.14.

In practice, therefore, the parol evidence rule is almost never an issue. It only applies **2.19** if the contract is intended to be wholly in writing; and, when deciding whether or not the parties intended the contract to be wholly in writing, the court must look at all the evidence—including evidence from outside the writing itself.[20]

The Law Commission concluded that:[21]　　　　　　　　　　　　　　　　　　　　　**2.20**

> in so far as any such rule of law can be said to have an independent existence, [it] does not have the effect of excluding evidence which ought to be admitted if justice is to be done between the parties … Evidence will only be excluded when its reception would be inconsistent with the intention of the parties. While a wider parol evidence rule seems to have existed at one time, no such wider rule could, in our view, properly be said to exist in English law today.

Even today, the parol evidence rule is very occasionally called in aid[22] but, in prac-　**2.21** tice, it is a dead letter.

The absence of the parol evidence rule has, however, left a gap. As Tindal CJ said **2.22** about the rule in *Shore v Attorney-General*:[23] 'If it were otherwise [i.e. if the rule did not exist], no lawyer would be safe in advising upon the construction of a written instrument.' Lord Hobhouse made the same point more recently, in *Shogun Finance v Hudson*,[24] when he said that: 'the bargain is the document; the certainty of the contract depends on it'. The High Court of Australia echoed these sentiments in *Equuscorp v Glengallan Investments*:[25]

> In a time of growing international trade with parties in legal systems having the same or even stronger deference to the obligations of written agreements … this is not the time to ignore the rules of the common law upholding obligations undertaken in written agreements. It is a time to maintain those rules.

The problem is this: the parties enter into long discussions about a transaction **2.23** and eventually negotiate and sign a written agreement. For good commercial reasons, they may want that document to represent their deal.[26] But there is nothing to prevent one of the parties from dredging up an email or conversation made in the course of the negotiations and claiming that it is part of the contract. The court then has to decide if that was the parties' intention—which is likely to be a time-consuming and expensive exercise with an uncertain outcome.

---

[20] See the discussion by McLauchlan in 'The Entire Agreement Clause: Conclusive or a Question of Weight?' (2012) 128 LQR 521, part 3.

[21] Law Com No. 154 at 2.45.

[22] Most notably by Lord Hobhouse in *Shogun Finance v Hudson* [2004] 1 AC 919 at [49].

[23] (1842) 9 Cl&F 355 at 366.

[24] [2004] 1 AC 919 at [49].

[25] (2004) 218 CLR 471 at [35].

[26] See the comments made in Law Com No. 154, 1.6.

2.24   Experience suggests that this is something which commercial parties want to avoid. And that is why so many commercial contracts contain what has become known as an 'entire agreement clause'.

D. Entire Agreement Clauses

2.25   As its name suggests, an entire agreement clause is intended to put beyond doubt the question as to what constitutes the contract between the parties.[27] At its simplest (and most are more complex than this), it will state that the document is the entire agreement between the parties, and therefore that any prior written or oral arrangements between the parties do not form part of the contract. In addition, it will also normally seek to ensure that any such statements will not give rise to any liability as non-contractual representations, whether in equity (to rescind the contract) or in tort.[28]

2.26   If a clause states that the document is to be the entire agreement between the parties, then that is what it is. The agreement is what the parties intend it to be, and the entire agreement clause makes it very clear what their intention is. In *Inntrepreneur Pub Co v East Crown*,[29] Lightman J said: 'Such a clause constitutes a binding agreement between the parties that the full contractual terms are to be found in the document containing the clause and not elsewhere ...' And, as Longmore LJ said in *North Eastern Properties v Coleman*:[30] 'If the parties agree that the written contract is to be the entire contract, it is no business of the courts to tell them that they do not mean what they have said.'[31]

2.27   Entire agreement clauses have therefore replaced the parol evidence rule as a mechanism for identifying the terms of the contract.

2.28   This approach has not gone without criticism. The Law Commission, in its Report on the Parol Evidence Rule, regarded an entire agreement clause as strongly persuasive, but not as conclusive.[32] And in the Law Quarterly Review,[33] David McLauchlan has

---

[27] See McMeel, *The Construction of Contracts* (2nd edn, Oxford University Press, 2011), Chapter 26; Lewison at 3.16.

[28] In principle, such a provision is effective (see *Peekay Intermark v Australia and New Zealand Banking Group* [2006] 1 CLC 582 at [56]–[57] and *Springwell Navigation v J P Morgan Chase* [2010] 2 CLC 705 at [143]–[171]), subject to any relevant statutory constraint, such as under the Unfair Contract Terms Act 1977 or section 3 of the Misrepresentation Act 1967. See Cartwright, 'Excluding Liability for Misrepresentation', Chapter 11 in Burrows and Peel (eds), *Contract Terms* (Oxford University Press, 2007).

[29] [2000] 2 Lloyd's Rep, 611 at 614.

[30] [2010] 2 EGLR 161 at [82].

[31] But it would probably not prevent the contract being rectified if it could be proved that the parties had omitted from the document a clause which they had intended to include: Law Com No. 154 at 2.15; McLauchlan (2012) 128 LQR 521, part 6. Rectification is discussed under Principle 9.

[32] Law Com No. 154 at 2.15.

[33] McLauchlan (2012) 128 LQR 521.

argued that an entire agreement clause, while usually being entitled to considerable weight, should not be regarded as being conclusive that the written agreement is the entire agreement between the parties. The clause may be part of the boiler-plate, and may simply be an untrue statement of what the parties have actually agreed. 'A writing has no magical power to cause statements of fact to be true when they are actually untrue.'[34] All evidence is relevant to the question of what the parties intended their contract to be. It is open to a party who signs a document containing an entire agreement clause to say that he simply did not agree to it.

There are two problems with this approach—the first conceptual, the second prac- **2.29** tical. The first is that the basic principle of contractual interpretation is that it is concerned with establishing the objective intention of the parties to the contract. And what could more clearly express their objective intention than what they have written?

The second problem is that it would undermine the commercial imperative of cer- **2.30** tainty. If the parties want to put beyond doubt what is the scope of their agreement, then why should they not be allowed to do so? The point is put very clearly by Lightman J in *Inntrepeneur Pub Co v East Crown*:[35]

> The purpose of an entire agreement clause is to preclude a party to a written agreement from thrashing through the undergrowth and finding in the course of negotiations some (chance) remark or statement (often long forgotten or difficult to recall or explain) on which to found a claim such as the present to the existence of a collateral warranty. The entire agreement clause obviates the occasion for any such search and the peril to the contracting parties posed by the need which may arise in its absence to conduct such a search.

The courts have recognized the efficacy of entire agreement clauses, and it is sug- **2.31** gested that this is correct in principle, and is justified in practice.

E. Parol Evidence, Entire Agreement Clauses, and Interpretation

In its primary sense, the parol evidence rule was about what a contract is, not what **2.32** it means. It was in the past extended to cover the interpretation of contracts[36] but, at least since the 1970s, it is clear that evidence of the background facts at the time the contract was entered into is available to interpret the contract. The extent of that evidence is discussed under Principle 4.

---

[34] McLauchlan (2012) 128 LQR 521 at 531.
[35] [2000] 2 Lloyd's Rep 611 at 614.
[36] See Law Com No. 154 at 1.2 and the speech of Lord Blackburn in *Inglis v Buttery* (1877) 3 App Cas 552 at 557, quoted earlier in para 2.05.

2.33 A traditional entire agreement clause is also concerned with what the contract is, rather than what it means, and it cannot therefore affect the question of whether evidence is admissible to aid the process of interpreting their contract.[37] But there is no reason in principle why the parties should not be able to restrict the background information available in the interpretation process. That is a subject which is discussed in the Epilogue.

F. Categorization and Shams

2.34 Although the text of the agreed document is the starting point for any discussion of the parties' obligations under their contract, there are circumstances in which what they have said in the document, in the light of the background facts at the time they entered into it, is not conclusive.

2.35 In the first place, there is a distinction between what the parties have actually agreed and how that agreement is categorized as a matter of law. This issue is discussed under Principle 5 at paras 5.83–5.90.

2.36 Second, in very rare cases, a document may be regarded as a sham. This will be the case if it does not express the real intention of the parties. If it is a sham, it will have no effect on third parties.[38]

2.37 In *Snook v London and West Riding Investments*,[39] Diplock LJ explained the sham doctrine in the following words:

> I apprehend that, if it has any meaning in law, it means acts done or documents executed by the parties to the 'sham' which are intended by them to give to third parties or to the court the appearance of creating between the parties legal rights and obligations different from the actual legal rights and obligations (if any) which the parties intend to create … for acts or documents to be a 'sham', with whatever legal consequences follow from this, all the parties thereto must have a common intention that the acts or documents are not to create the legal rights and obligations which they give the appearance of creating.

2.38 It is rare to come across a sham document in practice. A document will only be a sham if the parties are fraudulent—putting forward a document to a third party which does not represent their real agreement.

---

[37] See Robert Walker LJ in *John v PricewaterhouseCoopers* [2002] EWCA Civ 899 at [67].
[38] See McMeel at 27.36–27.45.
[39] [1967] 2 QB 786, 802.

3

PRINCIPLE 3: THE WHOLE TEXT

Principle 3: Contracts are read as a whole.

A. Two Concepts

The principle that contracts are read as a whole involves two concepts. The first, and **3.01** most important, is that words and phrases in a contract cannot be seen in isolation. They get their colour from the rest of the contract; and, if the contract is part of a wider transaction, from the other transaction documents.[1]

The second concept, which is less important in practice, is that the person interpret- **3.02** ing the contract should strive to give effect to each part of the contract.[2]

B. The Contract as a Whole

It may not be universally acknowledged, but it is a truth nevertheless, that you **3.03** cannot understand what the parties have undertaken to do in one part of a contract without looking at the context of the whole contract. Contractual obligations are assumed voluntarily, and the extent of each party's promises must be gauged from the contract as a whole.[3]

---

[1] See Lewison, *The Interpretation of Contracts* (6th edn, Sweet & Maxwell, 2015) at 7.02 and McMeel, *The Construction of Contracts* (2nd edn, Oxford University Press, 2011), Chapter 4. This is also the case in civil law jurisdictions. See article 4.4 of the *Unidroit Principles of International Commercial Contracts* (2010 edn): 'Terms and expressions shall be interpreted in the light of the whole contract or statement in which they appear.'

[2] See Lewison at 7.03 and McMeel, Chapter 4. This is also the case in civil law jurisdictions. See article 4.5 of the *Unidroit Principles of International Commercial Contracts* (2010 edn): 'Contract terms shall be interpreted so as to give effect to all the terms rather than to deprive some of them of effect.'

[3] See the illuminating discussion by Professor Brian Coote in *Contract as Assumption* (Hart, 2010), Chapter 6, in the context of exception clauses.

3.04 Lord Watson made this point clearly in relation to deeds in *Chamber Colliery Co v Twyerould*,[4] when he referred to:

> the well-known rule that a deed ought to be read as a whole, in order to ascertain the true meaning of its several clauses; and that the words of each clause should be so interpreted as to bring them into harmony with the other provisions of the deed, if that interpretation does no violence to the meaning of which they are naturally susceptible.

3.05 The musical analogy was adopted by Gibbs J in the High Court of Australia. In *Australian Broadcasting Commission v Australasian Performing Rights Association*,[5] he said:

> Of course the whole of the instrument has to be considered, since the meaning of any one part of it may be revealed by other parts, and the words of every clause must if possible be construed so as to render them all harmonious one with another.

3.06 In *Charter Reinsurance Co v Fagan*,[6] Lord Mustill used a visual metaphor, rather than an aural one: 'The words must be set in the landscape of the instrument as a whole.'

3.07 As well as reading the document as a whole, it may be necessary to read particular parts of the document as a whole. So, for instance, in *Chartbrook v Persimmon Homes*,[7] Lord Hoffmann[8] and Lord Walker[9] found it helpful to read particular words in a schedule in the context of the general structure of that schedule.

C. Limiting Words

3.08 Perhaps the most common effect of reading the contract as a whole is for words which are expressed to apply generally to be limited by reference to the rest of the contract. Four examples can show how this works in practice:

(1) *The Laura Prima*,[10] in the House of Lords;
(2) *Lion Nathan v Coopers Brewery*,[11] in the Federal Court of Australia;
(3) *Re Sigma Finance*,[12] in the Supreme Court;
(4) *Thorney Park Golf v Myers Catering*,[13] in the Court of Appeal.

---

[4] [1915] 1 Ch 268 (note) at 272 (1893).
[5] (1973) 129 CLR 99 at 109.
[6] [1997] AC 313 at 384.
[7] [2009] 1 AC 1101.
[8] [2009] 1 AC 1101 at [20].
[9] 2009] 1 AC 1101 at [79].
[10] *Nereide v Bulk Oil International* [1981] 3 All ER 737.
[11] (2006) 236 ALR 561.
[12] [2010] 1 All ER 571.
[13] [2015] EWCA Civ 19.

In *The Laura Prima*,[14] there was a dispute between shipowners and charterers in **3.09** relation to the demurrage payable on a voyage charterparty. When the vessel arrived in port to load, there was a significant delay because no berth was available. The question was whether the owner was entitled to demurrage for that period. That in turn depended on whether the period counted as 'used laytime'. If it did, the owner could recover. If not, the owner could not.

Clause 6 of the charterparty provided that, on arrival at the port, the master would **3.10** give the charterer notice that the vessel was ready to load, and laytime would commence shortly afterwards. It then went on to say: 'However, where delay is caused to vessel getting into berth after giving notice of readiness for any reason over which Charterer has no control, such delay shall not count as used laytime.' The master had given notice of readiness. The charterer therefore argued that, because it had no control over the availability of the berths, the period of delay would not count as used laytime under clause 6, and therefore demurrage would not be payable.

The owner argued that it was not possible to read clause 6 in isolation from clause 9, **3.11** which provided for the vessel to load at any safe place 'which shall be designated and procured by the Charterer'. The owner argued that, because the charterer had not designated and procured a safe berth, it was therefore in breach of clause 9, and the final sentence of clause 6 did not apply.

The House of Lords found in favour of the owner. The word 'berth' in the last sen- **3.12** tence of clause 6 did not mean 'any berth'. What it meant was a berth which had been designated and procured by the charterer under clause 9. The charterparty had to be read as a whole, and the apparent width of the word 'berth' in clause 6 was limited by reference to the obligation on the charterer in clause 9.

The second example is *Lion Nathan v Coopers Brewery*.[15] Article 38 of a company's **3.13** articles of association provided that: 'No member may make any transfer of shares and the Directors must not register any transfers of shares without complying with [the pre-emption rights contained in the articles].' The company entered into a share buy-back, and the question arose whether the words 'any transfer' in the article encompassed a transfer to anyone, including the company itself, or whether it only meant a transfer to a third party.

The Federal Court of Australia decided that the articles did not apply to a share **3.14** buy-back by the company itself. They were only intended to limit new membership in the company. When it was read in the context of the articles of association as a whole, it was apparent that article 38 was part of the pre-emptive rights regime, and was only meant to restrict dispositions from one member to another. This decision

---

[14] *Nereide v Bulk Oil International* [1981] 3 All ER 737.
[15] (2006) 236 ALR 561.

was reached by reading article 38 in the light of the company's articles of association as a whole.[16]

3.15 The third example is *Re Sigma Finance*.[17] Sigma was a structured investment vehicle which got into financial difficulties, as a result of which receivers were appointed over all of its assets under a security trust deed. Unusually, the company's obligations were not accelerated on the appointment of the receivers. Instead, the trustee had a sixty-day period to realize the company's assets and to divide them into pools for the benefit of its secured creditors. This was because the secured creditors were divided into various classes—including a short-term class and a number of long-term classes.

3.16 Under clause 7.6 of the security trust deed, the trustee had to use its reasonable endeavours to establish pools of assets to represent the various classes of creditor, and it had the power to deal with the charged assets in order to do so. The last sentence of clause 7.6 read:

> During the Realisation Period the Security Trustee shall so far as possible discharge on the due dates therefor any Short Term Liabilities falling due for payment during such period, using cash or other realisable or maturing Assets of [the company].

3.17 It proved impossible to save the company, and the short-term creditors argued that they were entitled to be paid before the long-term creditors in accordance with the final sentence of clause 7.6. The long-term creditors argued that the trust deed envisaged that all the secured assets would be segregated into the various pools and then applied *pari passu* within those pools, and that a literal reading of the last sentence of clause 7.6 would cut across that intention.

3.18 Sales J and a majority of the Court of Appeal gave that provision its literal meaning and found in favour of the short-term creditors. By a majority of four to one, the Supreme Court found in favour of the long-term creditors.

3.19 The principal judgment in the Supreme Court was given by Lord Mance. He considered that the decision in the lower courts attached too much weight to the natural meaning of the words in the final sentence of clause 7.6 and too little weight to the context in which that sentence appeared and to the scheme of the security trust deed as a whole.[18] A reading of the overall scheme of the security trust deed showed that clause 7.6 was drafted on the assumption that the company had enough assets to cover at least its secured liabilities. In other words, the apparent breadth of its effect had to be limited by the other provisions of the security trust deed. It only applied if the company were solvent.

---

[16] See, in particular, the decision of Kenny J at (2006) 236 ALR 561 at [103].
[17] [2010] 1 All ER 571.
[18] [2010] 1 All ER 571 at [12].

The final example is *Thorney Park Golf v Myers Catering*.[19] Myers agreed to provide **3.20** catering services at Thorney Park's golf club. It was a short contract, drafted by a non-lawyer. Clause 4 said that: 'In order for this contract to be reasonable for both parties to develop and invest in a viable business development plan an initial term of three years ... must be agreed.' Clause 6 provided that the club could terminate the agreement immediately on certain breaches by Myers. 'Otherwise either party may terminate this agreement without given reason in writing giving four months notice or any such period that is mutual to both parties.'

The judge at first instance considered that the termination provision in clause 6 was **3.21** clear, and that it applied at any time—even within the initial three-year period. The Court of Appeal disagreed. It seemed to them to be of significance that, at the forefront of the contract, in clause 4, the parties had identified the initial term of three years as being required in order for the contract to be reasonable (i.e. it would have been unreasonable without it) and that this was to enable both parties to develop and invest in a viable business development plan.[20] Although the court recognized the force of the contrary argument—based on the syntax of clause 6—in the end it seemed to them that the argument failed to give suitable effect to clause 4.[21]

In the result, a clause which was, in isolation, perfectly clear was held not to mean **3.22** what it said because it was in conflict with the rest of the agreement. By reading the contract as a whole, the court both created, and resolved, an ambiguity.

These four cases are illustrations of the principle that the apparently broad effect of **3.23** one particular clause in a contract can be impliedly limited by reference to the rest of the contract. A reading of the rest of the contract can show that the parties did not intend those words to be given their broad, literal meaning because that would conflict with the scheme of the contract as a whole.[22]

D. Extending Words

In an exceptional case, words in a contract can be given a broader meaning than **3.24** their natural meaning. This is what happened in *Charter Reinsurance Co v Fagan*.[23] This case concerned the interpretation of a reinsurance contract by which the reinsurer was to be liable for the losses of the insurer during the period of the reinsurance in excess of an ultimate net loss of a specified amount. 'Net loss' was defined as

---

[19] [2015] EWCA Civ 19.
[20] [2015] EWCA Civ 19 at [25].
[21] [2015] EWCA Civ 19 at [27].
[22] Other examples of the application of this principle are the decision of the Privy Council in *Vaswani v Italian Motors* [1996] 1 WLR 270 and, more recently, that of the Court of Appeal in *Kudos Catering v Manchester Central Convention Complex* [2013] EWCA Civ 38.
[23] [1997] AC 313.

meaning: 'the sum actually paid by the reinsured [i.e. the insurer] in settlement of losses or liability after making deductions for [recoveries and other reinsurances]'. The insurer was insolvent, and was not paying claims. The reinsurer denied liability under the reinsurance policy on the basis that it was only liable in respect of amounts 'actually paid' by the insurer. If the insurer was not paying claims, then no amount had been 'actually paid', and therefore the reinsurer was not liable.

3.25 The House of Lords decided that the reinsurers were liable nevertheless. The principal judgment was given by Lord Mustill. His initial reaction was that no sums had been 'actually paid'. But he recognized that the focus of this discussion was too narrow. The words had to be set in the landscape of the instrument as a whole. Having carried out a detailed study of the structure and terms of the reinsurance policy, he decided that the reference to the sum actually paid was not intended to impose an additional condition precedent to recovery under the policy, but was being used for the purpose of measurement—to establish the amount of the recovery by emphasizing that it is the ultimate outcome of the net loss calculation which determines the amount of liability. This was far from the ordinary meaning of the words, but, in the light of the policy as a whole, this was what they meant.

3.26 This case can be regarded as the high-water mark of the principle that contracts should be read as a whole.

E. The Transaction as a Whole

3.27 In modern transactions, it is common for one contract to form part of an overall suite of documents entered into by the parties in relation to one transaction. In such a case, it is necessary to read all the transaction documents together.[24]

3.28 An illustration of this principle is *Holding & Barnes v Hill House Hammond*.[25] This case involved the interpretation of a covenant by the landlord in a lease of a building by which it undertook 'to keep the foundations and the roof in good and tenantable repair and condition and to keep the structure and exterior of the Building (other than those parts comprised in the property) in good and tenantable repair and condition'. The tenant argued that the words in brackets must have been included in error, and should be deleted. They were relevant for a lease of part of a building, but not for a lease of the whole building. The Court of Appeal agreed. It was an obvious mistake and it was clear what was intended.[26] Their conclusion was reinforced by the fact that the parties had entered into six other leases as part of the same transaction,

---

[24] Jessel MR in *Smith v Chadwick* (1881–82) 20 ChD 27 at 62 and 63. *3869130 Canada Inc v ICB Distribution* 2008 CONCA 396 at [33] (Ontario Court of Appeal). See Lewison at 3.03.

[25] [2002] 2 P&CR 11.

[26] See Principle 7.

and that those words were included in those leases of parts of a building, but not included in the other lease of a whole building. Reading the transaction documents as a whole, it was clear that a mistake had been made.

It is common, in practice, for parties to enter into one principal document and then **3.29** into various subsidiary documents. Here, if there is a discrepancy, it is likely to be the principal contract which will govern the situation.

This is what happened in *Orion Finance v Crown Financial Management*.[27] The **3.30** owner of equipment let it on hire purchase to a hirer, who then, as part of the same transaction, leased it to a lessee. The hire purchase agreement between the owner and the hirer required the hirer to assign to the owner the rentals payable to it under the lease in order to secure the hirer's obligations to pay rent under the hire purchase agreement. But, when the assignment was actually entered into, it was expressed to be an absolute assignment, and there was no reference to the fact that it was intended to be by way of security. The Court of Appeal had no difficulty in deciding that this was a mistake. The principal document showed that it was intended to be by way of security.

In some cases, it is not clear which of a number of documents entered into by **3.31** the parties is the principal document. In such a case, the court has to decide which seems the most likely interpretation in the light of the documents as a whole.[28]

F. Dealing with Conflicting Provisions

In the cases discussed so far, apparently clear words have been given a different **3.32** meaning than would otherwise have been expected, because of the necessity to read them in the light of other clauses in the contract or in the other transaction documents. In other cases, the problem is more straightforward: two clauses are in conflict; how is that conflict to be resolved?

Some provisions are more important than others

Some parts of a contract can be seen to be more important than others, and will **3.33** therefore carry greater weight when weighing up conflicting provisions in the document.[29] So, for instance, recitals are likely to carry less weight than operative provisions.[30]

---

[27] [1996] BCC 621.
[28] See *State Street Bank & Trust Co v Sompo Japan Insurance* [2010] EWHC 1461 (Ch).
[29] See Lewison at 7.04 and 7.05.
[30] *Ex parte Dawes* (1886) 17 QBD 275 at 286.

3.34 The same principle can be seen to operate where the parties have used a standard form of contract and have adapted it. As Lord Bingham said in *The Starsin*:[31]

> [I]t is common sense that greater weight should attach to terms which the particular contracting parties have chosen to include in the contract than to pre-printed terms probably devised to cover very many situations to which the particular contracting parties have never addressed their minds.

3.35 In *The Starsin* itself, the House of Lords gave greater weight to the front page of a bill of lading, onto which details of the transaction had been entered, than to the standard printed conditions on the back. This was because that is what a reasonable person involved in the trade would do.[32]

3.36 In the days of word processors, printed forms are used less frequently, but it is very common for contracts to be based on standard terms. It is probably the case that, in the event of a conflict between the standard terms and terms specifically agreed for the transaction, the latter will prevail.

Specific and general clauses

3.37 In practice, it is quite common for contracts to contain clauses the content of which overlaps. For instance, a contract may contain certain specific indemnity provisions, and then a general indemnity clause. If the general indemnity is expressed to be subject to the specific indemnities, this creates no problem. But it is quite common for such clauses not to cross-refer to each other and therefore for them to appear to be stand-alone obligations. Nevertheless, reading the document as a whole, a court is likely to interpret the general indemnity in such a way that it does not impinge upon matters which are the subject of the specific indemnities.[33]

3.38 For instance, if a specific indemnity contains particular requirements for recovery, and there is no such limitation in the general indemnity, it is likely that a court would refuse to allow recovery under the general indemnity if the claim is of a type covered by the specific indemnity but the conditions which it lays down for recovery have not been complied with. Although, on its face, the general indemnity might cover the eventuality, a court would most likely decide that it was intended to be limited by reference to the specific indemnity.

3.39 The position was summed up by Hoffmann LJ when he said, in *William Sindall v Cambridgeshire City Council*:[34]

---

[31] *Homburg Houtimport v Agrosin* [2004] 1 AC 715 at [11].
[32] [2004] 1 AC 715 at [45] (Lord Bingham).
[33] See Lewison at 7.05.
[34] [1994] 1 WLR 1016 at 1024.

It is of course a principle of construction that words capable of bearing a very wide meaning may have to be given a narrow construction to reconcile them with other parts of the document.

The order of the clauses

In the past, the courts developed a large number of rules, which they applied in the **3.40** interpretation of contracts. They were known as 'canons of construction'. One such rule was described by Lord Wrenbury in 1922 in *Forbes v Git*,[35] when he said:

> The principle of law to be applied may be stated in few words. If in a deed an earlier clause is followed by a later clause which destroys altogether the obligation created by the earlier clause, the later clause is to be rejected as repugnant and the earlier clause prevails.

It is suggested that this formulaic process would no longer be applied by a court **3.41** today. As Lord Hoffmann said in *Investors Compensation Scheme v West Bromwich Building Society*:[36] 'Almost all the old intellectual baggage of "legal" interpretation has been discarded.'

This more modern approach is borne out by the decision of Chadwick J in *Re* **3.42** *Atlantic Computers*.[37] This case involved the interpretation of a comfort letter given by a parent company to a bank concerning a facility made available by the bank to a subsidiary of the parent. In paragraph (c) of the comfort letter, the parent company undertook to the bank that, if the subsidiary were unable to meet its commitment, the parent company 'will take steps to make arrangements for [the subsidiary's] present, future or contingent obligations to the bank both for capital and interest to be met'. In a later paragraph, the letter went on to say that this provision was 'an expression of present intention by way of comfort only'.

The question was whether the parent company was liable to the bank under the **3.43** clause. The bank argued that paragraph (c) created a legally binding obligation and that the later paragraph purported to destroy that obligation which had already arisen. It argued that, as a matter of construction, the final paragraph could not be allowed to have that effect and that it must be struck down on the grounds of repugnancy.

Chadwick J disagreed, and held that the parent company was not under a legal **3.44** obligation to the bank. He said:[38]

> The letter must be read as a whole. Reading the document as a whole, it cannot make any difference that the qualification ... appears where it does. The qualification

---

[35] [1922] 1 AC 256, at 259. See Lewison at 9.08.
[36] [1998] 1 WLR 896 at 962.
[37] [1995] BCC 696.
[38] [1995] BCC 696, 698.

might equally well have appeared immediately before para (c) … Those who enter into letters of this kind cannot be taken to have had a different intention because they choose to introduce the qualification immediately after rather than immediately before the relevant paragraph.

3.45 It is suggested that the order of the clauses in the document is of little significance. The document must be read as a whole.

G. Giving Effect to Each Part of the Contract

3.46 Reading a document as a whole is also said to require the reader to give effect to each part of the contract. Sir John Romilly MR stated the principle in these terms in *Re Strand Music Hall Company*:[39]

> The proper mode of construing any written instrument is to give effect to every part of it, if this be possible, and not to strike out or nullify one clause in a deed, unless it be impossible to reconcile it with another and more express clause in the same deed.

3.47 The problem with this approach is that it is a counsel of perfection. It assumes that the draftsman has carefully weighed every provision and not covered the same point more than once. Anyone who has had to review commercial contracts will know that this is more an aspiration than a reality.

3.48 This point was well made by Lord Hoffmann in *Beaufort Developments v Gilbert-Ash*:[40]

> [T]he argument from redundancy is seldom an entirely secure one. The fact is that even in legal documents (or, some might say, especially in legal documents) people often use superfluous words. Sometimes the draftsmanship is clumsy; more often the cause is a lawyer's desire to be certain that every conceivable point has been covered. One has only to read the covenants in a traditional lease to realise that draftsmen lack inhibition about using too many words.

3.49 If there is a presumption against superfluous language, it is a very weak one. It is perhaps best seen as something which the reader will have in mind as a possibility when reviewing the contract. This was the approach adopted by the Supreme Court in *Rainy Sky v Kookmin Bank*.[41] In that case, the court adopted an interpretation of words in the contract which effectively rendered another clause of the contract redundant. The case is discussed in more detail later, under Principle 6, paras 6.29–6.32.

---

[39] (1865) 35 Beav 153 at 159.
[40] [1999] 1 AC 266 at 274. And see the observations of Neuberger MR in *Macquarie Internationale Investments v Glencore UK* [2010] 1 CLC 1035 at [83].
[41] [2011] 1 WLR 2100.

H. Deleted Words

Words which have been deleted from a contract are not generally used to interpret **3.50**
it. Because the reasons for this are related to the principle that evidence of prior
negotiations is not admissible evidence in interpreting a contract, this point is discussed later, under Principle 4, paras 4.94–4.97.

I. When Contracts Are Not Read as a Whole

There are exceptional cases where it is not appropriate to read a document as a **3.51**
whole. An example is *The Starsin*.[42] This case involved a bill of lading. On the front
of the bill of lading it appeared that the carrier of the goods was the charterer of the
vessel concerned. But small print on the back of the bill indicated that the carrier
was the owner of the vessel. The House of Lords decided that the carrier was in fact
the charterer, and not the owner, and that it would not be appropriate to read the
document as a whole because a reasonable person, versed in the shipping trade,
would place more reliance on the front of the bill than on the standard conditions
on the back.

Lord Hoffmann, commenting on the contrary decision of the Court of Appeal, **3.52**
said:[43]

> [where they] went wrong is that they conscientiously set out trying, as lawyers natu-
> rally would, to construe the bill of lading as a whole. In fact the reasonable reader of a
> bill of lading does not construe it as a whole. For some things he goes no further than
> what it says on the front. If the words there are reasonably sufficient to communicate
> the information in question, he does not trouble with the back. It is only if the infor-
> mation on the front is insufficient, or the questions which concern the reader relate
> to matters which do not ordinarily appear on the front, that he turns to the back.
> And then he calls in his lawyers to construe the document as a whole.

Of course, this was an exceptional case, where the reasonable reader of the docu- **3.53**
ment would have concentrated on just one part of the document. That will hardly
ever be the case in commercial transactions.

The courts do occasionally fail to read documents as a whole in circumstances where **3.54**
there is no justification of this kind—particularly where the clause in question is one
which the court might find morally objectionable. Examples of this tendency can be
seen in the approach of the courts to exclusion clauses and clauses which limit the
rights of a person on its insolvency.

---

[42] *Homburg Houtimport v Agrosin* [2004] 1 AC 715.
[43] [2004] 1 AC 715 at [82].

3.55   The classic approach to exclusion clauses used to be that of Denning LJ in *Karsales v Wallis:*[44]

> The thing to do is to look at the contract apart from the exempting clauses and see what are the terms, express or implied, which impose an obligation on the party. If he has been guilty of a breach of those obligations in a respect which goes to the very root of the contract, he cannot rely on the exempting clauses.

3.56   Although the doctrine of fundamental breach was finally put to rest by the House of Lords in *Photo Production v Securicor,*[45] the temptation to see an exclusion clause as something other than just one of the terms of the contract is evident even in the judgment of Lord Diplock in that case. He said:[46]

> [A]n exclusion clause is one which excludes or modifies an obligation, whether primary, general secondary or anticipatory secondary, that would otherwise arise under the contract by implication of law ... Since the presumption is that the parties by entering into the contract intended to accept the implied obligations exclusion clauses are to be construed strictly and the degree of strictness appropriate to be applied to their construction may properly depend upon the extent to which they involve departure from the implied obligations.

3.57   In other words, although there is no longer a rule of law which can strike down an exclusion clause, they nevertheless have to be read differently from other clauses in the contract. You first look at the contract without the clause, and then consider how the clause should be interpreted.

3.58   Where the Unfair Contract Terms Act 1977 applies, this is still how the courts interpret exclusion clauses.[47] Such a construction is doubtless forced upon the courts by the way in which the Unfair Contract Terms Act is drafted. Whether the courts will continue to adopt this approach in commercial transactions which are not the subject of the Unfair Contract Terms Act is not entirely clear.[48] In principle, it is suggested that they ought to read the contract as a whole with a view to establishing what the actual obligations of the parties are, and that any other approach would be to favour form over substance.

3.59   Where insolvency intervenes, the courts can also be reluctant to read contracts as a whole. When a person enters into insolvency proceedings, its assets must be applied in accordance with the scheme of distribution set out in the insolvency legislation. This broadly provides for the debtor's assets to be applied in payment *pari passu* of its liabilities at the time of the insolvency. As a result, the courts will strike down a contract which provides for a person's property to go somewhere else on that

---

[44] [1956] 1 WLR 936 at 940.
[45] [1980] AC 827.
[46] [1980] AC 827 at 850.
[47] *Phillips Products v Hyland* [1987] 1 WLR 659 at 664.
[48] Exclusion clauses are discussed further under Principle 7 at paras 7.66–7.82.

person's insolvency. Such a provision would clearly defeat the purpose of the insolvency legislation.[49]

This is all unexceptionable. But, as the decision of the Supreme Court in *Belmont* **3.60** *Park Investments v BNY Corporate Trustee Services*[50] shows, the courts have extended this doctrine beyond its natural bounds by failing to read contracts as a whole.

The facts of the *Belmont* case were complicated but, in essence, they involved **3.61** a company granting security to two creditors—A and B. A was to have a first ranking security, with B ranking second, unless and until A went into insolvency proceedings, whereupon B would have first ranking security and A would rank second. A went into insolvency proceedings, and the validity of the provision was challenged. It was argued that the provision removed an asset from A on its insolvency.

On a normal interpretation of the contract, it is difficult to see how this transac- **3.62** tion could have offended against insolvency law. A had no right to the charged assets before the security was granted. Its rights were granted to it when it obtained its security interest in the charged assets. And, when the security was granted, A's rights over the charged assets were limited in a way which, on A's insolvency, postponed it to B. A never had the unfettered right to first ranking security, and therefore nothing had been removed from it on its insolvency. Reading the contract as a whole, A had obtained what in the vernacular is known as a 'flawed asset'.

In the *Belmont* case, the Supreme Court felt unable to interpret the contract in this **3.63** way. It decided that an asset had been removed from A in its insolvency although, on the facts, it went on to decide that the transaction was valid.

The court drew a distinction (which had been made in previous cases) between **3.64** the transfer of a proprietary interest in an asset which is limited by reference to the transferee's insolvency—which is valid—and the transfer of a proprietary interest in an asset which is determined on the transferee's insolvency—which is void.

It is suggested that this is a distinction without a difference. If the contract is read as **3.65** a whole, the scope of the transfer is limited by reference to the transferee's insolvency.

In summary, although the courts do generally accept that contracts need to be read **3.66** as a whole, they are not always prepared to carry this principle to its logical conclusion in the case of clauses which they find objectionable. This does no favours to the coherence and certainty of the law.

---

[49] *Ex Parte Jay* (1880) LR 14 Ch 19.
[50] [2012] 1 AC 383.

4

PRINCIPLE 4: THE CONTEXT

Principle 4: Contracts are read in the context of their background facts. These are the facts reasonably available to the parties which are relevant to establishing how a reasonable person would understand what the parties intended by the contract when it was entered into.

A. The Issue

The text is the starting point, but it is not the finishing point. When interpreting a **4.01** written contract, the court will do so in the light of the background facts.[1]

Principle 4 is one of the most difficult and controversial of the Principles. The issue **4.02** is this: apart from the contract itself, what else can the interpreter look at when deciding what it means?

The history of the law in this area consists largely of a fight for supremacy between **4.03** two opposing approaches. In one camp are those who wish to see a contract interpreted largely on the basis of what the document says. The arguments here are based more on pragmatism than on principle. If the debate is limited to the words actually used in the document, this will make the process of interpretation quicker, cheaper, and more certain than it would otherwise be. And that is what business people want.

The other camp consists of those who wish to see the contract read against the **4.04** background of its surrounding facts. They see the issue as a matter of principle. Words have no meaning in isolation from their surrounding facts. They are only given meaning if they are read in context. So, if you want to understand what the parties objectively intended, you have to read the words in context. And that means absolutely everything that might be relevant.

---

[1] See McMeel, *The Construction of Contracts* (2nd edn, Oxford University Press, 2011), Chapter 5; Lewison, *The Interpretation of Contracts* (6th edn, Sweet & Maxwell, 2015) at 3.17 and 3.18.

4.05   The law in this area is sometimes seen as a movement from one extreme (only read-ing the document) to the other (reviewing all the surrounding circumstances). The truth is more complex. There has always been a divergence of view amongst judges about the extent to which external evidence should be available to interpret a writ-ten contract. And there always will be.

4.06   The answer does not lie at either extreme. It lies somewhere in the middle. The problem is in finding the middle.[2]

4.07   When trying to do so, it is important to understand the opposing views. It is the tension between them which requires the line to be drawn; and understanding why the opposing views are taken is crucial for an understanding of where the line should be drawn.

4.08   The materials which are available to interpret a written contract have been referred to by various names over the years—the matrix of facts,[3] the surrounding circum-stances,[4] the background.[5] They are all synonyms. In this book, they are described as the 'background facts'.

B. One View: Stick to the Contract

4.09   The view that the person interpreting the contract should as far as possible restrict him- or herself to the contract itself is deeply ingrained in the psyche of many com-mercial lawyers. It is based on an understanding of what business people need in practice, and its guiding principle is Oliver Wendell Holmes' aphorism that: 'The life of the law has not been logic: it has been experience.'[6]

4.10   The main concern is the loss of certainty and the increase in the time and cost which would be involved in allowing all background information to be available as part of the interpretation exercise.[7] There is also a worry that third parties who acquire an interest in the contract (for instance, by assignment) will not have had access to the background information available to the original parties, and that to use that information could therefore prejudice them.[8]

---

[2] For a perceptive and even-handed discussion of the issues involved, see Mitchell, *Interpretation of Contracts* (Routledge Cavendish, 2007), Chapters 2–4.

[3] Lord Wilberforce in *Prenn v Simmonds* [1971] 1 WLR 1381 at 1384.

[4] Lord Wilberforce in *Reardon Smith Line v Yngvar Hansen-Tangen* [1976] 1 WLR 989 at 995.

[5] Lord Hoffmann in *Investors Compensation Scheme v West Bromwich Building Society* [1998] 1 WLR 896 at 913.

[6] Oliver Wendell Holmes, Jr, *The Common Law* (1881), 1.

[7] In *Wire TV v CableTel (UK)* [1998] CLC 244 at 257, Lightman J referred to 'the flood of evi-dence in the case on the factual matrix, much of which was legally inadmissible or totally unhelpful'.

[8] See Alan Berg's comments on the importance of taking account of the interests of third parties in 'Richard III in New Zealand' (2008) 124 LQR 6.

In *National Bank of Sharjah v Dellborg*,[9] Saville LJ expressed the view of many com-   **4.11**
mercial lawyers when he said:

> It is difficult to quarrel with the general proposition that when interpreting an agree-
> ment the court is trying to work out what the parties intended to agree, rather than
> analysing words in a vacuum. Thus where the words the parties have used are ambig-
> uous or, read literally, are meaningless or nonsensical, the surrounding circumstances
> must be considered in order to select the appropriate meaning or to try to give the
> words meaning or sense. However, where the words used have an unambiguous and
> sensible meaning as a matter of ordinary language, I see serious objections in an ap-
> proach which would permit the surrounding circumstances to alter that meaning.

Saville LJ identified two problems in particular in allowing too much evidence of   **4.12**
surrounding circumstances. In the first place, it would add to the cost and delay of
litigation and arbitration. And second, it could adversely affect the position of third
parties.

Kirby J made the same point in a dissenting judgment in the High Court of Australia   **4.13**
in *Royal Botanic Gardens and Domain Trust v South Sydney City Council*.[10] He was
concerned at the tendency for judges and others to look first at external sources for
guidance, before turning to the text. 'It is as if some who have the responsibility of
interpretation of legal words find the reading and analysis of the texts themselves
distasteful, like dentists happy to talk about the problem but loathe to pull a tooth.'[11]

Kirby J went on to justify the importance of looking primarily at the text. The   **4.14**
fundamental reason for observing restraint in the use of extrinsic evidence is that
the very purpose of a formal contract is to put an end to disputes and to discourage
expensive and time-consuming litigation. It is one thing to recognize that much
language is inherently ambiguous but, where the language is clear, it should be
applied.[12]

The issues here are very much the same as those discussed earlier in relation to the   **4.15**
parol evidence rule. As has been seen under Principle 2, that rule no longer has any
meaningful part to play in commercial law, but its absence has led commercial parties to find another way of limiting external evidence—by using an entire agreement
clause. There does seem to be a strong and consistent body of opinion amongst
those who deal with commercial contracts in practice that they would like, as far as
possible, to limit the scope of disputes about both the identity and the meaning of
written contracts.

---

[9] Unreported, 9 July 1997.
[10] (2002) 240 CLR 45 at [70]–[73] and [98] –[103].
[11] (2002) 240 CLR 45 at [70].
[12] In a similar vein, see the remarks of JJ Spigelman, former Chief Justice of New South Wales,
in 'From Text to Context: Contemporary Contractual Interpretation' (2007) 81 ALJ 322 and in
'Contractual Interpretation: A Comparative Perspective' (2011) 85 ALJ 412.

C. The Other View: Use the Context

4.16 The opposing view is that it is not possible to understand the words used in a written contract without at least some knowledge of the background. The most extreme view is that words do not have a meaning outside their context, and therefore the written contract just cannot be understood without reference to the background facts.

4.17 This point has been made forcefully by David McLauchlan: 'The truth is that no words have a fixed or settled meaning. Rather it is some *person* who gives a meaning to them.'[13] He adopts Corbin's view that the principle that words should be given their plain meaning is based on 'a great illusion ... that words, either singly or in combination, have a "meaning" that is independent of the persons who use them'.[14]

4.18 This approach has judicial support. In *Charrington & Co v Wooder*,[15] Lord Dunedin said that the court needs to:

> place itself in thought in the same position as the parties to the contract were placed, in fact, when they made it—or, as it is sometimes phrased, to be informed as to the surrounding circumstances.

4.19 The reason was explained by Lord Blackburn in *River Wear Commissioners v Adamson*:[16]

> In all cases the object is to see what is the intention expressed by the words used. But, from the imperfection of language, it is impossible to know what that intention is without inquiring farther, and seeing what the circumstances were with reference to which the words were used, and what was the object, appearing from those circumstances, which the person using them had in view; for the meaning of words varies according to the circumstances with respect to which they were used.

D. Where Are We Now?

4.20 We are all contextualists now. There is no doubt that it is necessary to read the words in a written contract in the context of its background facts. This has been made clear in three important judgments—two by Lord Wilberforce in the 1970s and one by

---

[13] McLauchlan, 'Contract Interpretation: What Is It About?' (2009) 31(1) Sydney Law Review 5. Emphasis in the original.

[14] A.L. Corbin, *Corbin on Contracts*, Vol 1 (West Publishing Co., St Paul, Rev. edn 1963), Article 106, p. 474, quoted in McLauchlan, 'Plain Meaning and Commercial Construction: Has Australia Adopted the *ICS* Principles?' (2009) 25 JCL 7. The same point is made by Lord Steyn, 'The Intractable Problem of the Interpretation of Legal Texts' (2003) 25(1) Sydney Law Review 5, reproduced in Worthington (ed.), *Commercial Law and Commercial Practice* (Hart, 2013) 123 at 124.

[15] [1914] AC 71 at 82.

[16] (1877) 2 App Cas 743 at 763.

Lord Hoffmann in the 1990s. All three are seminal judgments, and it is necessary to quote them.

In *Prenn v Simmonds*,[17] Lord Wilberforce said: **4.21**

> In order for the agreement ... to be understood, it must be placed in its context. The time has long passed when agreements, even those under seal, were isolated from the matrix of facts in which they were set and interpreted purely on internal linguistic considerations.

Lord Wilberforce returned to this theme in *Reardon Smith Line v Yngvar Hansen-* **4.22**
Tangen a few years later:[18]

> No contracts are made in a vacuum: there is always a setting in which they have to be placed. The nature of what is legitimate to have regard to is usually described as 'the surrounding circumstances' but this phrase is imprecise: it can be illustrated but hardly defined. In a commercial contract it is certainly right that the court should know the commercial purpose of the contract and this in turn presupposes knowledge of the genesis of the transaction, the background, the context, the market in which the parties are operating.

In the 1990s, Lord Hoffmann took up the theme again, in what has become the **4.23**
most-quoted judgment of all in relation to contractual interpretation— *Investors Compensation Scheme v West Bromwich Building Society*.[19] Lord Hoffmann summarized the law in five principles. For this purpose, it is sufficient to quote the first two:[20]

(1) Interpretation is the ascertainment of the meaning which the document would convey to a reasonable person having all the background knowledge which would reasonably have been available to the parties in the situation in which they were at the time of the contract.

(2) The background was famously referred to by Lord Wilberforce as the 'matrix of fact', but this phrase is, if anything, an understated description of what the background may include. Subject to the requirement that it should have been reasonably available to the parties and to the exception to be mentioned next [*prior negotiations—which are discussed later in paras 4.71–4.93*], it includes absolutely anything which would have affected the way in which the language of the document would have been understood by a reasonable man.[21]

---

[17] [1971] 1 WLR 1381 at 1383–4.
[18] [1976] 1 WLR 989 at 995–6.
[19] [1998] 1 WLR 896.
[20] [1998] 1 WLR 896 at 912–13.
[21] 'It is hard to imagine a ruling more calculated to perpetuate the vast cost of commercial litigation.' The words of Sir Christopher Staughton in 'How Do the Courts Interpret Commercial Contracts?' (1999) 58 CLJ 303, 307.

4.24 It is difficult to over-estimate the importance of this statement by Lord Hoffmann. Views differ as to the extent to which he was simply reminding us of the principles which had already been laid down by Lord Wilberforce in the 1970s (and, indeed, by Lord Blackburn a century earlier), but there can be no doubt that this decision has focused minds on the extent of the background evidence available to interpret written contracts.

4.25 It is therefore clear that every contract must be interpreted in the light of the relevant background facts which were reasonably available to the parties at the time the contract was entered into. The legal background against which the contract was entered into may itself be a relevant background fact.[22]

E. No Need for Ambiguity

4.26 One other thing is clear. This principle applies even if the words of the contract are unambiguous. It is possible to find quite a lot of statements in earlier cases to the effect that the surrounding circumstances are only relevant if the words in the written contract are ambiguous.[23] But, if there ever was such a limitation, it no longer exists in England.

4.27 Lord Steyn made the point in *R v National Asylum Support Service*:[24]

> The starting point is that language in all legal texts conveys meaning according to the circumstances in which it was used. It follows that the context must always be identified and considered before the process of construction or during it. It is therefore wrong to say that the court may only resort to evidence of the contextual scene when an ambiguity has arisen ... [In the *Investors Compensation Scheme* case], Lord Hoffmann made crystal clear that an ambiguity need not be established before the surrounding circumstances may be taken into account.

4.28 In New Zealand, it is also clear that ambiguity is not required in order to enable the court to consider the background facts.[25] The same is true in Singapore. In *Y.E.S. v Soup Restaurant*,[26] Andrew Phang Boon Leong JA said, in the Singapore Court of

---

[22] As in *Prenn v Simmonds* [1971] 1 WLR 1381, where the existing companies legislation was a relevant background fact. See Lewison at 4.06.

[23] See, for instance, the speech of Viscount Haldane LC in *Charrington & Co v Wooder* [1914] AC 71 at 77.

[24] [2002] 1 WLR 2956 at [5].

[25] This was settled by the New Zealand Court of Appeal in *Boat Park v Hutchinson* [1999] 2 NZLR 74 at 81–2, and in *Ansley v Prospectus Nominees* [2004] 2 NZLR 590 at [36]. It was recently reiterated by the New Zealand Supreme Court in *Firm PI v Zurich Australian Insurance* [2015] 1 NZLR 432 at [61].

[26] [2015] SGCA 55 at [35]. Emphasis in the original.

Appeal, that: 'the court is always to pay close attention to both the text *and* context in every case—noting that both *interact* with each other'.[27]

The position is less certain in Australia.[28] The starting point for any discussion of **4.29** contractual interpretation in Australia is the decision of the High Court of Australia in *Codelfa Construction v State Rail Authority of New South Wales*[29] and, in particular, the judgment of Justice Mason in that case. In *Western Export Services v Jireh*,[30] Justices Gummow, Heydon, and Bell confirmed that, until the High Court reconsiders *Codelfa*, it is binding throughout Australia. The problem comes in deciding what *Codelfa* is actually authority for.

Some Australian courts consider that *Codelfa* requires the contract to be ambiguous **4.30** before the background facts can be admitted in evidence. This was the view of the High Court in *Western Export Services v Jireh*.[31] It derives its strength from the following statement of Mason J in *Codelfa*:[32]

> The true rule is that evidence of surrounding circumstances is admissible to assist in the interpretation of the contract if the language is ambiguous or susceptible of more than one meaning. But it is not admissible to contradict the language of the contract when it has a plain meaning.

On the face of it, this requires ambiguity before the background facts can be admit- **4.31** ted. But a number of Australian courts have decided that, when Mason J's judgment is read as a whole, he is not intending to restrict the principle in this way. This is largely because Mason J quoted, with apparent approval, Lord Wilberforce's comments in *Prenn v Simmonds*[33] and the *Reardon Smith* case.[34] This was the view of the New South Wales Court of Appeal in *Franklins v Metcash Trading*[35] and of the Federal Court of Australia in *Lion Nathan Australia v Coopers Brewery*,[36] and it seems to garner some support from the judgments of the High Court of Australia in *Pacific Carriers v BNP Paribas*[37] and *Electricity Generation Corporation v Woodside Energy*.[38]

---

[27] And see *Zurich Insurance v B-Gold* [2008] 3 SLR(R) 1029 and *Sembcorp Marine v PPL Holdings* [2013] 4 SLR 193.

[28] See the discussion in McLauchlan, 'Plain Meaning and Commercial Construction: Has Australia Adopted the *ICS* Principles?' (2009) 25 JCL 7.

[29] (1981–1982) 149 CLR 337.

[30] (2011) 282 ALR 604 at [3]. And see *Royal Botanic Gardens and Domain Trust v South Sydney City Council* (2002) 240 CLR 45 at [39].

[31] [2011] 282 ALR 604 at [2] and [3]. Although that was only an application for special leave to appeal, and therefore only of persuasive authority.

[32] (1981–1982) 149 CLR 337 at 352.

[33] [1971] 1 WLR 1381.

[34] [1976] 1 WLR 989.

[35] (2009) 76 NSWLR 603.

[36] (2006) 236 ALR 561.

[37] (2004) 218 CLR 451 at [22].

[38] (2014) 251 CLR 640 at [35].

4.32 The New South Wales Court of Appeal has consistently maintained that ambiguity is not a requirement for taking account of the background facts. In *Mainteck Services v Stein Heurtey*,[39] Leeming JA said that 'language is unavoidably contextual' and that this is not inconsistent with what Mason J said in *Codelfa*.[40] Similarly in *Newey v Westpac*,[41] Gleeson JA denied that ambiguity is a precondition to examining the background facts,[42] and considered that the decision of the High Court of Australia in *Electricity Generation Corporation v Woodside Energy*[43] requires a contextual approach to interpretation. The Federal Court of Australia took a similar approach in *Stratton Finance v Webb*.[44]

4.33 There is therefore a powerful body of authority in Australia which supports the requirement to look at the context, whether or not the language of the contract is ambiguous on its face. But the law is still not clear in Australia because, in its most recent discussion of the issue in *Mount Bruce Mining v Wright Prospecting*,[45] the High Court left the point open. The issue was not relevant to the case, and the court declined to deal with it.[46]

4.34 In the result, whilst the High Court of Australia sits firmly on the fence, many of the lower courts in Australia continue to look at the background facts even where there is no ambiguity on the face of the document.[47] It is time that this issue was resolved by the High Court, but it is suggested that it is unlikely to resist the proposition that the background facts are admissible in all cases of interpretation. The real question, it is suggested, is not *whether* background facts are always admissible in evidence, but *the extent* of those background facts.

F. What Are the Relevant Background Facts?

4.35 If it is clear that a contract needs to be interpreted in the context of its background facts, what is less clear is what this means in practice. What is the extent of these background facts against which the contract needs to be interpreted?[48] As Catherine Mitchell has said: 'It is difficult to deny that all contracts require

---

[39] (2014) 89 NSWLR 633 at [72]–[86].
[40] (2014) 89 NSWLR 633 at [76] and [78].
[41] [2014] NSWCA 319.
[42] [2014] NSWCA 319 at [86].
[43] (2014) 251 CLR 640 at [35].
[44] (2014) 314 ALR 166 at [40].
[45] [2015] HCA 37.
[46] [2015] HCA 37 at [48]–[52] (French CJ, Nettle and Gordon JJ), [110]–[113] (Kiefel and Keane JJ), and [118]–[120] (Bell and Gageler JJ).
[47] The Western Australian courts are more circumspect: *Technomin Australia v Xstrata Nickel* (2014) 48 WAR 261 at [33]–[48], [144]–[158], and [171]–[217].
[48] For a clear discussion of the issues involved, see McMeel, Chapter 5.

contextual interpretation to some degree, but ... "context" can be broadly or narrowly defined.'[49]

Lord Hoffmann considered this issue in *Bank of Credit and Commerce International*   **4.36**
v Ali.[50] He said that:

> [W]hen [in *Investors Compensation Scheme v West Bromwich Building Society*[51]] I said that the admissible background included 'absolutely anything which would have affected the way in which the language of the document would have been understood by a reasonable man', I did not think it necessary to emphasise that I meant anything which a reasonable man would have regarded as *relevant*. I was merely saying that there is no conceptual limit to what can be regarded as background.

One might be forgiven for thinking that this takes us very little further. How do we   **4.37**
distinguish the relevant metal from the irrelevant dross? There are, in practice, two ways in which the courts have limited the admissibility of background facts. One is based on principle, the other on pragmatism; although they do sometimes overlap.

G. Limitations Based on Principle

The limitations based on principle ultimately derive from the guiding principle   **4.38**
of contractual interpretation, which is described in Principle 1. The purpose of contractual interpretation is to establish the intention of the parties to the contract. This is done objectively: what would a reasonable person understand their common intention to be from what they have written, said, and done?

How would a reasonable person go about trying to derive the parties' intention from   **4.39**
its external manifestations? He or she would start with what the parties have written, because that is the clearest objective evidence of their common intention. But it is now clear that the interpreter cannot stop there. He or she must look at the relevant background facts. So what, in principle, is relevant?

The first task of the person interpreting the contract is to determine what the   **4.40**
contract is. Is it just the writing, or has the contract been made partly in writing and partly orally or by conduct? This is an issue which has been discussed under Principle 2.

Having determined what the contract is, the task of the interpreter is then to es-   **4.41**
tablish what the words used by the parties mean. The crucial point is that the background facts do not provide independent evidence of what the parties intended.

---

[49] Mitchell, 43.
[50] [2002] 1 AC 251 at [39]. Emphasis in the original.
[51] [1998] 1 WLR 896 at [913].

They are there to assist in the interpretation of the words actually used by the parties in the contract. They therefore play a role which is subservient to that of the words used.

4.42 The limits on background facts which are derived from principle are essentially concerned with two aspects of Principle 1—the requirement to establish the intention of the parties to the contract objectively; and the requirement to do so at the time the contract is entered into. So one limit is concerned with objectivity, the other with timing.

4.43 The first limit on the admissibility of background facts derives from the basic principle that the intention of the parties is established objectively. We are concerned with how a reasonable person would view what has happened, not what the parties subjectively intended—with apparent intentions, not actual ones.

4.44 This principle manifests itself in three ways. In the first place, it makes statements of subjective intention inadmissible because they are irrelevant.

4.45 Second, it limits the background facts to those which the parties ought reasonably to be expected to have known. Those are the only facts which are relevant if the purpose of the exercise is to establish the parties' objective intention.

4.46 Third, it excludes prior negotiations—at least to the extent that they are concerned with the parties' aspirations. Negotiations are more concerned with subjective intentions than with objective facts. And in practice, it is almost impossible to distinguish between aspiration and agreement in the period running up to the signing of the contract. This is not to say that facts which become apparent to both parties during the negotiations are irrelevant, simply that the negotiations themselves are of no probative value.

4.47 The second limit on the admissibility of background facts is concerned with time. The purpose of the exercise is to establish the objective intention of the parties at the time the contract was entered into. It is information reasonably available to the parties at the time the contract was entered into which is primarily relevant to establish that intention. This principle has two important manifestations in practice—the limitations on the use of subsequent conduct and of prior negotiations in interpreting a contract.

4.48 If we are concerned with the intention of the parties at the time the contract was entered into, things happening later can generally have no relevance. What happens later might provide evidence of an amendment to an agreement, or possibly a waiver, but generally cannot establish what the parties intended at an earlier time. It is theoretically possible that the conduct of the parties might help to determine what they intended at the time the contract was entered into, but most common law jurisdictions prohibit even this evidence on the ground that a contract can only have one meaning, and that meaning cannot vary over time.

This is also another reason why there is a general prohibition on the use of evidence **4.49** obtained from prior negotiations in interpreting a contract. Although things which happen in the period running up to the contract might, in general terms, be relevant to what was intended at the time of the contract, the negotiations themselves cannot be relevant to the question of what was intended at the time the contract was entered into. Anyone who has negotiated a commercial contract will know that it is frequently the case that the parties change their positions right up to the moment of signing. What might have been agreed during negotiations is no guide to what was actually agreed when the contract was signed.

The result is that, as a matter of principle, there are excluded from those background **4.50** facts which can be used as an aid to interpretation:

(1) declarations of subjective intent;
(2) facts not reasonably available to the parties at the time the contract was entered into;
(3) prior negotiations;
(4) subsequent conduct.

In principle, all other background facts are relevant.

H. Limitations Based on Pragmatism

But that is not the end of the story. The tension between those who would broaden **4.51** the scope of admissible background facts, and those who would narrow it, has already been discussed. It is a recurrent problem. At the end of the twentieth century, it looked as if there would be very few pragmatic limits on the admissibility of background facts—particularly in the light of Lord Hoffmann's judgment in *Investors Compensation Scheme v West Bromwich Building Society*,[52] when he said that the background facts included 'absolutely anything which would have affected the way in which the language of the document would have been understood by a reasonable man'. Almost twenty years on, that statement seems more like an aspiration than a reality.

Pragmatism manifests itself in two ways in this context. In the first place, the courts **4.52** have recognized the need for certainty and the speedy resolution of disputes as a reason for limiting the amount of background facts which can be used in the

---

[52] [1998] 1 WLR 896 at 912.

interpretation process. This was recognized by Lord Hoffmann in *Chartbrook v Persimmon Homes*[53] as another reason for excluding prior negotiations.

4.53 The other way in which pragmatism has been used to limit the availability of background facts is concerned with contracts in which third parties might have an interest. It is one thing to delve into the background facts of which the parties were reasonably aware if they are the only ones affected by the outcome. But what if third parties become involved, who are unfamiliar with that background? Is it right that they should be affected by it?

4.54 This is a concern in relation to two types of contract—those which are frequently transferred, and those which are matters of public record.

4.55 Contracts which are matters of public record are relatively easy to deal with because it is normally clear whether or not a contract falls into this category. The other type of case—contracts which are frequently transferred—is more of a problem, because it is uncertain how far the category extends.

4.56 It includes contracts which are transferable by delivery (such as bills of exchange, promissory notes, and bills of lading) and also contracts the benefit of which is frequently assigned. There is a limited number of contracts which are transferable by delivery, but most contracts can be assigned in the absence of a restriction in the contract itself. Restrictions on assignment are common in commercial contracts, but it is also commonplace to assign the benefit of contracts in commercial practice— either outright (for instance, by way of sale) or by way of security. Important commercial contracts are very frequently assigned or charged in practice.[54]

4.57 The courts are aware of this, and are reluctant to admit evidence of background facts in such cases if they could not reasonably have been known by the third parties concerned. If the contract is of a type where it is likely that a third party will obtain an interest in it, the courts have restricted the use of background facts to those which the third parties concerned ought reasonably to have been aware of. This is a significant restriction. Facts which were reasonably available to the parties at the time the contract was entered into will not be admissible in such a case if they were not reasonably available to third parties. In practice, this restricts background facts to things such as basic market conditions known to those operating in the market concerned.

4.58 This restriction is sometimes seen as a matter of principle. In *Cherry Tree Investments v Landmain*,[55] Lewison LJ said that there is no conflict between this approach and the general principle that contracts must be read in the light of their background

---

[53] [2009] 1 AC 1101 at [36]–[37], quoted later at para 4.78.
[54] See the comments of Alan Berg in 'Thrashing Through the Undergrowth' (2006) 122 LQR 354.
[55] [2013] 2 WLR 481 at [128].

facts. The purpose of interpretation is to establish what a reasonable person would understand the document to mean against the relevant background facts. And the weight which a reasonable person would attribute to the background facts depends on the nature of the contract.

This principle had been expounded by Campbell JA in the New South Wales Court of Appeal in *Phoenix Commercial Enterprises v City of Canada Bay Council*:[56]   **4.59**

> [T]he way [the principles of interpretation] come to be applied to a particular contract can be affected by aspects of the contract such as whether it is assignable, whether it will endure for a longer time rather than a shorter time, and whether the provision that is in question is one to which indefeasibility attaches by virtue of the contract being embodied in an instrument that it registered [in a land registry]. All these are matters that will be taken into account by the reasonable person seeking to understand what the words of the document conveyed. That is because the reasonable person seeking to understand what the words convey would understand that the meaning of the words of the document does not change with time or with the identity of the person who happens to be seeking to understand the document. That reasonable person would therefore understand that the sort of background knowledge that is able to be used as an aid to construction, has to be background knowledge that is accessible to all the people who it is reasonably foreseeable might, in the future, need to construe the document.

This is an attractive argument. A reasonable person, interpreting the contract, would understand that fewer background facts would be relevant to the interpretation of a contract which is likely to be transferred, than one which is not.   **4.60**

The problem with this approach is that the basic principle of contractual interpretation (Principle 1) is that the purpose of contractual interpretation is to establish the intention of the parties to the contract. Although this is done objectively, it is still the intention of the parties to the contract that the court is ultimately striving for. And it is difficult to see how that can alter depending on the likelihood, or otherwise, of the benefit of the contract being transferred. It is therefore suggested that this limitation on admissibility of background facts is essentially a pragmatic one, which recognizes that not all contracts are the same and that the scope of admissible evidence where a dispute is likely to be between the parties to the contract may be broader than where it is not.   **4.61**

But this does create a problem in practice.[57] How do you decide when background facts are generally admissible, and when they are not? One answer would be to determine it on the basis of the parties to the litigation concerned: are they the parties   **4.62**

---

[56] [2010] NSWCA 64 at [151]. Cited with approval by Lewison LJ in *Cherry Tree Investments v Landmain* [2013] 2 WLR 481 at [128].

[57] The issues are discussed by Matthew Barber and Rod Thomas in 'Contractual Interpretation, Registered Documents and Third Party Effects' (2014) 77 MLR 597.

to the contract or is a third party involved? But this would have the undesirable effect that the contract could mean different things depending on who was suing on it. That cannot be acceptable.[58]

4.63 The alternative is to divide contracts into two categories: those which are normally transferred and those which are not. It is easy to say that some contracts fall into one category rather than the other, but it is very difficult to draw the line in the intermediate type of case. Very many commercial contracts are assigned. But many are not. How (and where) do you draw the line? Those cases which have restricted background facts have generally been concerned with contracts which either have some public function (because they are on a register) or which are routinely transferred (such as bills of lading). The extent to which this principle might be extended to other types of commercial contract has yet to be tested.

4.64 As can be seen from this discussion, it is clear that pragmatism does have an important part to play in limiting the availability of background facts in the interpretation process, but it is by no means clear how it should be manifested in practice. This is an area of the law which needs to develop, and this is an issue to which we will return later.

I. Summary of Limitations

4.65 In summary, the limits on admissibility of background facts fall into three categories, the first two of which are based on principle, the last on pragmatism. They are:

(1) objectivity (this prevents the admissibility of declarations of subjective intention and prior negotiations and limits the background information to that reasonably available to the parties at the time the contract was entered into);
(2) timing (this prevents the admissibility of prior negotiations and of subsequent conduct);
(3) pragmatism (this is more difficult to pin down, but it certainly prevents the admissibility of prior negotiations and is also concerned to limit the availability of background information where third parties are likely to be involved).

4.66 It will help to look at these issues under the following headings:

- the knowledge of the parties;
- declarations of subjective intention;
- prior negotiations;
- deleted words;

---

[58] See the comments of Diplock LJ in *Slim v Daily Telegraph* [1968] 2 QB 157 at 172: 'the unexpressed major premise [of lawyers] that any particular combination of words has one meaning'.

- subsequent conduct;
- third parties.

J. The Knowledge of the Parties

Background facts are only relevant if, in the words of Lord Hoffmann in *Investors* **4.67**
Compensation Scheme v West Bromwich Building Society, they[59] 'would reasonably
have been available to the parties in the situation in which they were at the time of
the contract'.

This is an aspect of the objective nature of the interpretation process. What is rele- **4.68**
vant is not what the parties actually knew, but what a reasonable person would
expect them to know.

K. Declarations of Subjective Intention

Declarations of subjective intention are not admissible in interpreting a contract **4.69**
because they are irrelevant to the question to be decided—what is the objective
intention of the parties? As Lord Wilberforce said in *Reardon Smith Line v Yngvar
Hansen-Tangen*:[60]

> When one speaks of the intention of the parties to the contract, one is speak-
> ing objectively—the parties cannot themselves give direct evidence of what their
> intention was …

In a similar light, Lord Hoffmann in *Chartbrook v Persimmon*[61] gave, as one of the **4.70**
reasons for excluding evidence of prior negotiations, the fact that they:

> will be drenched in subjectivity and may, if oral, be very much in dispute. It is often
> not easy to distinguish between those statements which (if they were made at all)
> merely reflect the aspirations of one or more of the parties and those which embody
> at least a provisional consensus which may throw light on the meaning of the con-
> tract which was eventually concluded.

L. Prior Negotiations

In England, and in some other common law jurisdictions, evidence of the negotia- **4.71**
tions between the parties in the period running up to the execution of the contract
is not generally admissible as part of the background facts.[62] This is in contrast

---

[59] [1998] 1 WLR 896 at 912.
[60] [1976] 1 WLR 989 at 996.
[61] [2009] 1 AC 1101 at [38].
[62] See Lewison at 3.09.

with the civil law tradition,[63] which places more emphasis on the parties' subjective intention. There are also moves afoot in some other common law jurisdictions to remove, or at least to reconsider, the prohibition on using prior negotiations as evidence.[64]

4.72 When, in the 1970s, it was accepted that the 'surrounding matrix of facts' was available as evidence when interpreting a contract, it was counter-balanced by an insistence that this did not extend either to prior negotiations[65] or to subsequent conduct.[66]

4.73 As far as prior negotiations were concerned, the reason why they were excluded was that they were unhelpful. In the words of Lord Wilberforce in *Prenn v Simmonds*:[67]

> The reason for not admitting evidence of [prior negotiations] is not a technical one or even mainly one of convenience (though the attempt to admit it did greatly prolong the case and add to its expense). It is simply that such evidence is unhelpful. By the nature of things, where negotiations are difficult, the parties' positions, with each passing letter, are changing and until the final agreement, though converging, still divergent. It is only the final document which records a consensus.

4.74 The law therefore became settled. Evidence of the background facts would be admitted, but not to the extent that it consisted of pre-contractual negotiations. There the matter lay until, in his third principle in *Investors Compensation Scheme v West Bromwich Building Society*,[68] Lord Hoffmann opened the question up:

> (3) The law excludes from the admissible background the previous negotiations of the parties and their declarations of subjective intent. They are admissible only in an action for rectification. The law makes this distinction for reasons of practical policy and, in this respect only, legal interpretation differs from the way we would interpret utterances in ordinary life. The boundaries of this exception are in some respects unclear. But this is not the occasion on which to explore them.

4.75 The implicit invitation to open the question of whether prior negotiations should be excluded was taken up by a number of judges and academics, chief amongst whom were Lord Nicholls[69] in England and Justice Thomas[70] and Professor David

---

[63] See, for instance, the *Unidroit Principles of International Commercial Contracts* (2010 edn), Article 4.3(a), which requires regard to be had to 'all the circumstances', including 'preliminary negotiations between the parties'.

[64] The utility of the prohibition on the use of prior negotiations was discussed in detail in the Supreme Court of New Zealand in *Vector Gas v Bay of Plenty Energy* [2010] 2 NZLR 444, but their Honours did not reach a consensus on the point. See McLauchlan, 'Contract Interpretation in the Supreme Court–Easy Case, Hard Law?' (2010) 16 NZBLQ 229.

[65] *Prenn v Simmonds* [1971] 1 WLR 1381.

[66] *Schuler v Wickman Machine Tool Sales* [1974] AC 235.

[67] [1971] 1 WLR 1381 at 1384.

[68] [1998] 1 WLR 896 at 913.

[69] Nicholls, 'My Kingdom for a Horse: The Meaning of Words' (2005) 121 LQR 577.

[70] *Yoshimoto v Canterbury Golf International* [2001] 1 NZLR 523 at 538–49.

McLaughlan[71] in New Zealand. In essence, they argued that there is no need to exclude prior negotiations for the following reasons:

(1) conceptually, evidence of negotiations is part of the relevant background;
(2) it is useful evidence of the parties' real intentions;
(3) in practical terms, it will come out anyway in a claim for rectification;
(4) case management can sort the useful wheat from the unhelpful chaff.[72]

4.76 The opportunity for the House of Lords to explore these issues came in 2009 in *Chartbrook v Persimmon Homes*.[73] The principal judgment was again given by Lord Hoffmann. He reviewed the arguments for and against, and reached the conclusion that the general exclusion of prior negotiations should be retained.[74]

4.77 Lord Hoffmann's reason for excluding prior negotiations was, however, rather different from that of Lord Wilberforce in *Prenn v Simmonds*.[75] Lord Wilberforce regarded them as unhelpful because they are irrelevant to the key question: what is the objective intention of the parties? Lord Hoffmann agreed that this would usually be the case, but not always. He therefore based his decision not just on principle, but also on pragmatism. To allow evidence of prior negotiations would reduce certainty and increase time and cost.

4.78 Lord Hoffmann recognized that:

> There is certainly a view in the profession that the less one has to resort to any form of background in aid of interpretation, the better.

This view:

> reflects what may be a sound practical intuition that the law of contract is an institution designed to enforce promises with a high degree of predictability and that the more one allows conventional meanings or syntax to be displaced by inferences drawn from background, the less predictable the outcome is likely to be.[76]

And to admit such evidence could adversely affect third parties.[77]

4.79 In the result, the House of Lords decided that the exclusion of prior negotiations should be retained in the interests of economy and predictability.

---

[71] McLauchlan, 'Contract Interpretation: What Is It About?' (2009) 31(5) Sydney Law Review 5.

[72] The abolition of the rule excluding prior negotiations was also advocated by Catherine Mitchell, 'Contract Interpretation: Pragmatism, Principle and the Prior Negotiations Rule' (2010) 26 JCL 134 and, on balance, by Gerard McMeel, 'Prior Negotiations and Subsequent Conduct—the Next Step Forward for Contractual Interpretation?' (2003) 119 LQR 272.

[73] [2009] 1 AC 1101.

[74] [2009] 1 AC 1101 at [28]–[47].

[75] [1971] 1 WLR 1381.

[76] [2009] 1 AC 1101 at [36]–[37].

[77] [2009] 1 AC 1101 at [40].

4.80 Lord Hoffmann's approach in the *Chartbrook* case[78] rather suggests that he is giving a broader meaning to the expression 'prior negotiations' than Lord Wilberforce did in *Prenn v Simmonds*.[79] To the extent that prior negotiations are concerned with the subjective intentions of the parties, they are excluded anyway. And if they are evidence of objective facts, why treat them differently from any other objective facts? Lord Hoffmann refused to limit the exclusion to those facts which were irrelevant (i.e. subjective)[80]—thereby indicating that the exclusion of prior negotiations covered objective facts as well as subjective intentions. But he then went on to say that:

> [t]he rule excludes evidence of what was said or done during the course of negotiating the agreement for the purpose of drawing inferences about what the contract meant. It does not exclude the use of such evidence for other purposes: for example, to establish that a fact which may be relevant as background was known to the parties …[81]

4.81 A similar distinction had been drawn by Mason CJ in the High Court of Australia in *Codelfa Construction v State Rail Authority of New South Wales*:[82]

> Obviously the prior negotiations will tend to establish objective background facts which were known to both parties and the subject matter of the contract. To the extent to which they have this tendency they are admissible.

4.82 It is hard to see how this approach differs from saying that prior negotiations are only excluded to the extent that they provide evidence of the parties' subjective intention. Lord Hoffmann clearly considered that he was excluding evidence for pragmatic reasons—not just on principle—but the extent of the exclusion is not entirely clear.

4.83 One question is what we mean by the expression 'prior negotiations'. In *Vector Gas v Bay of Plenty Energy*,[83] Tipping J said in the Supreme Court of New Zealand:

> Some of the difficulties in this area may derive from the concept of 'prior negotiations' being employed in a more or less expansive way. Sometimes the concept seems to be used as if it encompassed all conduct and circumstances associated with negotiations towards the formation of a contract. It is necessary, however, to distinguish between the subjective content of negotiations; that is, how the parties were thinking, their individual intentions and the stance they were taking at different stages of the negotiating process, on the one hand, and, on the other, evidence derived from the negotiations which shows objectively the meaning the parties intended their words to convey. Such evidence includes the circumstances in which the contract

---

[78] *Chartbrook v Persimmon Homes* [2009] 1 AC 1101.
[79] [1971] 1 WLR 1381.
[80] [2009] 1 AC 1101 at [32].
[81] [2009] 1 AC 1101 at [42]. And see the judgment of Mason J in *Codelfa Construction v State Rail Authority of New South Wales* (1981–1982) 149 CLR 337 at 354.
[82] (1981–1982) 149 CLR 337 at 352.
[83] [2010] 2 NZLR 444 at [27].

was entered into, and any objectively apparent consensus as to meaning operating between the parties.

4.84 Tipping J decided that the subjective content of negotiations was not admissible because it offended against the principle that contracts are interpreted objectively. But:

> Evidence of facts, circumstances and conduct attending the negotiations is admissible if it is capable of shedding objective light on meaning.[84]

4.85 One approach to the problem would therefore be to decide that the prohibition on the use of prior negotiations only prevents the subjective intentions of the parties from being prayed in aid. This would exclude the drafts which are circulated before the contract is signed, but relevant objective facts would be admissible even if they came to light during negotiations. Two cases can illustrate the issues involved— *Macdonald v Longbottom*[85] in the 1850s and *Bank of Scotland v Dunedin Property Investment Co*[86] in the 1990s.

4.86 In *Macdonald v Longbottom*,[87] a wool stapler wrote to a farmer offering to buy 'your wool' for a certain price. The written offer was accepted by the farmer, but the offer did not, itself, explain what was meant by the expression 'your wool'. Before the written offer was made, the parties had discussed the proposed purchase both of the wool which the farmer had on his own farm, and also of wool which he had bought from other farms. The Court of Queen's Bench had no difficulty in allowing evidence of those negotiations to be used for the purpose of establishing what was meant by the offer for 'your wool'. They were facts which were relevant to establishing what had been sold, and the fact that they came out of pre-contractual negotiations was of no concern.

4.87 A more recent example of a case where evidence obtained during negotiations was admissible is *Bank of Scotland v Dunedin Property Investment Co*.[88] A company raised money by issuing fixed rate loan stock to a bank. In order to protect itself against interest rate fluctuations, the bank entered into a swap contract with a third party. The loan stock deed enabled the company to redeem the stock early, subject to reimbursing the bank for all expenses incurred by it 'in connection with' the stock.

The company gave notice to redeem the stock early. The bank therefore terminated the swap contract and then claimed the (substantial) cost of doing so from the company, on the basis that it was an expense incurred 'in connection with' the stock.

---

[84] [2010] 2 NZLR 444 at [29].
[85] (1859) 1 El & El 997.
[86] [1998] SC 657.
[87] (1859) 1 El & El 977.
[88] 1998 SC 657.

4.88   The court decided that the expense was recoverable by the bank. It was reinforced in its conclusion by reference to evidence of the negotiations between the parties before the loan stock was issued. That evidence established that the company was aware that the bank would borrow money to subscribe for the loan stock and that the bank intended to hedge the transaction; and that, if the loan stock was redeemed early, there would be a cost of an uncertain amount associated with the hedge.

4.89   Lord President Rodger said:[89]

> [T]he rule which excludes evidence of prior communings as an aid to interpretation of a concluded contract is well-established and salutory. The rationale of the rule shows, however, that it has no application when the evidence of the parties' discussions is being considered, not in order to provide a gloss on the terms of the contract, but rather to establish the parties' knowledge of the circumstances with reference to which they used the words in the contract.

4.90   These cases indicate that prior negotiations are relevant to the extent that they identify objective facts which the parties must have had in mind when they entered into the contract.[90] They are certainly consistent with the view that the prohibition on the use of prior negotiations only extends to the subjective aspirations of the parties. But then that was not how it was expressed by Lord Hoffmann in *Chartbrook*. He saw the pragmatic limitation as extending further than the limitation based on principle. It is not at all clear how these issues will be resolved.

4.91   One point has been settled. If the prior negotiations are admissible in accordance with these principles, they will continue to be admissible even if they are made in the course of 'without prejudice' negotiations. The fact that they are without prejudice does not affect their admissibility.[91]

4.92   And it is also clear that prior negotiations continue to be admissible to support a claim for rectification or estoppel by convention.[92] See Principles 9 and 10.

4.93   It is hard to believe that *Chartbrook* is the last word on this matter, even in England.[93] The problem is that, by focusing on the extent of an exclusion from the basic principle that all external evidence should be admitted, we have been diverted from the real question, which is the extent to which external evidence should be admitted in the first place. The pragmatic reasons for restricting the admissibility of prior negotiations which were cited by Lord Hoffmann in *Chartbrook* are exactly the reasons why many commercial lawyers would suggest that there needs to be some general

---

[89]   1998 SC 657 at 665.

[90]   This was the approach of the New Zealand Court of Appeal in *New Zealand Carbon Farming v Mighty River Power* [2015] NZCA 605 at [100].

[91]   *Oceanbulk Shipping & Trading v TMT Asia* [2011] 1 AC 662 at [39–40].

[92]   *Chartbrook v Persimmon Homes* [2009] 1 AC 1101 at [42].

[93]   See the criticism of it by Professor David McLauchlan in '*Chartbrook Ltd v Persimmon Homes Ltd*: Commonsense Principles of Interpretation and Rectification?' (2010) 126 LQR 8.

limitation on the availability of external evidence. The real question is not the extent to which prior negotiations should be excluded, but the circumstances in which external evidence generally should be admitted. This is discussed further below.

M. Deleted Words

In these days of word processors, contracts containing deleted words are less common, but they do surface occasionally. Where they do, the general approach has been to ignore them on the ground that they are part of the negotiations and do not help in interpreting what is left.[94] **4.94**

The courts do, nevertheless, occasionally use deleted words as an aid to interpretation.[95] In *Mopani Copper Mines v Millennium Underwriting*,[96] Christopher Clarke J considered that there were circumstances in which deleted words could be used, and this approach was followed by the Court of Appeal in *Narandas-Girdhar v Bradstock*.[97] Here, the Court of Appeal was prepared to use deleted words to interpret an ambiguity in a contract. Briggs LJ said[98] that: 'if the fact of deletion shows what it is the parties agreed that they did not agree and there is ambiguity in the words that remain, then the deleted provision may be an aid to construction, albeit one that must be used with care.' **4.95**

A convincing argument can be made that the striking out of words from a printed form should be capable of being taken into account in the interpretation of the contract. This was certainly the view of Lord Reid in *Timber Shipping Co v London & Overseas Freighters*.[99] Although he did not have to decide the point in the case, Lord Reid was clearly of the view that a distinction should be drawn between the deletion of words inserted by the draftsman and the deletion of words in a printed form. In the former case, the deletion would be part of the negotiations and would not be admissible in evidence. In the latter case, the words which were struck out would not have been inserted by the parties, and their deletion should be relevant in interpreting the contract. **4.96**

In principle, it is suggested that deleted words can be used in the interpretation process if they are relevant in establishing the objective intention of the parties—but not if they are part of the negotiations leading up to the execution of the contract. **4.97**

---

[94] *Inglis v Buttery* (1878) 3 App Cas 552. See Lewison at 3.04.

[95] For instance, in *Caffin v Aldridge* [1895] 2 QB 648 and in *Mediterranean Salvage & Towage v Seamar Trading & Commerce* [2009] 1 CLC 909 at [38]. See McLauchlan, 'Deleted Words, Prior Negotiations and Contract Interpretation' (2010) 24 NZULR 277.

[96] [2008] 2 All ER (Comm) 976 at [102]–[125].

[97] [2016] EWCA Civ 88.

[98] [2016] EWCA Civ 88 at [20].

[99] [1972] AC 1 at 15–16.

N. Subsequent Conduct

4.98 The purpose of contractual interpretation is to establish the objective intention of the parties when entering into the contract. That needs to be tested at the time the contract is entered into. It must follow, at least as a general proposition, that the background facts which are used to assist in interpreting a contract are limited to those which existed at the time the contract was entered into. What is relevant in interpreting the contract is the background facts at the time it was entered into, not anything which may subsequently happen.[100]

4.99 The principle that subsequent conduct cannot be taken into account in interpreting a contract was determined by the House of Lords in two cases in the 1970s—*James Miller v Whitworth Street Estates*[101] and *Schuler v Wickman Machine Tool Sales*.[102]

4.100 In *James Miller v Whitworth Street Estates*,[103] Lord Reid said:

> [I]t is not legitimate to use as an aid in the construction of the contract anything which the parties said or did after it was made. Otherwise one might have the result that a contract meant one thing the day it was signed, but by reason of subsequent events meant something different a month or a year later.

4.101 In *Gibbons Holdings v Wholesale Distributors*,[104] Tipping J in the Supreme Court of New Zealand criticized Lord Reid's reasoning on the basis that subsequent conduct can be relevant in helping to establish the parties' objective intentions at the time of the contract, not subsequently.[105] Although this is true, it is suggested that Lord Reid is nevertheless correct in the sense that, if subsequent conduct were available, the result could vary, depending on when the question was raised—whether before or after the relevant conduct had taken place.

4.102 In *Schuler v Wickman Machine Tool Sales*,[106] Lord Simon gave two additional reasons why subsequent conduct should not be considered—that it had no greater probative value than prior negotiations, and that it was only really evidence of subjective intentions. It is suggested that neither of those reasons is particularly compelling. Subsequent conduct can be objective evidence of how the parties are carrying out

---

[100] *Wasa International Insurance v Lexington Insurance* [2010] 1 AC at [45]. See Lewison at 3.19.
[101] [1970] AC 583.
[102] [1974] AC 235 by Lord Reid at 252, Lord Morris at 260, Lord Wilberforce at 261–2, Lord Simon at 265–70, and Lord Kilbrandon at 272–3.
[103] [1970] AC 583 at 603.
[104] [2008] 1 NZLR 277.
[105] [2008] 1 NZLR 277 at [59].
[106] [1974] AC 235 at 265–70.

the contract. It is not necessarily concerned with subjective intentions. It is evidence on which a reasonable person might draw to establish the parties' objective intention.

The best justification for the exclusion of subsequent conduct is that a contract has **4.103** an objectively ascertainable meaning when it is entered into, and that to take account of subsequent conduct would result in the possibility of the contract meaning different things at different times.

This continues to be the position in England and in Australia,[107] but not in New **4.104** Zealand. In *Gibbons Holdings v Wholesale Distributors*,[108] four of the five judges in the Supreme Court of New Zealand considered that evidence of subsequent conduct is admissible, although only two of them considered it was relevant on the facts of the case itself.

Tipping J considered that, as a matter of principle, the court should not deprive **4.105** itself of any material which might be helpful in ascertaining the parties' objective intention unless there are sufficiently strong policy reasons to limit it. The purpose of looking at the subsequent conduct is not to find the subjective intentions of the parties, but their objective shared intention. He said that:[109]

> If some mutual or shared post-contract conduct of the parties is objectively capable of shedding light on the meaning they themselves placed on the words in dispute, I consider more is to be gained than lost by allowing the Court to take it into account.

Thomas J[110] took a rather broader approach to the issue:[111] **4.106**

> When the courts approach a fork in the road, and one road leads to a presumed intent based on the meaning of words and the other road leads to the meaning actually intended, the courts must take that road which leads the parties' actual intention.

Although Thomas J's approach is unlikely to find favour in many common law **4.107** jurisdictions because it cuts across the basic principle of objectivity in the law of contract, the approach of Tipping J has more to recommend it. The subsequent conduct of the parties may well provide useful evidence of their shared, objective, intention. But it would result in the possibility of the contract meaning different things at different times and, for that reason, it may find difficulty in gaining acceptance in other common law jurisdictions.

---

[107] *Agricultural and Rural Finance v Gardiner* (2008) 238 CLR 570 at [35].
[108] [2008] 1 NZLR 277.
[109] [2008] 1 NZLR 277 at [53].
[110] [2008] 1 NZLR 277 at [111]–[122].
[111] [2008] 1 NZLR 277 at [97].

4.108 If the subsequent conduct is sufficiently clear, it can be used to show that the parties had subsequently varied the contract.[112] It can also be used as evidence for a claim for estoppel by convention. See Principle 10.

4.109 More controversially, it has been suggested that subsequent conduct can be used to determine whether a charge is a fixed charge or a floating charge.[113] This is an issue relating to characterization, rather than interpretation, of the contract concerned,[114] but the court can only characterize the transaction once it knows what the parties intended. The courts use what happens after the contract is entered into in order to establish what the parties intended. They are therefore concerned with the first stage of the process (interpretation), rather than the second stage (characterization).

4.110 In principle, this is difficult to justify: subsequent conduct is being taken into account to determine the parties' intention. But in practice, it is likely that what the courts are really doing is deciding whether, at the time the transaction was entered into, the parties were likely to comply with the requirements of the relevant clause of the document. If it can be established that, at the time the contract was entered into, it was impracticable to comply with that clause, then the courts are entitled to decide that the parties are unlikely objectively to have intended the clause to have its apparent effect.[115]

O. Third Parties

4.111 The courts are less ready to accept detailed evidence from outside the written contract in circumstances where people are likely to have interests in the contract who were not involved at the time it was entered into. The reason is obvious. If third parties might obtain an interest in the contract, it may not be appropriate for the contract to be interpreted in the light of the facts available to the parties at the time the contract was entered into if the third parties would not have had access to those facts.

4.112 This principle applies to public documents,[116] such as companies' constitutional documents[117] and contracts registered at an asset registry.[118] It also applies to documents which are negotiated, transferred, or assigned in the ordinary course.[119]

---

[112] *Phillip Collins v Davis* [2000] 3 All ER 808 at 822.

[113] *Re Brumark Investments, Agnew v Commissioner of Inland Revenue* [2001] 2 AC 710 at [48]–[49].

[114] See Principle 5, paras 5.83–5.90.

[115] In doing so, they can rely on Principle 7: if the clause as drafted is unworkable in practice, the parties cannot have intended it.

[116] *Opua Ferries v Fullers Bay of Islands* [2003] 3 NZLR 740 at [20].

[117] *Attorney General of Belize v Belize Telecom* [2009] 1 WLR 1988 at [36].

[118] *Cherry Tree Investments v Landmain* [2012] 2 P&CR 10.

[119] *Dairy Containers v Tasman Orient* at [12].

It is also the case where the contract concerned envisages that other people will **4.113** become parties to it in the future. Lord Collins made this point in *Re Sigma Finance*[120] in relation to a security trust deed, which secured a variety of creditors who held different instruments issued at different times and in different circumstances. Lord Collins considered that:[121]

> this is not the type of case where the background or matrix of fact is or ought to be relevant, except in the most generalised way ... Where a security document secures a number of creditors who have advanced funds over a long period it would be quite wrong to take account of circumstances which are not known to all of them. In this type of case it is the wording of the instrument which is paramount.

Even in the case of documents of this kind, background facts are sometimes admit- **4.114** ted as an aid to interpretation. An example is the decision of the Court of Appeal in *Caresse Navigation v Office National de l'Electricité*.[122] Beatson LJ stressed the need for certainty that follows from the negotiable nature of a bill of lading, which may come into the hands of a person in another jurisdiction who has no ready means of ascertaining the terms of the underlying charterparty,[123] but he was nevertheless prepared to hold that the reference in a bill of lading to a 'law and arbitration clause' was a reference to a 'law and jurisdiction' clause because a reading of the associated charterparty would make it clear that that must have been what was meant.

In *BNY Mellon v LBG Capital*,[124] the Supreme Court has recently had to consider **4.115** the extent to which background facts can be used when interpreting transferable bonds. The court split three to two on the interpretation of the clause in question, but it does not seem that they disagreed on the principle of the extent to which the background facts were available.

One of the key questions in the case was the extent to which it was possible to in- **4.116** terpret a transferable instrument in the light of associated documents which were issued at the same time. And, because the instrument was intended (and this was clear from its face) to count as part of the capital of the issuer, the case also raised the question of the extent to which the regulations which prompted it and the regulatory policy of the relevant financial body (in this case the Financial Services Authority) could be taken into account.

In the event, the court was prepared to take account of the general thrust and effect **4.117** of the regulatory material which was published at around the time the security was issued, because the bonds could not be understood without some appreciation of

---

[120] [2010] BCC 40 at [36]–[37].
[121] [2010] BCC 40 at [37].
[122] [2015] QB 366.
[123] [2015] QB 366 at [15].
[124] [2016] 2 Lloyd's Rep 119.

the regulatory policy at the time.[125] But they did not take account of the associated documents issued by the issuer at the same time.[126] The majority decided that these documents were not of any relevance in interpreting the instrument itself, and it is not entirely clear whether, as a matter of principle, they would have refused to admit the evidence in any event.

4.118 Lord Neuberger said[127] that the weight to be given to the background facts must be highly dependent on the facts of the particular case but, where a negotiable instrument is concerned, very considerable circumspection is appropriate before the contents of other documents are taken into account.

4.119 It is suggested that the correct approach is to consider what a reasonable person who acquired the instrument would expect to look at when interpreting it. This depends on the market concerned. If a reasonable purchaser in the market concerned should be aware of certain background facts, then they should be taken into account. If not, then they should not be taken into account. The criterion should be the practice in the market concerned.

4.120 Third parties frequently acquire rights under commercial contracts by assignment or charge. Similar arguments could be applied to these contracts, although these issues have yet to be tested in court.

4.121 In *Mannai Investment Co v Eagle Star Life Assurance Co*,[128] Lord Hoffmann said that:

> There are documents in which the need for certainty is paramount and which admissible background is restricted to avoid the possibility that the same document may have different meanings for different people according to their knowledge of the background.

This suggests a broader reason why the background might be restricted—where the need for certainty is paramount.

4.122 In an article in the Modern Law Review in 2014, Matthew Barber and Rod Thomas said:[129] 'There is an essential conflict between the contextual approach to contractual interpretation and third party reliance on the apparent meaning of contractual documents . . . .' The difficulty in drawing the line in practice between those cases where the background facts are admissible, and those where they are not, rather suggests that the rule itself needs to be reconsidered.

---

[125] [2016] 2 Lloyd's Rep 119 at [33].

[126] [2016] 2 Lloyd's Rep 119 at [34].

[127] [2016] 2 Lloyd's Rep 119 at [30].

[128] [1997] AC 749 at 779.

[129] Barber and Thomas, 'Contractual Interpretation, Registered Documents and Third Party Reliance' (2014) 77 MLR 597 at 617.

P. What Background Facts Should be Admissible?

The problem

In England at least, *ICS* and *Chartbrook* have, in theory, settled the position. All **4.123** background facts are admissible if they go to prove the objective intention of the parties at the time the contract was entered into, but prior negotiations are not generally admissible, and nor is subsequent conduct.

It has been suggested earlier that the problem with the way in which this area of the **4.124** law has developed over the past few years is that it has done so by reference to the scope of an exception to the basic principle concerning background facts, rather than by reference to the scope of the principle itself. Neither of the extreme views (no admissibility/total admissibility) has many adherents. There is a spectrum between these two extremes and, somewhere on that spectrum a line must be drawn. Some would draw it closer to one end of the spectrum and others closer to the other end.

Lord Nicholls, for instance, will always want to widen the available evidence, **4.125** on the basis that it might be useful and that problems can be dealt with by case management. Sir Christopher Staughton will always see the practical problems involved in this and will wish to draw the line more narrowly: 'what the parties must have had in mind' at the time they made the contract. 'But it must still be the immediate context, and not facts in the past, distant or even recent.'[130]

Doherty JA put it mildly when he said, in the Court of Appeal for Ontario in **4.126** *Dumbrell v The Regional Group of Companies*:[131] 'There is some controversy as to how expansively context should be examined for the purposes of contractual interpretation.' This is a conflict which it is difficult to resolve. Where you draw the line is a matter of judgement on which individual judges do have, and will continue to have, different views. Some will place certainty, speed of decision, and cost more at the forefront than others. That has always been the case, and it always will be the case.

But the law does need to be clarified. Over the next few years what is needed is a **4.127** developing jurisprudence of precisely what is encompassed within the expression 'background facts' and what is not—and the extent to which it depends on the nature of the contract concerned.

---

[130] Staughton, 'How Do the Courts Interpret Commercial Contracts?' (1999) 58 CLJ 303 at 308.
[131] (2007) 279 DLR (4th) 201 at [55].

A possible approach

4.128 How might these uncertainties be resolved? In trying to resolve them, it is always important to have in mind the underlying principle of contractual interpretation—that it is concerned with the objective intention of the parties (Principle 1). How can this help to resolve the uncertainty?

4.129 There are two principles which are clear and largely uncontroversial. The first is that the requirement to establish the objective intention of the parties means that their subjective intentions must be excluded. Declarations of subjective intention are not admissible in evidence, and nor is the course of the parties' negotiations in the period running up to the execution of the contract. Some commentators would challenge this approach,[132] but it is generally accepted that this is a necessary consequence of the objective theory of interpretation.

4.130 The second uncontroversial principle is also based on the objective principle: the background facts are limited to those reasonably available to the parties.

4.131 A decision then has to be taken whether subsequent conduct should be taken into account. It is generally agreed that it cannot be taken into account unless it helps to establish the objective intention of the parties at the time the contract is entered into. Some jurisdictions (such as England and Australia) generally prohibit the use of subsequent conduct, even to establish the intention of the parties at the time the contract was entered into. In New Zealand, such evidence is admissible. The real issue here is whether it should be possible for a contract to mean different things at different times. In principle, it is suggested that this is undesirable.

4.132 It is then that the real difficulties manifest themselves. To what extent does the understandable desire to do justice between the parties conflict with three key imperatives of contract law:

(1) the need for certainty in commercial transactions;
(2) the importance of reducing the time and cost of the resolution of commercial disputes;
(3) the protection of third parties who obtain an interest in a commercial contract, whether outright or by way of security.

4.133 The starting point in resolving this problem is to recognize that it is not just concerned with prior negotiations. The focus on the extent to which prior negotiations can be used in interpreting a contract has diverted us from the real question—the extent to which it is commercially sensible to allow too much evidence of the background facts to be available in the interpretation process.

---

[132] Particularly, and eloquently, Lord Nicholls, Justice Thomas, and Professor David McLauchlan.

The question, then, is whether it is possible to find a clear and objective basis for **4.134** establishing what is, and is not, a relevant background fact. As Lord Wilberforce acknowledged in *Reardon Smith Line v Yngvar Hansen-Tangen*,[133] the expression 'surrounding circumstances' is imprecise, and of course this is also true of its synonyms. They can be illustrated, but hardly defined.

But this is such an important question that some attempt should be made to answer **4.135** it. Ideally, there should be one rule for all contracts. Any attempt to apply different rules to different types of contract will only result in confusion.[134] One approach would be to limit background facts by reference to their nature. For instance, the search could be limited to matters such as:

(1) the identity of the parties;
(2) the nature and purpose of the transaction;
(3) the market in which the transaction took place.

These are all broad concepts, and can themselves be interpreted more or less widely. **4.136** But they can nevertheless help in determining which background facts are relevant, particularly if there is kept in mind the necessity to protect the certainty of commercial transactions, the speedy resolution of commercial disputes, and the protection of the interests of third parties.

In practice, it is suggested that the most important background fact in most com- **4.137** mercial transactions is the market in which the transaction took place. If you are interpreting a loan agreement, you need to understand the market norms by which loan agreements are normally negotiated. The same is true of a charterparty, an insurance policy, and any other commercial contract.

Two recent cases can illustrate this point—one in the United Kingdom Supreme **4.138** Court and the other in the New Zealand Supreme Court. In *Firm PI v Zurich Australian Insurance*,[135] the New Zealand Supreme Court had to interpret the terms of an insurance policy. When doing so, they were conscious of the need to place the policy in the context of the way in which the insurance market operated.[136] Similarly, in *Marks and Spencer v BNP Paribas*,[137] the United Kingdom Supreme Court had to consider whether a term should be implied into a commercial lease to allow the apportionment of rent. The court decided that no such term should be implied, and the key determinant of that decision was the understanding in the commercial property market that rent paid in advance is not apportionable unless

---

[133] [1976] 1 WLR 989 at 995–6.
[134] How do you decide which contracts are only likely to involve the parties and which might concern third parties?
[135] [2015] 1 NZLR 432.
[136] [2015] 1 NZLR 432 at [66].
[137] [2016] AC 742. This case is discussed in more detail under Principle 8.

the lease contains an express provision to that effect. It would therefore be contrary to the understanding in the market to imply such a term.[138]

4.139 In *Chartbrook*,[139] the House of Lords recognized the pragmatic necessity of limiting the scope of background facts in an interpretation dispute. What is now needed is to find a way of putting that insight into practice.

---

[138] [2016] AC 742 at [46] and [50].
[139] *Chartbrook v Persimmon Homes* [2009] 1 AC 1101.

Part III

UNDERSTANDING WORDS

Principle 5: Words are nearly always given their ordinary meaning in their context.

Principle 6: If words are ambiguous in their context, they are given the meaning the parties are most likely objectively to have intended.

Principle 7: Very occasionally, it is clear that the parties cannot objectively have intended words they have used to have their ordinary meaning. If so, they are given the meaning which the parties must objectively have intended. The more unreasonable the result, the more unlikely it is that the parties can have intended it.

The purpose of Part II was to establish the materials which are available for the interpretation process. This Part is about what the words used in the contract actually mean. **Pt 3.01**

This sounds as if it should be rather a simple task. The reason it has proved not to be is largely caused by a tension between two different ways of approaching the issue; and it is impossible to understand how contracts are interpreted in practice without appreciating what it is which drives these two approaches. **Pt 3.02**

One approach is simply to give the words used their ordinary meaning. It is expressed in a number of different ways—natural, plain, conventional, commonsense, popular—but the underlying concept is the same. Words are given the meaning which would be understood by reasonable people of the kind who will read the contract concerned.[1] **Pt 3.03**

---

[1] See the approach of Lord Bingham in *The Starsin, Homburg Houtimport v Agrosin* [2004] 1 AC 715 at [45].

Pt 3.04   This school of thought would accept that, in order to do this, it is necessary to read the document as a whole. Most would even recognize the necessity to put the document in the context of the basic background facts which existed at the time—the identity of the parties concerned, the nature of the transaction on which they are embarking, the market in which they are involved. But, having done that, they feel confident that words generally have an ordinary meaning, and it is that meaning which they must be given, unless they are ambiguous.

Pt 3.05   The other approach is to recognize that words do not have an 'ordinary' meaning— they can only have a meaning in context by reference to the parties who wrote them. One of the beauties of the English language is its almost infinite potential for ambiguity, and to pursue an ordinary meaning is to pursue a chimera.

Pt 3.06   Those in the first camp take the view that the parties have written the contract, and the duty of the court is to give effect to what they have written. The result may seem very odd—even totally unreasonable—but that is what they have agreed, and that is what they must be held to. He who lives by the pen, dies by the pen.

Pt 3.07   In the other camp are those who want to make sense of what the parties have written. Surely they cannot have intended a result so unreasonable or absurd? They must have meant something else. And it would be lacking in common humanity not to listen to the cry to temper justice with mercy.

Pt 3.08   At their extremes, these are, of course, caricatures. We none of us fall wholly into one camp or the other. We all have to decide where we draw the line between the two extremes. And, in this respect, judges are no different from the rest of us. Their characters and backgrounds will determine whether they draw the line towards one end of the spectrum or the other.

Pt 3.09   It is also important to appreciate that this debate will always be with us. It is tempting to see contractual interpretation as a slow move from a literal to a purposive approach. Tempting, but wrong.[2] This debate has always existed, and it always will exist. Those who have to decide questions of interpretation will draw their lines in different places. And those of us who need to understand what contracts mean have to understand that.

Pt 3.10   That is what Part III is about. We move from natural meanings in Principle 5 to unnatural meanings in Principle 7, pausing to consider ambiguity in Principle 6.

Pt 3.11   Because interpretation is an art, not a science, we will never always be able to second-guess the judge or the arbitrator. But we will be better prepared for the task if we understand the reasons for these opposing approaches to contractual interpretation.

---

[2] To apply, in a different context, a warning by Lord Bingham about the dangers of implying terms: see *Philips Electronique v British Sky Broadcasting* [1995] EMLR 472 at 482 (discussed in Chapter 8).

5

PRINCIPLE 5: NATURAL MEANINGS

Principle 5: Words are nearly always given their ordinary meaning in their context.

A. Do Words Have an Ordinary Meaning?

The idea that words should be given their 'natural and ordinary meaning' in context **5.01** has a very long pedigree.[1] In recent years, two eminent commercial lawyers—Sir Christopher Staughton and Lord Mustill—have made the point very eloquently.

In *Charter Reinsurance Co v Fagan*,[2] Lord Mustill said: **5.02**

> I believe that most expressions do have a natural meaning, in the sense of their pri-
> mary meaning in ordinary speech…. Subject to [words which have a technical mean-
> ing] … the inquiry will start, and usually finish, by asking what is the ordinary
> meaning of the words used.

Sir Christopher Staughton made the same point even more bluntly in an article in **5.03** the Cambridge Law Journal,[3] when he said:

> [I]n my opinion business men would prefer a general rule that words mean what they
> say in ordinary English, rather than a rule that contracts shall mean what the House
> of Lords, or some of its members, think they ought to mean.

These are powerful sentiments, and they appeal to a broad cross-section of com- **5.04** mercial lawyers.[4] But there is another approach, which tells us that words do not have a meaning which is independent of the persons who use them. Professor David

---

[1] For a recent example of the use of this expression, see the judgment of Lord Bingham in *Bank of Credit and Commerce International v Ali* [2001] 1 AC 251 at [8]. See Lewison, *The Interpretation of Contracts* (6th edn, Sweet & Maxwell, 2015), Chapter 5.

[2] [1997] AC 313 at 384.

[3] Staughton, 'How Do the Courts Interpret Commercial Contracts?' (1999) 58 CLJ 303 at 310. Prefigured in the (dissenting) judgment of Staughton LJ in *Charter Reinsurance Co v Fagan* [1997] AC 313 at 368.

[4] They are, for instance, reflected in the opinion of the Privy Council in *Melanesian Mission Trust Board v Australian Mutual Provident Society* (1997) 74 P&CR 297 at 301 and in Brian Davenport's note in (1999) 115 LQR 11 on *Total Gas Marketing v Arco British* [1998] 2 Lloyd's Rep 209.

McLauchlan has said:[5] 'The truth is that words have no fixed or settled meaning. Rather it is some *person* who gives a meaning to them.' In this he follows Corbin who, in his American textbook *Corbin on Contracts*, referred to the 'great illusion ... that words, either singly or in combination, have a "meaning" that is independent of the persons who use them'.[6]

5.05 This concept was expressed with typical elegance by Oliver Wendell Holmes when, in *Towne v Eisner*,[7] he said:

> A word is not a crystal, transparent and unchanged, it is the skin of a living thought and may vary greatly in colour and context according to the circumstances and the time in which it is used.

5.06 In England, Lord Blackburn made the same point in *River Wear Commissioners v Adamson*:[8] 'the meaning of words varies according to the circumstances with respect to which they were used'. This idea was developed more recently by Lord Hoffmann in two cases in 1997. In *Mannai Investment Co v Eagle Star Life Assurance Co*,[9] he said that 'words do not in themselves refer to anything; it is people who *use* words to refer to things'. And in *Charter Reinsurance Co v Fagan*[10] he said:

> I think that in some cases the notion of words having a natural meaning is not a very helpful one. Because the meaning of words is so sensitive to syntax and context, the natural meaning of words in one sentence may be quite unnatural in another.

5.07 How do you reconcile the seemingly irreconcilable? The answer may lie in the fact that one approach (that of David McLauchlan, Oliver Wendell Holmes, and Lord Hoffmann) is concerned primarily with theory, whereas the other (that of Lord Mustill and Sir Christopher Staughton) finds its roots in pragmatism and experience. It may be theoretically correct that a word can only have a meaning in the context of background facts, but most words are pretty easy to understand in the context of the few words which surround them. But then again there are some words which can only sensibly be given a meaning if one looks more broadly, to the document as a whole and to the surrounding facts.

5.08 Slade J made this point in *Earl of Lonsdale v Attorney-General*:[11]

> Of many, perhaps the majority, of words used by English speaking people there can be little doubt as to the ordinary meaning ... To take an example at random, the court

---

[5] McLauchlan, 'Contract Interpretation: What Is It About?' (2009) 31(1) Sydney Law Review 5, in part 4. Emphasis in the original.

[6] Quoted by McLauchlan in 'Plain Meaning and Commercial Construction: Has Australia adopted the *ICS* principles?' (2009) 25 JCL 7 at 9. And see Carter at 11.18–11.21.

[7] (1918) 245 US 418 at 425.

[8] (1877) 2 App Cas 743 at 763.

[9] [1997] AC 749 at 778.

[10] [1997] AC 313 at 391.

[11] [1982] 1 WLR 887 at 901–2.

would not, I conceive, find much difficulty in attaching a literal or primary meaning to the word 'elephant', if it found it in a written instrument. In contrast, however, some English words and phrases fall into a second, quite different category. There are words and phrases which are readily capable of bearing two or more alternative meanings ...

The second category can contain words which seem straightforward—for instance, **5.09** 'summer': a period, the starting point and length of which is very much dependent on its context.

B. The Context

It is certainly the case that words which appear on their face clearly to mean one **5.10** thing can, in context, be shown to mean something quite different.

An example is *The Aragon*.[12] A charterparty only allowed the charterer to use the **5.11** vessel within 'USA East of Panama Canal'. The question at issue was whether the US Gulf was within that limit. By referring to an atlas, it transpired that the US Gulf is in fact to the west of the meridian of longitude on which the Panama Canal stands. On the face of it, therefore, a trip to the US Gulf would be outside the charterer's limits. In fact, Donaldson J decided, and the Court of Appeal agreed, that the US Gulf was within the limits. The purpose of the charter was to carry out a round trip from Europe to the east coast of North America and then back. In this context, what was meant by the words 'USA East of Panama Canal' was a port in the United States of America which did not entail going through the Panama Canal. The meaning of the words could only properly be understood in context.

What is interesting about this case is that the court was able to interpret the words **5.12** concerned in context without trawling through a great deal of background information. The relevant context was that the voyage started in Europe—to the east of the US Gulf. Once that was understood, the contextual meaning of the words 'East of Panama Canal'—and the reason why they had been used—became clear. The use of context does not necessarily require the court to take into account a great deal of information in addition to the contract itself.

C. The Context at the Time of the Contract

The purpose of contractual interpretation is to determine the objective intention of **5.13** the parties. In principle, this must be established at the time the contract is entered into. What is important is to establish what their intention was at that time, in the light of the background facts which existed at that time.[13]

---

[12] *Segovia Compagnia Naviera v R Pagnan & Fratelli* [1977] 1 Lloyd's Rep 343.
[13] See Lewison at 5.15.

5.14 This point is illustrated by the decision of the Supreme Court in *Lloyds TSB Foundation for Scotland v Lloyds Banking Group*.[14] It concerned the interpretation of an undertaking by Lloyds Bank to a charitable foundation which it had set up. Lloyds Bank had undertaken in a Deed to pay to the Foundation a certain percentage of 'the Pre-Tax Profits (after deduction of Pre-Tax Losses)' for each relevant accounting reference period. 'Pre-Tax Profits' and 'Pre-Tax Losses' were defined to mean:

> in relation to any Accounting Reference Period … respectively the 'group profit before taxation' and the 'group loss before taxation' (as the case may be) shown in the Audited Accounts for [the relevant period].

5.15 When the Deed was entered into, profits could only lawfully be included in a profit and loss account once they had been realized. But the law was subsequently changed and, following an acquisition by Lloyds Bank, its consolidated accounts required it to state a 'gain on acquisition' of over £11bn, although this gain was neither distributable nor taxable. As a result, in the consolidated accounts of the bank, a loss of £10bn was converted into a profit of £1bn.

5.16 The Foundation argued that the 'group profit before taxation' in the Audited Accounts was, as a result, £1bn, and that was therefore the figure by reference to which the payment should be made.

5.17 The Supreme Court decided that this was not what the Deed meant. It was not sufficient simply to read off the figure in the relevant line in the Audited Accounts. The Deed had to be read against the background facts existing at the time—which were that it was 'unthinkable'[15] that unrealized profits or losses would be taken into account. The change was wholly outside the parties' original contemplation, and the question was therefore how the language best operated in fundamentally changed and entirely unforeseen circumstances. The court decided that the answer was evident. It operated best, and quite naturally, by ignoring the unrealized gain on acquisition and treating the loss which existed apart from that as the relevant figure for the purpose of the Deed.[16]

5.18 This case demonstrates two things—first, that the document has to be read in the context of its background facts; and second, that the relevant background facts are those which existed at the time the document was entered into. In the light of the large number of long-term contracts which exist, this is an important principle.

---

[14] [2013] 1 WLR 366.

[15] [2013] 1 WLR 366 at [1].

[16] [2013] 1 WLR 366 at [22]–[23].

D. The Ordinary Meaning in Context, However Odd the Result

The basic principle, therefore, is that words will be given their ordinary meaning in **5.19** context. And this is the case, however odd the result may be. This can be illustrated by three cases:

(1) *William Hare v Shepherd Construction*[17] in the Court of Appeal;
(2) *Enviroco v Farstad Supply*[18] in the Court of Appeal;
(3) *Fitzhugh v Fitzhugh*[19] in the Court of Appeal.

In *William Hare v Shepherd Construction*,[20] there was a dispute about a 'pay when **5.20** paid' clause in a construction sub-contract. An amount of money was due from the head contractor to the sub-contractor, but the head contractor denied liability on the basis of a clause in the sub-contract which said that if the employer was 'insolvent', the head contractor was not obliged to pay the sub-contractor unless the head contractor had received payment from the employer.

The employer had gone into administration. The head contractor said that, be- **5.21** cause the employer was now insolvent, the head contractor was not liable to pay the sub-contractor until it had been paid itself. The sub-contractor argued that the 'pay when paid' clause did not apply because the employer's administration did not amount to 'insolvency' for the purpose of the clause. That clause defined insolvency to include 'the making of an administration order' against the employer, but did not, on the face of it, cover a case where the employer had gone into administration by filing documents with the court, rather than by applying for an administration order—which is what had happened in this case.

The head contractor argued that the parties cannot have intended an administra- **5.22** tion to amount to 'insolvency' only if an administration order was made. It would make no commercial sense. It pointed to the fact that practically all administrations are entered into by the filing of documents, rather than by the making of a court order. So administration would very rarely trigger the clause if this is what it meant.

The Court of Appeal had no truck with this approach. The clause required an ad- **5.23** ministration order to be made. An administration order had not been made. And that was the end of it.

---

[17] [2010] All ER (D) 168 (Mar).
[18] [2011] 1 WLR 921.
[19] [2012] 2 P&CR 14.
[20] [2010] All ER (D) 168 (Mar).

5.24   The second example is *Enviroco v Farstad Supply*.[21] This case involved a charterparty under which the owner was obliged to indemnify the charterer and its 'affiliates' in respect of certain claims. The expression 'affiliate' was defined as including any 'subsidiary' within the meaning of the Companies Act 1985.

5.25   The charterer claimed an indemnity against the owner in respect of a company which would, in normal commercial parlance, be understood as being a subsidiary. But, because it had transferred the shares in the subsidiary to a bank as security for a loan, it did not technically comply with the definition of 'subsidiary' in the companies legislation.

5.26   The charterer argued that the parties must have intended the word 'subsidiary' to be given a normal commercial meaning, but the House of Lords held that the parties had used the definition in the companies legislation and since, for technical reasons, it did not apply, the company was not a subsidiary for the purpose of the charterparty.

5.27   The third example is *Fitzhugh v Fitzhugh*.[22] This was a family dispute. Harry and Anthony were brothers and were the surviving administrators of the estate of their late father. They granted a licence to Anthony and his partner Karen to use various farm outbuildings and fields in consideration for an annual licence fee of £1.

5.28   The licence was a short document. It defined the 'Licensor' to mean Harry and Anthony, and the 'Licensee' to mean Anthony and Karen. Under clause 4(b), the licence immediately terminated if: 'the Licensee commits any grave or persistent breaches of this Licence and the Licensor having given written notice to the Licensee of such breach or breaches the Licensee fails ... to rectify such breaches ....'

5.29   Anthony and Karen failed to pay the annual licence fee of £1 for seven years. Solicitors acting for Harry served a notice on Anthony and Karen requiring them to remedy those persistent breaches by paying the arrears of £7. Anthony and Karen failed to do so. Harry therefore contended that the licence had terminated under clause 4(b). Anthony argued that the notice was not a valid notice under clause 4(b) because that could only have been given by both Harry and Anthony as the 'Licensor'.

5.30   Morgan J decided that the notice had validly been given. Although, on the face of it, the 'Licensor' meant both Harry and Anthony, this would produce a curious result under clause 4(b) because Anthony, as a joint Licensee, would not willingly join in the giving of the notice. The solution was therefore to interpret the reference

---

[21]   [2011] 1 WLR 921.
[22]   [2012] 2 P&CR 14.

to 'Licensor' in clause 4(b) as referring to all those persons who together were the Licensor apart from any person who was also a Licensee.

The Court of Appeal disagreed. They held that the notice was invalid because it had **5.31** not been given by both Harry and Anthony as the 'Licensor'. The contract defined 'Licensor' as being Harry and Anthony, and that was clearly the case in other clauses of the licence. It would be improbable that, in a short, simple and professionally drawn document, the expression 'Licensor' was intended to have one meaning in clause 4(b) and another meaning in the rest of the document.[23]

The Court of Appeal accepted that this would give rise to practical difficulties, and **5.32** perhaps unwarranted expense, but it would not render clause 4(b) unworkable.[24] The words meant what they said.

There are plenty of cases in which the courts have given words their ordinary mean- **5.33** ing, even though the result seems curious in a commercial context. But there are also cases where the courts have refused to do so. The circumstances in which this is done are the subject of Principle 7, which deals with unnatural meanings.

E. Definitions Clauses

Most commercial contracts contain definitions clauses. In major transactions, there **5.34** is sometimes a separate document which contains the definitions for all the transaction documents. Where definitions clauses are used, the defined term is the ordinary meaning which the court will apply.[25] That is clear from the three cases which have just been discussed—*William Hare v Shepherd Construction*[26], *Enviroco v Farstad Supply*,[27] and *Fitzhugh v Fitzhugh*.[28]

Definitions clauses are sometimes expressly limited. They will sometimes say that **5.35** the definitions apply 'unless the context requires otherwise'. This requires the person interpreting the document to decide whether the defined meaning cannot have been intended to apply in the particular circumstances concerned. Even more un-certain, although less common these days, are definitions clauses which only apply 'where the context so admits'. There is much to be said for the draftsman having the courage of his or her convictions and avoiding the use of either of these expressions.

---

[23] [2012] 2 P&CR 14 at [20].

[24] [2012] 2 P&CR 14 at [21]. For a criticism of the decision, see McLauchlan, 'The Lingering Confusion and Uncertainty in the Law of Contract Interpretation' [2015] LMCLQ 406 at 432–4.

[25] See Lewison at 5.11. Unless Principle 7 applies: see *The Alexandros T, Starlight Shipping v Allianz Marine and Aviation* [2014] 2 CLC 503, discussed under Principle 7 at paras 7.135–7.137.

[26] [2010] All ER (D) 168 (Mar).

[27] [2011] 1 WLR 921.

[28] [2012] 2 P&CR 14.

F. Private Dictionaries

5.36 David McLauchlan has argued that the parties should also be free to have their own private agreement as to the meaning of the words they have used. So the words can say one thing, but the parties actually mean something else.[29] He cites with approval an illustration contained in Article 212 of the United States Restatement (2nd) of Contracts:

> A and B are engaged in buying and selling shares of stock from each other, and agree orally to conceal the nature of their dealings by using the word 'sell' to mean 'buy' and using the word 'buy' to mean 'sell'. A sends a written offer to B to 'sell' certain shares, and B accepts. The parties are bound in accordance with the oral agreement.

5.37 There is no doubt that this approach gives effect to the actual agreement of the parties. The problem with it is that it cuts across the basic objective approach of English law. What is important is what a reasonable person would regard the parties to have agreed, rather than what they have actually agreed. If both parties are in agreement, and no third party is involved, there is no reason why they should not abide by their actual agreement, rather than what they have written. The courts will only become involved if the parties disagree or a third party becomes involved. In such a case, should the actual agreement of the parties prevail?

5.38 If a third party is involved, the parties will not be allowed to say anything other than what the document says—because otherwise the document would be a sham.[30]

5.39 But what if no third party is involved? Should the objective nature of the contractual arrangement be tempered by a degree of subjectivity? The issues involved are illustrated by the *Karen Oltmann*.[31] A time charterparty allowed the charterers to redeliver the vessel 'after 12 months trading'. The issue was whether the charterers could only exercise the option to redeliver at the end of the twelve-month period, or whether they could do so at any time after the first twelve months of the charterparty. Kerr J decided that the word 'after' was ambiguous. It could either mean 'on the expiry of' or 'at any time after the expiry of'. And in order to resolve the ambiguity, he looked at the prior negotiations of the parties, which showed that the parties had agreed that the charterer would only be entitled to redeliver on the expiry of the twelve-month period.

5.40 In *Chartbrook v Persimmon Homes*,[32] Lord Hoffmann disapproved of the reasoning in the *Karen Oltmann* on the basis that that prior negotiations should not be used

---

[29] McLauchlan, 'Contract Interpretation: What Is It About?' (2009) 31(1) Sydney Law Review 5, in part 4. And see Lewison at 5.10.

[30] See Chapter 2, paras 2.36–2.38.

[31] *Partenreederei MS Karen Oltmann v Scarsdale Shipping Co* [1976] 2 Lloyd's Rep 708.

[32] [2009] 1 AC 1101 at [43]–[47].

as part of the background facts in interpreting a contract.[33] But he did consider that rectification or estoppel by convention might have been an alternative basis on which the case could have been decided in the same way. If the parties had proceeded on a common assumption about what the charterparty meant, it might have been unjust to allow them to go back on that assumption.[34]

It can be argued that this is an artificial approach to the issue, and that there is **5.41** little point in denying the use of the prior negotiations for the purpose of interpretation, if they are then to be allowed in through the back door of estoppel by convention.[35] Indeed, if the parties had reached agreement on what the words meant, it would be more appropriate to give effect to it by a collateral contract than an estoppel. These are cogent arguments, but there are two answers to them. In the first place, it is a good discipline to require clear proof of the parties' assumption as to meaning—and this is more likely to be achieved if the claimant has to prove an estoppel by convention or a collateral contract. And, second, an estoppel by convention or collateral contract is personal to the parties, and cannot affect third parties. In the case of contracts which are likely to be assigned (and this is true of many commercial contracts), it would not be appropriate for a third party to be adversely affected by a side agreement or assumption between the parties.

In summary, a side agreement or a common assumption between the parties as to **5.42** the meaning of the contract should not affect the interpretation of the contract. But, if it can be proved that a side agreement or a common assumption do exist, then they can take effect between the parties as a collateral contract or as an estoppel by convention, respectively. But neither can affect third parties.

G. Technical Terms

Contracts sometimes contain technical terms. They may also contain terms which **5.43** have a specialized legal meaning (in other words, 'legal jargon').

There is a presumption that, if the parties use such words, they are using them **5.44** in their technical sense.[36] So, for instance, in *Infiniteland v Artisan*,[37] the expression 'actual knowledge' was held to have its conventional legal meaning, as was

---

[33] Prior negotiations are discussed under Principle 4, paras 4.69–4.91.
[34] Rectification is the subject of Principle 9. Estoppel by convention is the subject of Principle 10.
[35] McLauchlan, 'Common Intention and Contract Interpretation' [2011] LMCLQ 30.
[36] See Lewison at 5.08; McMeel, *The Construction of Contracts* (2nd edn, Oxford University Press, 2011), Chapter 13.
[37] [2006] 1 BCLC 632 at [82] (Chadwick LJ) and [87]–[88] (Carnwath LJ); Pill LJ dissented ([89]–[94]).

'licence' in *IDC Group v Clark*.[38] In *Lloyds TSB Bank v Clarke*,[39] the expression 'sub-participation agreement' was given its conventional meaning in the market in which it was used. This will particularly be the case where the draftsman appears to have used legal or technical words intentionally.

5.45 But this is only a presumption. It may be clear from the contract as a whole and the context that the draftsman is not using the word in its technical sense. This was the case in *Schuler v Wickman Machine Tool Sales*.[40] In a long-term contract, one clause provided that it was a 'condition' of the agreement that one of the parties send its representatives to visit the six largest United Kingdom motor manufacturers at least once in every six weeks. No other clause of the agreement was described as a condition. One of the parties argued that the expression 'condition' was used in its technical legal meaning of a provision, any breach of which would give the innocent party the option to terminate the agreement. The House of Lords decided that it could not have been intended that any minor breach of an undertaking of this kind could have been intended to give the other party the ability to terminate the contract.

5.46 The best that can be said is that, where technical terms or legal jargon are used in a contract, the starting point is that the parties are likely to have used them in their technical or legal sense, but the context may indicate otherwise.

H. Common Expressions

5.47 Some expressions are used frequently in contracts and have, over time, been the subject of analysis in a number of cases. Examples include: 'best endeavours' and 'reasonable endeavours',[41] and 'consequential loss'.[42] The cases describe the sorts of issues which arise when these words are used and attempt to guide the reader as to the meaning of the clause.

5.48 To a certain extent, these glosses on the words can be useful, but they cannot be taken too far. Such words, like any others, take their colour from their context, and previous judicial pronouncements on their meaning are at best presumptions as to the meaning the parties are likely to have intended—particularly in cases where the contract has been drafted by a lawyer, and the lawyer can be taken to have written the contract with knowledge of the cases concerned.

---

[38] [1992] 2 EGLR 187.
[39] [2002] 2 All ER (Comm) 992 at [15].
[40] [1974] AC 235.
[41] See, for instance, *Rhodia International v Huntsman International* [2007] ICLC 59 and *Jet2.com v Blackpool Airport* [2012] 1 CLC 605.
[42] See, for instance, *Hotel Services v Hilton International Hotels* [2002] 1 All ER (Comm) 750.

Lord Morris made the point in *Schuler v Wickman Machine Tool Sales*,[43] when **5.49**
he said:

> If it is correct to say, as I think it is, that where there are problems of the construction
> of an agreement the intention of the parties to it may be collected from the terms
> of their agreement and from the subject matter to which it relates, then I doubt
> whether, save insofar as guidance on principle is found, it is of much value (although
> it may be of much interest) to consider how courts have interpreted various differing
> words in various differing contracts. Nor is it of value to express either agreement or
> disagreement with the conclusions reached in particular cases.

This point has recently been reiterated by a number of experienced commercial **5.50**
judges. In *Transocean Drilling v Providence Resources*,[44] Moore-Bick LJ had to consider the cases concerning the meaning of 'consequential loss'. He said:[45] 'It is ques-
tionable whether some of [these cases] would be decided in the same way today,
when courts are more willing to recognise that words take their meaning from their
particular context and that the same word or phrase may mean different things in
different documents.' In *Khanty-Mansiysk Recoveries v Forsters*,[46] Sir Bernard Eder
considered that: 'reference to earlier authorities as to the meaning of a particular
word or phrase is often unhelpful and sometimes dangerous ...'. A similar point
has recently been made by the Supreme Court of Ireland in *Reid v Health Service
Executive*.[47]

I. Standard Form Contracts

The approach is different when it comes to standard form contracts—which are quite **5.51**
common in commercial and financial transactions.[48] Printed forms of contract are
less common than they used to be, but they have been replaced by standard forms of
contract, which can be downloaded and then used as a starting point for individual
transactions. Standard forms have been used in commercial transactions for a very
long time, as anyone dealing with charterparties, construction, or conveyancing will
be aware. They have now become increasingly important in financial transactions—
for instance, ISDA (International Swaps and Derivatives Association) documentation in relation to swaps and LMA (Loan Market Association) documentation in
relation to loans.

---

[43] [1974] AC 235 at 256. And see the typically forthright comments of Sir George Jessel MR
in *Aspden v Seddon* (1874) LR 10 Ch App 394 at 396n–399n; and Carter, *The Construction of
Commercial Contracts* (Hart, 2013) at 13.09.
[44] [2016] 2 Lloyd's Rep 51.
[45] [2016] 2 Lloyd's Rep 51 at [15].
[46] [2016] EWHC 522 (Comm) at [40].
[47] [2016] IESC 8 at [21].
[48] See Carter at 13.12–13.15.

5.52   The importance of these standard forms is that they promote uniformity of approach, and therefore consistency and certainty in the markets concerned. Lord Diplock made this point, in relation to charterparties, in *Federal Commerce and Navigation Co v Tradax Export*,[49] when he said that standard clauses:

> become the subject of exegesis by the courts so that the way in which they will apply to the adventure contemplated by the charterparty will be understood in the same sense by both the parties when they are negotiating its terms and carrying them out. It is no part of the function of a court of justice to dictate to charterers and shipowners the terms of the contracts into which they ought to enter on the freight market; but it is an important function of a court … to provide them with legal certainty at the negotiation stage as to what it is that they are agreeing to.

5.53   Lord Diplock elaborated on this point in *The Nema*: [50]

> It is only if parties to commercial contracts can rely upon a uniform construction being given to standard terms that they can prudently incorporate them in their contracts without the need for detailed negotiation or discussion.

5.54   What is true of the freight market is equally true of the swaps market and the loan market. Litigation over particular provisions of the ISDA documentation is important to everyone in that market because the determination of what the words mean in the standard form is expected to apply across the board to all cases in which that form is used.[51] The parties are assumed to have used the standard form on the basis of judicial explanations of the meaning of its words, and there is therefore a presumption that the words should be given the same meaning in all cases.[52] The great benefit of this approach is the necessary certainty it provides in commercial transactions.

5.55   This is only a presumption. In an appropriate case, it can be displaced by evidence that, in context, the words had a different meaning.[53] But it is a strong presumption, for the reasons discussed above.

J. Canons of Construction

5.56   Lawyers are brought up on canons of construction—often expressed in Latin. They lay down rules as to how words are to be interpreted. Common examples include:

---

[49] [1978] AC 1 at 8.

[50] *Pioneer Shipping v BTP Tioxide* [1982] AC 724 at 737.

[51] Hence the importance to the market of the judgments of the Court of Appeal in *Lomas v JFB Firth Rixson* [2012] 1 CLC 713 and in *Re Lehman Brothers International (Europe)* [2013] EWCA Civ 188.

[52] See the approach of Lord Hoffmann in *Beaufort Developments (NI) v Gilbert-Ash (NI)* [1999] 1 AC 266.

[53] See the discussion by Palmer J in the New South Wales Supreme Court in *Brooks v NSW Grains Board* [2002] NSWSC 1049 at [32]–[40].

- *contra proferentem*: if a person puts forward a document, it is to be construed strictly against him (this is discussed under Principle 6, paras 6.43–6.51);
- *eiusdem generis*: if a list of things of the same class is followed by general words, the general words will be interpreted in a limited way, by reference to the class (this is discussed at paras 5.71–5.82);
- *expressio unius est exclusio alterius*: if some items in a class are expressly provided for, other items of that class are excluded and cannot, therefore, be implied.[54]

How important are these canons of construction today?[55] The simple answer is: not **5.57** very important at all. It is generally accepted that they are at best guidelines, not rules to be slavishly followed. But there is still a tendency for lawyers to cling to them for support, rather like a plank in a shipwreck (*tabula in naufragio*). Perhaps this is because lawyers like to feel that they are deciding matters of interpretation on the basis of sound legal principle, rather than simply by intuition. But, whatever the reason, they are still frequently pleaded in aid in interpretation cases.

An important recent example is *Bank of Credit and Commerce International v Ali*.[56] It **5.58** concerned a different canon of construction—how to interpret a release. Employees of the bank had been made redundant and, in consideration of a payment by the bank, they entered into a release of 'all and any claims … of whatsoever nature that exist or may exist' against the bank except pension claims. The bank later went into liquidation and it transpired that it had been run fraudulently. The employees brought a claim against the bank on the basis that this had damaged their employment prospects. Did the release preclude the claim?

The House of Lords held that the release did not cover the claim. Some members **5.59** of the House of Lords relied on what Lord Bingham described as 'a long and … salutary line of authority … that, in the absence of clear language, the court will be very slow to infer that a party intended to surrender rights and claims of which he was unaware and could not have been aware'.[57] He described it not as 'a rule of law' but as 'a cautionary principle'.[58]

Other members of the House of Lords found this less helpful. In the words of Lord **5.60** Nicholls:[59] 'part of the object was that the release should extend to any claims which might later come to light. The parties wanted to achieve finality.' He decided in favour of the employees on a different ground.

---

[54] *Miller v Emcer Products* [1956] Ch 304. See Lewison at 7.06; McMeel at 8.26–8.33. Implied terms are discussed under Principle 8.

[55] See Lewison at 2.09 and Chapter 7.

[56] [2002] 1 AC 251.

[57] [2002] 1 AC 251 at [10].

[58] [2002] 1 AC 251 at [17].

[59] [2002] 1 AC 251 at [27].

5.61 What is interesting about this case is that a line of old cases was dredged up and dissected by the House of Lords with a view to deciding what the release meant.

5.62 Lord Hoffmann, who dissented in the case, found this reference to old authority perplexing. He said:[60]

> If interpretation is the quest to discover what a reasonable man would have understood specific parties to have meant by the use of specific language in a specific situation at a specific time and place, how can that be affected by authority? How can the question of what a reasonable man in 1990 would have thought the bank and [the employee] meant by using the language of an Acas form be answered by examining what Lord Keeper Henley said in 1758 …?

5.63 He continued:[61]

> The disappearance of artificial rules for the construction of exemption clauses seems to me in accordance with the general trend in matters of construction, which has been to try to assimilate judicial techniques of construction to those which would be used by a reasonable speaker of the language in the interpretation of any serious utterance in ordinary life. In *Investors Compensation Scheme Ltd v West Bromwich Building Society* [1998] 1 WLR 896, 912, I said with the concurrence of three other members of the House: 'Almost all the old intellectual baggage of "legal" interpretation has been discarded'. But if [counsel's] submissions on the rules of construction are accepted, a substantial piece of baggage will have been retrieved. Lord Keeper Henley's ghost … will have struck back. I think it would be an unfortunate retreat into formalism if the outcome of this case were to require employers using the services of Acas to add verbiage to the form of release in order to obtain the comprehensiveness which it is obviously intended to achieve.

5.64 Although Lord Hoffmann was in the minority in this case, it is hard to disagree with the principle that words used today in one context cannot be affected by the way in which the same words were used two hundred years ago (or even yesterday) in a different context. The risk in using these canons of construction is that the interpreter will make decisions by rote—following a formula—and will, as a result, take his eye off the ball—which is what the words mean in their particular context.

5.65 At best, canons of construction can be seen as commonsense starting points in determining what the parties are likely to have meant. They are not an alternative to reading the words in context.

5.66 An example of the problems which can occur by relying too heavily on canons of construction is *JRTT v Haycraft*.[62] A sold his shares in a company to B. The contract of sale gave A an option to repurchase the shares, which he exercised. The option agreement provided that completion of the option should take place on a particular

---

[60] [2002] 1 AC 251 at [51].
[61] [2002] 1 AC 251 at [62].
[62] [1993] BCLC 401.

date, which was defined as the 'Option Completion Date'. In fact, completion did not take place then because A was unable to pay the option price. B did not treat this as a repudiation of the agreement and sought completion of the agreement.

Clause 8.5 of the agreement provided that: **5.67**

'All rights attaching to the Shares shall on the Option Completion Date accrue to [A]' and that 'following the Option Completion Date [B] shall ... exercise all voting and other rights in respect of the Shares at the direction of [A]'.

A argued that the Option Completion Date had now occurred, and that he was **5.68** therefore entitled to have the shares voted in accordance with his directions. B accepted that the Option Completion Date had occurred, but relied on a canon of construction. He argued that there was a presumption that it was not the intention of the parties that either should be entitled to rely on his own breach in order to obtain a benefit and therefore that B should not be deprived of his right to vote the shares as a result of A's default.

Chadwick J accepted B's contention and decided that, as a matter of construc- **5.69** tion, A was not entitled to the voting rights. He should not benefit from his own wrongdoing.

The problem in this case was that the expression 'Option Completion Date' was the **5.70** date on which completion was to occur. But the same definition was then used in clause 8.5, on the assumption that this would also be the date on which completion did actually occur. So, in other words, there was a (pretty elementary) drafting error. It is difficult to see how it was possible to apply a presumption that a party cannot take advantage of its own wrong to override the clear wording of clause 8.5.[63]

K. *Eiusdem Generis*

Where a list of things of the same class is followed by general words, the general **5.71** words may be interpreted as being limited to members of that class.[64] There is still life in the *eiusdem generis* principle, even after Lord Hoffmann's criticism of 'intellectual baggage' in *Investors Compensation Scheme v West Bromwich Building Society*.[65]

Its purpose is to 'read down' general words. If there is a list of things, followed by **5.72** general words, the general words will be read in the context of the list. That may reflect an assumption that the parties have used the general words in the light of the previous ones, and that they intended them to be restricted accordingly. But what it fails to recognize is that the parties often use general words with the very purpose

---

[63] Unless Principle 7 applies.
[64] See Lewison at 7.13.
[65] [1998] 1 WLR 896 at 912.

of expanding the scope of their more specific words, and that to limit them defeats the object of the exercise. The parties might equally well have intended the words to be a catch-all. For every judge who finds the canon useful,[66] there is another who is wary of it.[67]

5.73 The latter approach is exemplified by the judgment of Devlin J in *Chandris v Isbrandtsen-Moller Co*,[68] when he said:

> A rule of construction cannot be more than a guide to enable the court to arrive at the true meaning of the parties. The *ejusdem generis* rule means that there is implied into the language which the parties have used words of restriction which are not there. It cannot be right to approach a document with the presumption that there should be such an implication. To apply the rule automatically in that way would be to make it the master and not the servant of the purpose for which it was designed—namely, to ascertain the meaning of the parties from the words they have used ... The so-called rule is, in short, really only a recognition of the fact that parties with their minds concerned with the particular objects about which they are contracting are apt to use words, phrases or clauses which, taken literally, are wider than they intend.

5.74 Fry LJ made a similar comment in *Earl of Jersey v Neath*,[69] when he wryly observed that the *eiusdem generis* principle: 'has often been urged for the sake of giving not the true effect to the contracts of parties, but a narrower effect than they were intended to have'.

5.75 The artificiality of the rule can also be seen from the fact that the addition of the word 'whatsoever' after the general words generally means that the presumption will not apply. As Devlin J said in *Chandris v Isbrandtsen-Moller Co*:[70]

> Legal draftsmen are all familiar with the existence of the rule, and familiar too with the proper signals to hoist if they do not want it to apply. Phrases such as 'whether or not similar to the foregoing' and 'without prejudice to the generality of the foregoing' are often employed in legal draftmanship; and if the draftsman has read the report of *Larsen v Sylvester & Co*,[71] he will know that the addition of 'whatsoever' generally serves the same purpose. Commercial draftsmen are not usually taught these rules.

5.76 As Lord Devlin illustrates, it is easy enough to get round the rule. Even more sensible for a draftsman is to start with the general principle and then to illustrate it by examples. If that is done, the rule can have no application at all. There is no list followed by general words. There are general words followed by a list of examples.

---

[66] Grose J in *Cosco Bulk Carrier Co v Team Up Owning Co* [2010] 1 CLC 919.
[67] Devlin J in *Chandris v Isbrandtsen-Moller Co* [1951] 1 KB 240.
[68] [1951] 1 KB 240 at 244.
[69] (1889) 22 QBD 555 at 566.
[70] [1951] 1 KB 240 at 245.
[71] [1908] AC 295.

Some judges do apply the *eiusdem generis* rule, and others do not. The difference in **5.77** approach can be seen by contrasting two cases—*Cosco Bulk Carrier Co v Team-Up Owning Co*[72] and *Chandris v Isbrandtsen-Moller Co*.[73]

In *Cosco Bulk Carrier Co v Team-Up Owning Co*,[74] a charterparty provided that: **5.78**

> in the event of a loss of time from default and/or deficiency in men including strike of Officers and/or crew or deficiency of … stores, fire, breakdown or damages to hull, machinery or equipment, grounding, detention by average accidents to ship or cargo, dry-docking for the purpose of examination or painting bottom, or by any other cause preventing the full working of the vessel, the payment of hire shall cease for the time thereby lost …

The vessel was seized by Somali pirates and the question was whether the seizure fell **5.79** within the words 'any other cause' in this clause. Grose J held that it did not. If it had said 'any other cause whatsoever' then it would have done. But since it did not, the seizure by Somali pirates was outside the contemplation of the clause.

Chandris v Isbrandtsen-Moller Co[75] was also a charterparty case. Here, the question **5.80** was whether the words 'acids, explosives, arms, ammunition or other dangerous cargo' included turpentine. In other words, was turpentine a 'dangerous cargo', even if it was not of the same kind as acids, explosives, arms, and ammunition? Devlin J decided that it was. He found the *eiusdem generis* rule of no value in reaching his conclusion: 'It seems to me that the only reason why the owner is objecting to acids, explosives, arms or ammunition is because they are dangerous; and that being so he may be presumed to have the same objection to all other dangerous cargo.'[76]

In the light of contrasting cases like these, it is difficult to be definitive about the **5.81** *eiusdem generis* rule but, whether or not it runs contrary to the more commercial approach to interpretation favoured in the Supreme Court, there is no doubt that it is still being used in the Commercial Court.

Perhaps, over time, judges will feel more confident about the nature of the interpre- **5.82** tation process, and will no longer feel the need for these props.

L. Distinguishing Interpretation from Categorization

It is important to distinguish between the interpretation of a contract and its cat- **5.83** egorization. It is sometimes necessary to decide whether a particular contracts falls within one legal category or another. This is because the law deals with different

---

[72] [2010] 1 CLC 919.
[73] [1951] 1 KB 240.
[74] [2010] 1 CLC 919.
[75] [1951] 1 KB 240.
[76] [1951] 1 KB 240 at 246.

categories of contract in different ways. So, for instance, it may be necessary to decide whether a person is an employee or an independent contractor because of the greater protections given to employees.[77] Or it may be necessary to decide whether a person is, or is not, a partner in a business because of the rights and duties conferred on partners.[78]

5.84 This involves a two-stage process. It is first necessary to decide what the rights and duties are of the parties under the contract. This is simply a matter of interpretation of the contract—establishing the objective intention of the parties. The second stage is then to decide into which category the contract falls. This is a matter of law, to which the objective intention of the parties is irrelevant. Once the court has established what the contract means, it then needs to determine whether that agreement falls into one category or another, according to the legal rules concerned.

5.85 Two examples[79] can illustrate how this happens in practice—the decision of the House of Lords in *Street v Mountford*[80] and that of the Privy Council in *Re Brumark Investments (Agnew v Commissioner of Inland Revenue).*[81]

5.86 In *Street v Mountford,*[82] Mr Street had granted Mrs Mountford the right to occupy two rooms, on the basis that she and her husband had the exclusive occupation of those rooms. The agreement contained a declaration by Mrs Mountford that she understood that the agreement she had entered into (which was described as a licence agreement) did not grant her a tenancy. The question at issue was whether Mrs Mountford was a licensee or a tenant of the property. The House of Lords decided that she was a tenant. A person is a tenant if he or she has the exclusive possession of property for a period of time, and the fact that Mrs Mountford had agreed that she was not a tenant was immaterial.

5.87 Lord Templeman put the point in this way:[83]

> In the present case, the agreement … professed an intention by both parties to create a licence and their belief that they had in fact created a licence. It was submitted on behalf of Mr Street that the court cannot in these circumstances decide that the agreement created a tenancy without interfering with the freedom of contract enjoyed by both parties … Both parties enjoyed freedom to contract or not to contract and both parties exercised that freedom by contracting on the terms set forth in the written agreement and on no other terms. But the consequences in law of the agreement, once concluded, can only be determined by consideration of the effect of the agreement. If the agreement satisfied all the requirements of a tenancy, then the

---

[77] *Autoclenz v Belcher* [2011] ICR 1157.
[78] *Pawsey v Armstrong* (1881) 18 ChD 698.
[79] A third example is the penalty doctrine, which is discussed under Principle 1 at paras 1.35–1.51.
[80] [1985] 1 AC 809.
[81] [2001] 2 AC 710.
[82] [1985] 1 AC 809.
[83] [1985] 1 AC 809 at 819.

agreement produced a tenancy and the parties cannot alter the effect of the agreement by insisting that they only created a licence. The manufacture of a five-pronged implement for manual digging results in a fork even if the manufacturer, unfamiliar with the English language, insists that he intended to make and has made a spade.

The question at issue in *Re Brumark Investments*[84] was whether a particular charge **5.88** was a fixed charge or a floating charge. It was important to determine this question because of the greater rights accorded to the holder of a fixed charge over the holder of a floating charge on the chargor's insolvency. In this case, the charge was expressed to be a fixed charge, but the House of Lords decided that this was not determinative. In a previous case, the Court of Appeal had decided that the parties were free to make whatever agreement they liked, and that whether or not the charge was a fixed charge or a floating charge was a matter of interpretation of the contract.[85] The Privy Council rejected this approach.

Lord Millett gave the judgment of the Board:[86]   **5.89**

> The question is not merely one of construction. In deciding whether a charge is a fixed charge or a floating charge, the court is engaged in a two-stage process. At the first stage it must construe the instrument of charge and seek to gather the intentions of the parties from the language they have used. But the object at this stage of the process is not to discover whether the parties intended to create a fixed or a floating charge. It is to ascertain the nature of the rights and obligations which the parties intended to grant each other in respect of the charged assets. Once these have been ascertained, the court can then embark on the second stage of the process, which is one of categorisation. This is a matter of law. It does not depend on the intention of the parties. If their intention, properly gathered from the language of the instrument, is to grant the company rights in respect of the charged assets which are inconsistent with the nature of a fixed charge, then the charge cannot be a fixed charge however they may have chosen to describe it.

In summary, if the court has to decide whether a contract falls within one legal cat- **5.90** egory or another, it must do two things. First, it must interpret the contract in the normal way. Then, once the rights and duties of the parties are clear, it must decide which category the contract falls into. The parties' views as to that characterization are irrelevant.

---

[84] *Agnew v Commissioner of Inland Revenue* [2001] 2 AC 710.
[85] *Re New Bullas Trading* [1994] 1 BCLC 485.
[86] [2001] 2 AC 710 at [32].

6

PRINCIPLE 6: AMBIGUITIES

Principle 6: If words are ambiguous in their context, they are given the meaning the parties are most likely objectively to have intended.

A. The Principle

The courts have always had to resolve ambiguities. If words are ambiguous, the **6.01** court can decide which of the possible meanings is the most likely objectively to have been intended.[1]

B. Is Ambiguity Still Important?

In the light of the developments in contractual interpretation since *Investors* **6.02** *Compensation Scheme v West Bromwich Building Society*,[2] it is legitimate to question whether there is any longer any need for a separate principle concerned with ambiguity. Is ambiguity subsumed within the wider principle (Principle 7) that words can be given an unnatural meaning as part of the interpretation process?

It is suggested that ambiguity still has an important, and separate, part to **6.03** play in the process of interpretation. The precise scope of Principle 7 is still unclear, and the extent of its application may differ from jurisdiction to jurisdiction. What is clear—especially since the decision of the Supreme Court in *Arnold v Britton*[3]—is that, to the extent that it does apply, it only does so in exceptional cases.

---

[1] See, generally, Lewison, *The Interpretation of Contracts* (6th edn, Sweet & Maxwell, 2015), Chapter 8; Burton, *Elements of Contract Interpretation* (Oxford University Press, 2009), Chapters 4 and 5.
[2] [1998] 1 WLR 896.
[3] [2015] AC 19.

6.04   Ambiguity is quite different. There is no doubt that ambiguities have to be resolved or, generally, about the way in which that should be done. And the result of the process is not to give the words an unnatural meaning, but to attribute to them one of their alternative meanings.

6.05   For these reasons, it is suggested that it is still important to understand how the courts resolve ambiguities.

6.06   The distinction between the two principles was acknowledged by Lord Clarke in *Rainy Sky v Kookmin Bank*.[4] The question in that case was whether, unless the most natural meaning of the words produces a result so extreme as to suggest that it was unintended, the court must give effect to that meaning.[5] The court rejected this approach. 'Where the parties have used unambiguous language, the Court must apply it.'[6] But where there is ambiguity, the court is entitled to prefer a sensible construction to one which is not.[7]

6.07   Lord Clarke put it this way:[8]

> The language used by the parties will often have more than one potential meaning. I would accept the submission ... that the exercise of construction is essentially one unitary exercise in which the court must consider the language used and ascertain what a reasonable person, that is a person who has all the background knowledge which would reasonably have been available to the parties in the situation in which they were at the time of the contract, would have understood the parties to have meant. In doing so, the court must have regard to all the relevant surrounding circumstances. If there are two possible constructions, the court is entitled to prefer the construction which is consistent with business common sense and to reject the other.

6.08   The distinction is clear. If the words used are unambiguous, the court can only read them in an unnatural way in an exceptional case. This is the province of Principle 7. But if the words are ambiguous, the court must decide which of the possible meanings is most likely to have been intended, and the more sensible the result, the more likely it is to have been intended. This is the province of Principle 6.

6.09   When considering ambiguities, there are essentially two key questions:

(1) When are words ambiguous?
(2) How do you resolve the ambiguity?

---

[4] [2011] 1 WLR 2900.
[5] [2011] 1 WLR 2900 at [20].
[6] [2011] 1 WLR 2900 at [23].
[7] [2011] 1 WLR 2900 at [21].
[8] [2011] 1 WLR 2900 at [21].

C. When Are Words Ambiguous?

Ambiguity is itself ambiguous.[9] Does it just encompass verbal or grammatical ambiguity, or does it extend to any case in which words can have more than one meaning? In practice, it is suggested that judges normally use the expression in its broader sense.[10] According to the Shorter Oxford Dictionary, words are ambiguous if they are uncertain or admit of more than one interpretation. That is the approach which will be adopted here.   **6.10**

There has been a debate about whether the principle only applies if the ambiguity is clear on the face of the document, or whether ambiguity can be established by reference to the background facts.   **6.11**

The cases contain a number of judgments which indicate that it is only if words are ambiguous on their face that the court can choose which meaning to apply. In the absence of ambiguity on the face of the document, the background facts cannot be used to create an ambiguity.   **6.12**

An example of this approach is the judgment of Viscount Haldane LC in *Charrington & Co v Wooder*:[11]   **6.13**

> If the language of a written contract has a definite and unambiguous meaning, Parol evidence is not admissible to shew that the parties meant something different from what they have said. But if the description of the subject-matter is susceptible of more than one interpretation, evidence is admissible to shew what were the facts to which the contract relates.

But, in the same case, Lord Dunedin expressed the principle rather differently:[12]   **6.14**

> Now, in order to construe a contract the Court is always entitled to be so far instructed by evidence as to be able to place itself in thought in the same position as the parties to the contract were placed, in fact, when they made it—or, as it is sometimes phrased, to be informed as to the surrounding circumstances.

So, even in the early years of the twentieth century, there was a conflict as to whether evidence of the background facts was only available in the case of ambiguity on the face of the document.   **6.15**

As has been seen in the discussion of Principle 4, it is now clear beyond doubt in England and New Zealand (though not yet in Australia) that the background facts   **6.16**

---

[9] See the discussion of ambiguity by the Hon JJ Spigelman in 'From Text to Context: Contemporary Contractual Interpretation' (2007) 81 Australian Law Journal 322.

[10] See the approach of the Supreme Court in *Rainy Sky v Kookmin Bank* [2011] 1 WLR 2900, discussed above at paras 6.06 and 6.07.

[11] [1914] AC 71 at 77.

[12] [1914] AC 71 at 82.

are always available for the purpose of interpreting the contract. It follows that, if the background facts show that the words used are ambiguous, the court is able to choose the meaning which most likely reflects the intention of the parties.

6.17 Two examples can illustrate how the current approach is applied in practice. They are both decisions of the Court of Appeal—*Batey v Jewson*[13] and *Napier Park v Harbourmaster.*[14]

6.18 *Batey v Jewson*[15] involved the interpretation of an assignment of 'any sums of money recoverable from the dispute with' a company. The question was whether it was an assignment of the proceeds of the dispute or whether it could be interpreted more broadly as an assignment of all of the assignor's rights against the company in relation to the dispute.

6.19 The Court of Appeal decided that, if read in isolation from the context, it appeared only to assign the proceeds of the dispute. But, when the background facts were examined, it became clear to the court that the purpose of the assignment was that the assignee would have the benefit of the assignor's rights of action against the company. In the result, therefore, the assignment was given the broader interpretation because the court examined the background facts.

6.20 *Napier Park v Harbourmaster*[16] was concerned with the interpretation of secured notes issued as part of a structured finance transaction. The way in which money would be applied depended on whether 'the ratings of the class A1 Notes have not been downgraded below their Initial Ratings'. After the notes had been issued, they were downgraded but, subsequently, they had been upgraded to the rating which they had held when the notes were issued. The question, therefore, was whether or not the notes 'have been downgraded'.

6.21 At first instance, the Chancellor, Sir Terence Etherton, decided that the rating had been downgraded. The fact that it had subsequently been upgraded again was irrelevant. The draftsman had made a conscious selection of the tense used, and the paragraph was clear and unambiguous.

6.22 The Court of Appeal disagreed, the principal judgment being given by Lewison LJ. He decided that, grammatically, a test or question expressed in the past tense is capable of referring to the historical past, the immediate past or, indeed, the present. Commercial considerations do have a part to play in deciding whether a particular interpretation is or is not ambiguous. Here, the wording was ambiguous. The

---

[13] [2008] EWCA Civ 18.
[14] [2014] All ER (D) 197 (Jun).
[15] [2008] EWCA Civ 18.
[16] [2014] All ER (D) 197 (Jul).

words were capable in normal English usage of referring to something which is continuing or something that has continuing effect. The question then is which is the most likely meaning, and the court decided that the most likely meaning was that the clause would only apply if, at the time it was tested, the notes were then downgraded.

One note of caution. It is not difficult to appear to create ambiguity where it does **6.23** not really exist. The mere fact that words might have a possible meaning different from their natural meaning in an extreme case does not make them ambiguous. A court will not go out of its way to create uncertainty. Lord Hope put it this way, when giving the opinion of the Privy Council in *Melanesian Mission Trust Board v Australian Mutual Provident Society*:[17] 'it is not the function of the court, when construing a document, to search for an ambiguity'. The ordinary meaning will be applied even if there is another possible meaning unless, as Rimer LJ said In *Prophet v Huggett*,[18] 'the language of the provision is truly ambiguous and admits of clear alternatives'.

Whether a phrase is ambiguous does not, therefore, depend on a literal interpre- **6.24** tation, but on a common-sense one. It is a question of judgment whether something is ambiguous. As Lord Wilberforce said in *Schuler v Wickman Machine Tool Sales*:[19] 'ambiguity ... is not to be equated with difficulty of construction'.

D. How is Ambiguity Resolved?

If words are ambiguous, they need to be interpreted in the way which is most **6.25** likely to give effect to the objective intention of the parties. This derives from the guiding principle of contractual interpretation (Principle 1), but it is only of limited practical use in determining which of the available options to adopt. In practice, there are two sources from which the parties' likely intention can be drawn:

(1) the rest of the contract and the background facts;
(2) the tribunal's view of the common sense of the alternative formulations.[20]

The best evidence of what the parties intended will come from the rest of the docu- **6.26** ment, set against its background facts. Failing that, the tribunal needs to turn to its own view of 'business common sense'.[21]

---

[17] (1997) 74 P&CR 297, 301.
[18] [2014] EWCA Civ 1013 at [33].
[19] [1974] AC 235 at 261.
[20] *Rainy Sky v Kookmin Bank* [2011] 1 WLR 2900. See Lewison at 7.17.
[21] The words are those of Lord Diplock in *The Antaios, Antaios Compania Naviera v Salen Rederierna* [1985] 1 AC 191 at 201.

6.27 An example of how this is done in practice is provided by *Lion Nathan Australia v Coopers Brewery*.[22] This case involved the interpretation of one of the articles of association of a company, which provided that: 'No member may make any transfer of shares and the Directors must not register any transfers of shares without complying with [the pre-emption rights provisions of the articles].' The question at issue was whether a share buy-back by the company constituted a 'transfer' within that article. The Federal Court of Australia decided that it did not. Reading the articles as a whole, it was apparent that this particular article was part of a regime providing for the disposition of shares from one member to another person who would thereby acquire membership. And it would make no sense to make the pre-emptive rights regime a condition precedent to the company buying its own shares. So, by putting the ambiguous clause in the context of the articles as a whole, and by reference to considerations of common sense, the court had no difficulty in deciding which of the alternative meanings to adopt.

E. Examples

6.28 An idea of the way in which the courts approach these issues in practice can be seen from five cases—one decision of the House of Lords, two of the Supreme Court of the United Kingdom, one of the Supreme Court of New Zealand, and one of the Singapore Court of Appeal:

(1) *Rainy Sky v Kookmin Bank*;[23]
(2) *Multi-Link Leisure Developments v North Lanarkshire Council*;[24]
(3) *Gibbons Holdings v Wholesale Distributors*;[25]
(4) *Y.E.S. v Soup Restaurant*;[26]
(5) *Prenn v Simmonds*.[27]

6.29 *Rainy Sky v Kookmin Bank*[28] concerned the interpretation of an advance payment bond issued by a bank to the buyer of a vessel. The buyer had contracted with a shipbuilder for the construction and purchase of the vessel. It had to pay instalments of the purchase price during construction of the vessel. The purpose of the advance payment bond was to secure the repayment of the instalments. The shipbuilder got into financial difficulties during the construction of the vessel, but it refused to

---

[22] [2006] FCAFC 144, on appeal from [2005] FCA 1812.
[23] [2011] 1 WLR 2900.
[24] [2011] 1 All ER 175.
[25] [2008] 1 NZLR 277.
[26] [2015] SGCA 55.
[27] [1971] 1 WLR 1381.
[28] [2011] 1 WLR 2900.

repay the instalments paid by the buyer; and the buyer therefore claimed repayment from the bank. The bank denied liability.

Paragraph 1 of the bond referred to the shipbuilding contract. Paragraph 2 then said **6.30** that pursuant to the terms of the shipbuilding contract:

> you [the buyer] are entitled, upon your rejection of the vessel in accordance with the terms of the contract, your termination, cancellation or rescission of the contract or upon a total loss of the vessel, to repayment of the pre-delivery instalments of the contract price paid by you prior to such termination or a total loss of the vessel (as the case may be) …

Paragraph 3 then said that 'In consideration of your [the buyer's] agreement to make the pre-delivery instalments under the contract … we [the bank] hereby, as primary obligor, irrevocably and unconditionally undertake to pay to you [the buyer] … all such sums due to you under the contract …'

There was no reference in paragraphs 1 or 2 to any 'sums' due under the contract. **6.31** The buyer argued that the reference to 'such sums' in paragraph 3 must be to the 'pre-delivery instalments' referred to in the opening words of paragraph 3, and that the bank was therefore liable to repay all pre-delivery instalments which the buyer had paid. The bank argued that the reference to 'such sums' must have been to the 'pre-delivery instalments' referred to in paragraph 2. The importance of this was that paragraph 2 only referred to some of the circumstances in which pre-delivery instalments could be recovered under the shipbuilding contract. Importantly, it did not refer to the ability of the buyer to recover pre-delivery instalments under the shipbuilding contract in the event of financial difficulties of the shipbuilder. The bank argued that paragraph 2 must have been inserted for a purpose and therefore it was intended to limit the amount of recovery under paragraph 3. Although the shipbuilder was liable to repay the instalments in this event under the shipbuilding contract, the bank was not liable to do so under the bond.

The Supreme Court decided that the buyer was entitled to recover from the bank. **6.32** Where the parties have used unambiguous language, the court must apply it.[29] But here, both constructions were arguable.[30] The strength of the bank's interpretation was that the contract had to be read as a whole (Principle 3), and it was not easy to see the point of paragraph 2 if the buyers' interpretation was correct.[31] The competing arguments were finely balanced, but: 'Since the language of paragraph 3 is capable of two meanings it is appropriate for the court to have regard to considerations of commercial common sense in resolving the question what a reasonable person would have understood the parties to have meant.'[32]

---

[29] [2011] 1 WLR 2900 at [23].
[30] [2011] 1 WLR 2900 at [31].
[31] [2011] 1 WLR 2900 at [32].
[32] [2011] 1 WLR 2900 at [40].

6.33 The second example is *Multi-Link Leisure Developments v North Lanarkshire Council*.[33] This case involved the interpretation of an option clause in a lease under which the landlord granted the tenant an option to purchase the property for an option price 'equal to the full market value of the [property] as at the date of entry for the proposed purchase ... of agricultural land or open space suitable for development of a golf course'. The question at issue was whether the full market value was the value of the land with 'hope value' (i.e. for development) or whether it was only the value on the basis that it continued to be agricultural land or a golf course. Although the clause prescribed the payment of 'the full market value of the property', it was 'of' agricultural land or a golf course. What did that mean?

6.34 The Supreme Court decided that the value should not be restricted by reference to the value of agricultural land or a golf course. Once the option was exercised, the tenant would be able to do whatever it wished with the land, and therefore that limited approach to valuation would be an artificial one.

6.35 This is a difficult case. The wording may not have been elegantly expressed, but the intention of the parties was clearly to link the option price to agricultural land or a golf course. The Supreme Court's interpretation effectively ignored this. It is tempting to suggest that they conflated difficulty of construction with ambiguity, which is what Lord Wilberforce warned against in *Schuler v Wickman Machine Tool Sales*.[34]

6.36 In *Gibbons Holdings v Wholesale Distributors*,[35] the question at issue was whether an assignee of leasehold premises which had undertaken to pay the rent 'during the remainder of the term of the lease' was under an obligation to pay only the rent due under the current lease or the rent due under the whole arrangement between the parties, which involved the creation of a new lease. The Supreme Court of New Zealand decided that it meant the latter. In context, the expression 'the lease' was capable of bearing either meaning. Looking at the transaction as a whole, the objective intention of the parties was that the expression 'the lease' was intended to cover both the term of the original lease and the term of the new lease.

6.37 A similar issue arose in *Y.E.S. v Soup Restaurant*.[36] YES and Soup both operated chains of Chinese restaurants in Singapore. At the time of the dispute, they were competitors but, when the transaction had been entered into, they were related companies within the same group. Soup took a lease of a unit in a shopping mall, part of which was intended to be used by YES, which had the adjoining unit. Soup therefore subleased part of the unit to YES on the terms of a short agreement drafted

---

[33] [2011] 1 All ER 175.
[34] [1974] AC 235 at 261.
[35] [2008] 1 NZLR 277.
[36] [2015] SGCA 55.

by a non-lawyer which provided that the agreement survived as long as Soup's 'lease' was not terminated.

Soup's lease expired and was replaced by a new lease. YES and Soup then ceased to **6.38** be members of the same group and became competitors. Soup purported to terminate the sub-lease. It claimed that its lease had terminated because the expression 'lease' in the termination clause meant the lease which was in existence at the time of the sub-lease. YES argued that it meant the lease which Soup had from time to time of the unit concerned, and therefore that it had not terminated.

The Singapore Court of Appeal found in favour of YES. The word 'lease' was not **6.39** defined and it was ambiguous. In context, the court decided that it meant the lease that Soup had from time to time of the unit, not the specific lease which it had at the time the sub-lease was entered into. There were three important aspects of context:

- the agreement was not drafted by lawyers;
- at the time the agreement was entered into, the companies were in the same group and it was therefore reasonable to infer that they had expected their close commercial partnership to continue for the foreseeable future; and
- both parties were aware that the premises which were being sub-leased were an integral part of YES's business and that the cost of renovation would be high, so it would be unlikely that the parties would have considered that YES would have to move out after a relatively short period.

This case is an illustration of the fact that it is often possible to resolve an ambiguity **6.40** in one clause by reference to the rest of the contract or the relevant background facts.

The last example is *Prenn v Simmonds*.[37] Here, the question at issue was whether, **6.41** in a commercial agreement, a reference to the 'profits' of a holding company was a reference to its solo accounts or to its consolidated accounts. Since the company was a holding company of a group, its own profits would depend on distributions made by subsidiaries. In the light of the agreement as a whole and the surrounding circumstances, the House of Lords decided that the reference to profits must have been to those of the group, not to the company individually. Only in this way would the clause make commercial sense.

These five cases are simply illustrations of the approach which the courts adopt. It **6.42** can be seen that, once an ambiguity has been identified, the approach is to look at the transaction as a whole and to the background facts to see if they provide a clue to the likely meaning, and then, if there is still uncertainty, to adopt the meaning which seems to the court to be the one which most accords with business common sense.

---

[37] [1971] 1 WLR 1381.

F. The *Contra Proferentem* Rule

6.43 The *contra proferentem* rule is one of those canons of construction referred to in the discussion of Principle 5. It finds its roots in Roman law,[38] and the basic principle is that an ambiguity in a contract will be construed against the person who put the contract forward.[39]

6.44 The rule only applies if the contract is genuinely ambiguous—in other words, if it is equally capable of bearing two distinct meanings.[40] Although the rule is frequently referred to, eminent judges have doubted its existence.[41] Like all canons of construction, it might well be regarded as being a piece of intellectual baggage.[42]

6.45 The real problem with applying it in practice in commercial transactions is that it is impossible to know in most cases who is the 'proferens' against whom any ambiguities have to be resolved. Most major commercial agreements are negotiated and are not simply produced by one party, in which event the rule should not be applied.[43] There is therefore a suggestion that, in order to apply the rule, you need to look at each clause separately, and apply it against the person who drafted it or who benefits from it.[44] But that ignores the basic proposition that a contract has to be read as a whole (Principle 3). It would require the person interpreting the contract to look at each clause in isolation, and that makes no commercial sense at all.

6.46 The rule is often seen as a rule of last resort. It is perhaps the most frequently referred to of all the canons of construction, but it is suggested that its role is now quite limited in negotiated commercial contracts.

6.47 There is one type of case where the *contra proferentem* rule is used even in negotiated contracts. This is in relation to certain types of clause which courts look on with suspicion. They include:

---

[38] In the *Unidroit Principles of International Commercial Contracts* (2010 edn), it is expressed in article 4.6 in the following way: 'If contact terms supplied by one party are unclear, an interpretation against that party is preferred.'

[39] See Lewison at 7.08; McMeel, *The Construction of Contracts* (2nd edn, Oxford University Press, 2011) at 8.04–8.15; Peel, 'Whither *Contra Proferentem?*', Chapter 4 in Burrows and Peel (eds), *Contract Terms* (Oxford University Press, 2007).

[40] *St Edmunsbury and Ipswich Diocesan Board of Finance v Clark (No. 2)* [1975] 1 WLR 468 at 477; *Transocean Drilling v Providence Resources* [2016] 2 Lloyd's Rep 51 at [20] (Moore-Bick LJ).

[41] See the observations of Sir George Jessel MR in *Taylor v Corporation of St Helens* (1877) LR 6 ChD 264 at 270–1.

[42] To use the expression coined by Lord Hoffmann in *Investors Compensation Scheme v West Bromwich Building Society* [1998] 1 WLR 896 at 912.

[43] See Hirst J's comments in *Kleinwort Benson v Malaysia Mining* [1988] 1 WLR 799 at 808–9. The decision was overruled in the Court of Appeal ([1989] 1 WLR 379), but not on this point.

[44] See Lewison at 7.08.

- exclusion and limitation clauses;
- clauses which limit liability for fraud or negligence;
- clauses which enable a party to terminate a contract for a minor breach.

These types of clause are discussed under Principle 7 as examples of cases where the **6.48** courts bend over backwards to read down clauses of a type which they consider to be so unreasonable that to apply them would be to produce a result which the parties are unlikely to have intended.

Exclusion clauses are a good example. As a general principle, they are now inter- **6.49** preted in the same way as any other clause of the contract, but there is a clear tendency (particularly in England) to interpret them 'strictly'. It is not entirely clear what this means in practice, but what seems to lie behind it is a tendency to give the benefit of the doubt to the person who is trying to get round the exclusion clause by interpreting any ambiguity in their favour.[45]

This is in reality another example of the use of the *contra preferentem* rule. Instead of **6.50** being applied to a document as a whole, it is applied to individual clauses which the courts regard as being objectionable. It is not a very logical stance—not least because it ignores the principle that contracts should be read as a whole. But it does seem to be ingrained in judicial attitudes.

These issues are discussed in more detail when we come to Principle 7. **6.51**

---

[45] *Nobahar-Cookson v Hut Group* [2016] EWCA Civ 128 at [12]–[21] (Briggs LJ).

7

PRINCIPLE 7: UNNATURAL MEANINGS

Principle 7: Very occasionally, it is clear that the parties cannot objectively have intended words they have used to have their ordinary meaning. If so, they are given the meaning which the parties must objectively have intended. The more unreasonable the result, the more unlikely it is that the parties can have intended it.

A. The Issue

Principle 7 is perhaps the most controversial of all of the Principles. As was seen in the discussion of Principle 4, there is still considerable doubt about the extent of the extrinsic evidence which is available as background to interpret a written contract, and there is a wide divergence of views about the extent to which it should be available. But Principle 7 is, if anything, even more divisive.   **7.01**

Principle 5 demonstrates that the basic approach is to give words their ordinary meaning in the context of the contract as a whole and of the background facts. Their ordinary meaning in context may not necessarily be the meaning which would first occur to the reader viewing them in isolation. Principle 6 shows that the courts have to decide the most appropriate meaning of ambiguous words, and that the ambiguity can arise from viewing the words in their context.   **7.02**

The combination of these two principles can by no standards be regarded as arid literalism, but Principle 7 carries further the search for what might be described as a purposive or commercial interpretation. There is no doubt that the courts do, on occasion, give words unnatural meanings. This is not a new development. They have always done so. The new development is that, over the past forty years, and increasingly so in the past twenty years, there has been a tendency for the courts to carry the process further than they did in the past.   **7.03**

7.04 The real question, therefore, is not whether Principle 7 exists, but how broadly it extends.[1] As Catherine Mitchell has said: 'As with so much in interpretation, it is all a matter of degree.'[2]

7.05 Even more than in relation to Principle 4, the battle-lines can clearly be seen to be drawn up between those who favour a broad application of Principle 7, and those who would restrict it to a more narrow application.[3]

B. The Expansive View

7.06 The expansive view is perhaps best described by Lord Hoffmann in *Investors Compensation Scheme v West Bromwich Building Society*.[4] The last two of Lord Hoffmann's principles of interpretation need to be read in their entirety:[5]

> (4) The meaning which a document (or any other utterance) would convey to a reasonable man is not the same thing as the meaning of its words. The meaning of words is a matter of dictionaries and grammars; the meaning of the document is what the parties using those words against the relevant background would reasonably have been understood to mean. The background may not merely enable the reasonable man to choose between the possible meanings of words which are ambiguous but even (as occasionally happens in ordinary life) to conclude that the parties must, for whatever reason, have used the wrong words or syntax ...
>
> (5) The 'rule' that words should be given their 'natural and ordinary meaning' reflects the common sense proposition that we do not easily accept that people have made linguistic mistakes, particularly in formal documents. On the other hand, if one would nevertheless conclude from the background that something must have gone wrong with the language, the law does not require judges to attribute to the parties an intention which they plainly could not have had. Lord Diplock made this point more vigorously when he said:[6]

If detailed semantic and syntactical analysis of words in a commercial contract is going to lead to a conclusion that flouts business commonsense, it must be made to yield to business commonsense.

7.07 This is a very wide-ranging statement. Words cannot be understood in isolation from their users. And if the courts believe that the users have used the wrong words, then they will be treated as if they had used the words which they must have intended. In other words, the court will change the words the parties have used.

---

[1] See Lewison, *The Interpretation of Contracts* (6th edn, Sweet & Maxwell, 2015) at 2.07 and 2.08.
[2] Mitchell, *Interpretation of Contracts* (Routledge Cavendish, 2007), 39.
[3] See Mitchell, Chapter 1.
[4] [1998] 1 WLR 896.
[5] [1998] 1 WLR 898 at 913.
[6] In *The Antaios, Antaios Compania Naviera v Salen Rederierna* [1985] AC 191 at 201.

This statement reflects the belief that, if one is searching for the objective intention **7.08** of the parties, it will sometimes be necessary to dispense with the words they have used because they could not have meant them.

This idea draws upon a much-quoted statement by Lord Reid in *Schuler v Wickman* **7.09** *Machine Tool Sales:*[7]

> The fact that a particular construction leads to a very unreasonable result must be a relevant consideration [in the interpretation process]. The more unreasonable the result the more unlikely it is that the parties can have intended it, and if they do intend it the more necessary it is that they shall make the intention abundantly clear.

This is a perfectly understandable view, and it is mirrored in Lord Mustill's com- **7.10** ment in *Torvald Klaveness v Arni Maritime Corporation*,[8] where he said: 'Naturally, no judge will favour an interpretation which produces an obviously absurd result unless the words used drive him to it, since it is unlikely that this is what the parties intended.'

The basic principle is clear. There is a spectrum. The more outrageous the result, the **7.11** less likely it is that the parties can have intended it. And if the court can read words in a way which makes business common sense, then they will bend over backwards to do so.

C. The Restrictive View

One person's commercial common sense is another's unjustified interference with **7.12** the parties' bargain.[9] Bending over backwards is one thing; performing a backward somersault is quite another. And for every judge who adopts an expansive view of Principle 7, there is another who would treat it more narrowly.

Two very clear examples are contained in *Charter Reinsurance Co v Fagan*.[10] In the **7.13** Court of Appeal, Staughton LJ (dissenting) said:[11] 'There must come a time when efforts to bend meanings (or, as I would say, reverse it) have to stop.' But perhaps the clearest expression of the concerns of commercial judges about carrying Principle 7 too far is contained in a speech of Lord Mustill in the same case. After citing the words of Lord Reid in *Schuler v Wickman Machine Tool Sales*,[12] that the more

---

[7] [1974] AC 235 at 251. Lord Diplock took a similar approach in *Photo Production v Securicor Transport* [1980] AC 827 at 850.

[8] [1994] 1 WLR 1465 at 1473.

[9] See the comments of Gleeson CJ, Gummow, and Hayne JJ in the High Court of Australia in *Maggbury v Hafele Australia* (2001) 210 CLR 181 at [43].

[10] [1997] AC 313.

[11] [1997] AC 313 at 368.

[12] Quoted above, para 7.09.

unreasonable the result the more unlikely it is that the parties can have intended it, Lord Mustill went on to say:[13]

> This practical rule of thumb (if I may so describe it without disrespect) must however have its limits. There comes a point at which the court should remind itself that the task is to discover what the parties meant from what they have said, and that to force upon the words a meaning which they cannot fairly bear is to substitute for the bargain actually made one which the court believes could better have been made. This is an illegitimate role for a court. Particularly in the field of commerce, where the parties need to know what they must do and what they can insist on not doing, it is essential for them to be confident that they can rely on the court to enforce their contract according to its terms ... In the end ... the parties must be held to their bargain.

7.14   This goes to the heart of English commercial law. Business people from all over the world choose English law because English law holds the parties to their bargains. No ifs, no buts. The courts enforce what has been agreed, not what they think might better have been agreed. It is the great strength of English commercial law.

7.15   Another concern with the expansive approach is that it risks confusing interpretation with rectification. Interpretation is concerned with establishing the meaning of a contract. Rectification, which is discussed under Principle 9, is about amending the terms of the contract if it does not reflect the parties' common intention at the time it was entered into. In other words, interpretation is concerned with reading the contract, rectification with changing it.[14]

7.16   The danger with the expansive approach to interpretation is that it risks confusing these two very different things. Sir Richard Buxton made the point very clearly in an article in the Cambridge Law Journal,[15] when he said:

> Principle 5 in *ICS* starkly departs from [principle], by confusing the meaning of what the parties said in their document with what they meant to say but did not say; then substitutes for the meaning of the document an intention of the parties that was not manifested in or by the document.

7.17   As will be seen in paras 7.53–7.61, the courts have always been able to amend obvious errors as a matter of interpretation, but, unless the error really is obvious, would it not be better to correct it by a process which is designed for the job, rather than one which is not?

---

[13] [1997] AC 313 at 387–8.

[14] See Burrows, 'Construction and Rectification', Chapter 5 in Burrows and Peel (eds), *Contract Terms* (Oxford University Press, 2007).

[15] Buxton, ' "Construction" and Rectification after *Chartbrook*' (2010) 69 CLJ 253 at 256–7. And see Paul Davies, 'Rectification Versus Interpretation' (2016) 75 CLJ 62.

D. So Where Are We?

There is no doubt that the courts do have the power to change words in contracts by **7.18** a process of interpretation, without going to the time and expense of a rectification claim.[16] Those in favour see this as a good thing because it gives effect to what they assume is the intention of the parties. There is also no doubt that English judges use interpretation as a back-door way of bringing concepts such as reasonableness and good faith into English law. English law does not have a general good faith principle, and nor is there any requirement for contractual rights to be exercised reasonably. But by interpretation, the courts can require parties to spell it out very clearly if they are intending to be unreasonable. In this light, Principle 7 can be seen as a safety valve to freedom of contract.

On the other hand, there is also no doubt that English law does hold dear the **7.19** principle of holding parties to their bargain. If parties have got the words wrong, they have only themselves to blame. If they can prove that the document does not accurately record their final agreement, then it can be rectified. But in the absence of such evidence, it is not appropriate for judges to second-guess the intentions of the parties. This latter point was well summed up by Neuberger LJ in *Skanska Rashleigh Weatherfoil v Somerfield Stores*,[17] when he said that:

> the court must be careful before departing from the natural meaning of the provision in the contract merely because it may conflict with its notions of commercial common sense of what the parties may must or should have thought or intended. Judges are not always the most commercially-minded, let alone the most commercially experienced, of people, and should, I think, avoid arrogating to themselves overconfidently the role of arbiter of commercial reasonableness or likelihood.

Arnold J expressed the point even more succinctly when, giving the judgment of the majority of the New Zealand Supreme Court in *Firm PI v Zurich Australian Insurance*,[18] he said that: 'there is reason to be cautious in this area because commercial absurdity tends to lie in the eye of the beholder'.

This dichotomy can also be seen in Canada, in two contrasting decisions of the **7.20** Supreme Court of Canada. In *Consolidated-Bathurst v Mutual Boiler*,[19] an insurance policy covered accidents to certain equipment, but specifically excluded corrosion. The majority of the Supreme Court managed to interpret the contract in such a way that it did cover losses resulting from corrosion. The court did so by searching for an interpretation which 'would appear to promote or advance the true intent

---

[16] See Lewison at 2.11. Rectification is discussed under Principle 9.
[17] [2006] EWCA Civ 1732 at [22].
[18] [2015] 1 NZLR 432 at [90].
[19] [1980] 1 SCR 888.

of the parties at the time of entry into the contract'.[20] They said that 'an interpretation which defeats the intentions of the parties and their objective in entering into the commercial transaction in the first place should be discarded in favour of an interpretation of the policy which promotes a sensible commercial result'.[21] This is a court striving to rewrite the contract in order to produce what seems to it a more sensible result.

7.21　Contrast this with the decision of the Supreme Court of Canada in *Eli Lilly v Novopharm*.[22] Here, the court said:

> When there is no ambiguity in the wording of a document, the notion in *Consolidated-Bathurst* that the interpretation which produces a 'fair result' or a 'sensible commercial result' should be adopted is not determinative. Admittedly, it would be absurd to adopt an interpretation which is clearly inconsistent with the commercial interests of the parties, if the goal is to ascertain their true contractual intent. However, to interpret a plainly worded document in accordance with the true contractual intent of the parties is not difficult, if it is presumed that the parties intended the legal consequences of their words.

7.22　A line therefore needs to be drawn between these opposing approaches. Different judges will reach different conclusions as to where to draw the line. And approaches can change from time to time and from jurisdiction to jurisdiction. So where are we now?

7.23　It is almost twenty years since Lord Hoffmann gave judgment in the *Investors Compensation Scheme* case.[23] Recently, there have been signs that the Supreme Court will no longer countenance too much 'judicial distortion of the English language'—to use the expression coined by Lord Diplock in *Photo Production v Securicor Transport*.[24] This was foreshadowed by Lord Neuberger in *Marley v Rawlings*[25] and it came to a head in *Arnold v Britton*.[26]

7.24　The facts and the decision in *Arnold v Britton* are discussed in more detail in paras 7.139–7.142. For present purposes, what is important is that the case involved the interpretation of a provision for the payment of service charge under a lease. The wording of the provision may have left a little to be desired, but it was pretty clear what it meant. The problem was that, if this meaning was applied, the result was surprising. The question for the court was whether the wording of the clause

---

[20] [1980] 1 SCR 888 at 901.
[21] [1980] 1 SCR 888 at 901.
[22] [1998] 2 SCR 129 at [56].
[23] *Investors Compensation Scheme v West Bromwich Building Society* [1998] 1 WLR 896. Strong support for the approach in this case is provided by McLauchlan, 'The Lingering Confusion and Uncertainty in the Law of Contract Interpretation' in [2015] LMCLQ 406.
[24] [1980] AC 827 at 851.
[25] [2015] AC 129 at [36]–[41].
[26] [2015] AC 1619.

could be overridden by a more 'commercial' interpretation which would avoid this surprising result.

Lord Carnwath would have followed the *Investors Compensation Scheme* approach. **7.25** In his view, something had gone wrong with the drafting and the relevant provision therefore had to be amended to make commercial sense.[27] But he was in the minority. By a majority of four to one, the Supreme Court gave effect to the wording of the clause even though that produced an odd result.

Lord Neuberger gave the principal judgment.[28] He accepted that the relevant words **7.26** must be read in their documentary, factual, and commercial context, but his primary focus was on the natural and ordinary meaning of the words used, and he was cautious about using 'commercial common sense' to override that meaning.[29] Whilst commercial common sense is important, a court should be very slow to reject the natural meaning of a provision as correct simply because it appears to be a very imprudent term for one of the parties to have agreed.[30] The less clear the words are, the more ready the court can be to depart from their natural meaning; but the converse is that the clearer the natural meaning, the more difficult it is to justify departing from it.[31] 'The reliance placed in some cases on commercial common sense and surrounding circumstances … should not be invoked to undervalue the importance of the language of the provision which is to be construed.'[32]

Like any other utterances, court judgments need to be read in context. The context **7.27** of the decision of the Supreme Court in *Arnold v Britton* is the series of cases in the House of Lords and the Supreme Court—discussed in section P of this chapter—from the *Investors Compensation Scheme* case[33] in 1998 to *Chartbrook v Persimmon*[34] in 2009 (and beyond), in which the courts have twisted the meaning of the words used to reach the desired result. The point that the Supreme Court was making in *Arnold v Britton* is that the courts should be wary of doing this except in an extreme case. That this was a deliberate change of emphasis is clear from the subsequent decision of the Supreme Court in *Marks and Spencer v BNP Paribas*,[35] which is discussed under Principle 8.

In recent years, most judgments concerning contractual interpretation have quoted, **7.28** or at least referred to, the judgment of Lord Hoffmann in the *Investors Compensation*

---

[27] [2015] AC 1619 at [125].
[28] [2015] AC 1619 at [14]–[23].
[29] [2015] AC 1619 at [17].
[30] [2015] AC 1619 at [20].
[31] [2015] AC 1619 at [18].
[32] [2016] AC 16219 at [17].
[33] *Investors Compensation Scheme v West Bromwich Building Society* [1998] 1 WLR 896.
[34] [2009] 1 AC 1101.
[35] [2016] AC 742.

Scheme case. More recently, the decision of Lord Clarke in the *Rainy Sky*[36] case has often been cited. In the future, it is likely the decision in *Arnold v Britton* will be cited at least as frequently.[37]

7.29 *Arnold v Britton*[38] is a defining case, but there are plenty of other recent cases in which experienced commercial judges have expressed concern about placing too much reliance on 'commercial common sense'. Whenever there is a dispute about the interpretation of a particular provision, each party will seek to demonstrate that its interpretation makes more business sense than that of the other party.[39] In many cases, the draftsman will intend what he has written, but will not have thought clearly enough about what he ought to have intended.[40]

7.30 Christopher Clarke LJ made the point very clearly in *Wood v Sureterm Direct*,[41] when he said:

> Businessmen sometimes make bad or poor bargains for a number of different reasons such as a weak negotiating position, poor negotiating or drafting skills, inadequate advice or inadvertence. If they do so it is not the function of the court to improve their bargain or make it more reasonable by a process of interpretation which amounts to rewriting it.

7.31 A similar concentration on what the words actually say has informed recent decisions of the Supreme Courts of Ireland and New Zealand.[42]

7.32 Since the *Investors Compensation Scheme* case was decided, the Irish courts have consistently followed it. In *Analog Devices v Zurich Insurance*,[43] Geoghegan J, delivering the judgment of the Supreme Court of Ireland, approved Lord Hoffmann's statement of principle in the *Investors Compensation Scheme* case. But, more recently, Fennelly J, giving the judgment of the Supreme Court of Ireland in *ICDL v European Computer Driving Licence Foundation*,[44] has emphasized that the *Investors Compensation Scheme* case does not warrant 'a loose and unpredictable path to interpretation', that the court will always commence with an examination of the words used in the contract, and that it will normally give them their natural and ordinary meaning. Business people are assumed to know what they are doing, and will

---

[36] *Rainy Sky v Kookmin Bank* [2011] 1 WLR 2100.
[37] *Ennismore Fund Management v Fenris Consulting* [2016] UKPC 9 is a recent example in the Privy Council.
[38] [2015] AC 19.
[39] *Cottonex v Patriot Spinning Mills* [2014] EWHC 236 (Comm) at [53]–[57] (Hamblen J).
[40] See the observations of Rimer LJ in *Prophet v Huggett* [2014] EWCA Civ 1013 at [36].
[41] [2015] EWCA Civ 839 at [30].
[42] And Canada: see the decision of the Supreme Court of Canada in *Sattva Capital v Creston Moly* [2014] 2 RCS 633 at [57].
[43] [2005] IESC 12.
[44] [2012] IESC 55 at [68].

normally be bound by what they have signed. There is a strong flavour here of the approach in *Arnold v Britton*.

The New Zealand courts have also staunchly followed the approach of Lord   **7.33**
Hoffmann in the *Investors Compensation Scheme* case.[45] But, in 2014, in what could be seen as a pre-echo of *Arnold v Britton*, the Supreme Court of New Zealand took a more cautious approach in *Firm PI v Zurich Australian Insurance*.[46] In this case, the majority[47] were clearly reluctant to carry too far the idea that the court could change the meaning of the words in the contract: '[The] language of many commercial contracts will have features that ordinary language … is unlikely to have, namely that it will result from a process of negotiation, will attempt to record in a formal way the consensus reached and will have the important purpose of creating certainty, both for the parties and third parties (such as financiers).'[48] And 'the reasons underlying the compromises that typically occur in commercial negotiations may not be easily perceived or understood by a court'.[49] The text therefore remains centrally important.[50]

The majority recognized that there is an obvious tension between the two opposing   **7.34**
positions of giving effect to the natural meaning of the words and producing a commercially sensible result, and that it will often be difficult to determine whether the particular case falls within one category or the other.[51] In conclusion:[52]

> All this means that if contractual language, viewed in the context of the whole contract, has an ordinary and natural meaning, a conclusion that it produces a commercially absurd result should be reached only in the most obvious and extreme of cases.[53]

Firm PI remains the leading New Zealand case, and is frequently cited and followed.   **7.35**
In *Air New Zealand v New Zealand Airline Pilots' Association*,[54] the New Zealand Court of Appeal commented on the similarity of approach with *Arnold v Britton*,[55] each of which emphasized that: 'central to the interpretation task is the natural and ordinary meaning of the words in question'.[56]

---

[45] See, for instance, *Vector Gas v Bay of Plenty Energy* [2010] 2 NZLR 444.
[46] [2015] 1 NZLR 432 at [60]–[79] and [88]–[93].
[47] McGrath, Glazebrook, and Arnold JJ.
[48] [2015] 1 NZLR 432 at [62].
[49] [2015] 1 NZLR 432 at [91].
[50] [2015] 1 NZLR 432 at [63].
[51] [2015] 1 NZLR 432 at [89].
[52] [2015] 1 NZLR 432 at [93].
[53] Reliance on the natural and ordinary meaning of the words is also stressed in the recent decision of the Supreme Court of New Zealand in *Mobil Oil New Zealand v Development Auckland* [2016] NZSC 89 at [75].
[54] [2016] NZCA 131.
[55] [2015] AC 1619.
[56] [2016] NZCA 131 at [40]; and *SFAI Money v Crawley* [2016] NZCA 219 at [50]–[54].

7.36 In the early years of this century there was a tendency, particularly in England but also in some other common law jurisdictions, to twist the meaning of words in contracts in order to produce what was considered to be a more commercial result. The pendulum had swung. There was then a backlash from those who considered that the courts had gone too far, and there can be no doubt that the recent cases in England and other jurisdictions show that the pendulum has swung back at least some of the way.

7.37 As has been seen in the Prologue, that is the nature of contractual interpretation. There will always be a tension between these two different approaches to interpretation. But, if we know what the options are, we can take account of them. As Hamlet said: 'The readiness is all.'[57]

7.38 In summary, there are clear links between Principles 4 and 7. Principle 4 has been seen as involving a debate between two opposing camps as to where to draw the line as to the extent of the background facts. The position is exactly the same in relation to Principle 7. Some judges are more comfortable about bending meanings than others; and this is true of lawyers generally. The question, therefore, is where you draw the line. And that is what the rest of the discussion of Principle 7 will attempt to establish.

E. Requirements

7.39 The starting point is that it will be a rare case in which the court will decide that the parties meant something different from what they said. A tribunal having to decide whether it should give words an unnatural meaning is, therefore, in a position rather similar to that faced by the Captain of the HMS Pinafore:

> What, never?
> No, never!
> What, *never?*
> Well, *hardly* ever![58]

7.40 Principle 7 will only apply if two things are satisfied:

(1) Something has clearly gone so wrong with the language used in the document that the parties cannot objectively have intended it.

(2) It is clear to a reasonable person what the parties actually objectively intended.[59]

---

[57] Shakespeare, *Hamlet*, 5.2.200 (The Arden Shakespeare Third Series, 2006).
[58] Gilbert and Sullivan, *HMS Pinafore*.
[59] Lord Hoffmann in *Chartbrook v Persimmon Homes* [2009] 1 AC 1101 at [25]; Chadwick LJ in *City Alliance v Oxford Forecasting Services* [2001] 1 All ER (Comm) 233 at [13]; Lord Hodge in *Arnold v Britton* [2015] AC 1619 at [78].

F. Something Has Gone Wrong

7.41 The first requirement is expressed in various ways. One way, favoured by Lord Hoffmann, is that it should be clear that 'something must have gone wrong with the language'.[60] Another way of expressing the point is illustrated in the judgment of Lord Diplock in *The Antaios*,[61] which was quoted by Lord Hoffmann in the *ICS* case[62] as being an alternative formulation:

> If detailed semantic and syntactical analysis of words in a commercial contract is going to lead to a conclusion that flouts business commonsense, it must be made to yield to business commonsense.

7.42 There is nothing explicit in either of these statements about the intention of the parties. In *City Alliance v Oxford Forecasting Services*,[63] Chadwick LJ made the link with the objective intention of the parties when he said that:

> It is not for the party who relies upon the words actually used to establish that those words effect a sensible commercial purpose. It should be assumed, as a starting point, that the parties understood the purpose which was effected by the words they used; and that they used those words because, to them, that was a sensible commercial purpose. Before the Court can introduce words which the parties have not used, it is necessary to be satisfied (i) that the words actually used produce a result which is so commercially nonsensical that the parties could not have intended it, and (ii) that they did intend some other commercial purpose which can be identified with confidence. If, and only if, those two conditions are satisfied, is it open to the court to introduce words which the parties have not used in order to construe the agreement. It is then permissible to do so because, if those conditions are satisfied, the additional words give to the agreement or clause the meaning which the parties must have intended.

7.43 This, then, is the test: something must have gone wrong because the obvious meaning of the words produces a result which is so absurd that it cannot have been intended.

7.44 The cases are peppered with variations of the adjective used to describe the nature of the result which is to be avoided. It has been described as:

- absurd,[64] obviously absurd,[65] commercially absurd;[66]
- flouting business common sense,[67] commercially nonsensical;[68]

---

[60] *Investors Compensation Scheme v West Bromwich Building Society* [1998] 1 WLR 896 at 913; *Chartbrook v Persimmon Homes* [2009] 1 AC 1101 at [25].

[61] *The Antaios, Antaios Compania Naviera v Salen Rederierna* [1998] 1 AC 191 at 205.

[62] *Investors Compensation Scheme v West Bromwich Building Society* [1988] 1 WLR 896 at 913.

[63] [2001] 1 All ER (Comm) 233 at [13].

[64] Dixon CJ in *Fitzgerald v Masters* (1956) 95 CLR 420 at 426–7.

[65] Lord Mustill in *Torvald Klaveness v Arni Maritime Corporation* [1994] 1 WLR 1465 at 1473.

[66] Lord Hoffmann in *Chartbrook v Persimmon* [2009] 1 AC 1101 at [15].

[67] Lord Diplock in *The Antaios, Antaios Compania Naviera v Salen Rederierna* [1985] 1 AC 191 at 201.

[68] Chadwick LJ in *City Alliance v Oxford Forecasting Services* [2001] 1 All ER (Comm) 233 at [13].

- bizarre;[69]
- irrational;[70]
- utterly fantastic;[71]
- arbitrary;[72]
- aberrant;[73]
- inconceivable;[74] and so on.

7.45 These expressions give some idea of the size of the hill to be climbed by some-one who wishes to deny that words are to be given their ordinary meaning in context. But no one has expressed the point more tellingly than Lord Reid in *Schuler v Wickman Machine Tool Sales Limited* [75] when he said that: '[t]he more unreasonable the result, the more unlikely it is that the parties can have intended it'. The important point is that it shows that there is a sliding scale of absurdity/fantasy/unreasonableness. The test can be stated relatively clearly, but where the line is drawn in practice depends on the personal reactions of the arbitrator or the judge to the issue in hand. One person's absurd result is another's good deal.[76]

7.46 Lord Hoffmann has been at the forefront of the move to bring the interpretation of legal documents more into line with the interpretation of ordinary speech. In *Investors Compensation Scheme v West Bromwich Building Society*,[77] he prefaced his five principles of interpretation by saying that the effect of the new approach to con-tractual interpretation is: 'to assimilate the way in which [contractual] documents are interpreted by judges to the common sense principles by which any serious ut-terance would be interpreted in ordinary life'. If Mrs Malaprop can make mistakes but still be understood, then so can the draftsman of a legal document.[78] But even Lord Hoffmann accepts that 'we do not easily accept that people have made lin-guistic mistakes, particularly in formal documents',[79] and that '[i]t clearly requires

---

[69] Lord Jauncey in *Alghussein Establishment v Eton College* [1988] 1 WLR 587 at 595.
[70] Lord Hoffmann in *Chartbrook v Persimmon* [2009] 1 AC 1101 at [15].
[71] Lord Morris in *Schuler v Wickman Machine Tool Sales* [1974] AC 235 at 255–6.
[72] Lord Neuberger MR in *Pink Floyd Music v EMI Records* [2010] EWCA Civ 1429, [20].
[73] Giles JA in *Kooee Communications & Primus Telecommunications* [2008] NSWCA 5 at [2].
[74] Millet LJ in *Barclays Bank v Weeks Legg & Dean* [1999] QB 309 at 328.
[75] [1974] AC 235 at 251.
[76] See Spigelman, 'Extrinsic Material and the Interpretation of Insurance Contracts' (2011) 22 Insurance Law Journal 143 at 143.
[77] [1998] 1 WLR 896 at 912.
[78] See Lord Hoffmann's comments in *Mannai Investment Co v Eagle Star Life Assurance Co* [1997] AC 749 at 774.
[79] *Investors Compensation Scheme v West Bromwich Building Society* [1998] 1 WLR 896 at 913.

a strong case to persuade the court that something must have gone wrong with the language'.[80]

The same point is made in the Scottish Law Commission's Discussion Paper **7.47** on Interpretation of Contracts:[81] 'In construing a contract drafted by lawyers, the words may be expected to have been chosen with care and to be intended to convey the meaning which the words chosen would convey to a reasonable person.'

Chadwick LJ summed up the point in *Bromarin v IMD Investments*,[82] when he said **7.48** that it should be 'an exceptional case' in which the words used do not express the meaning which the parties intended.

G. It is Clear What Was Intended

If it is established that something has gone wrong with the words used, the other **7.49** requirement is that it is clear to a reasonable person what the parties actually intended.[83]

In *Chartbrook v Persimmon Homes*,[84] Lord Hoffmann said that: 'it should be clear **7.50** what a reasonable person would have understood the parties to have meant', whilst at the same time acknowledging that: 'there is not, so to speak, a limit to the amount of red ink or verbal rearrangement or correction which the court is allowed'.

In some ways, the second requirement can be more difficult to satisfy than the first. **7.51** It may be pretty clear that something has gone wrong with the document, but by no means clear what the parties objectively intended to do. There may just be too many possible variants. The approach of the court in such a case is similar to that which it uses when resolving ambiguities. It needs to look at two things: (a) the document as a whole in the light of the background facts; and (b) what seems to it to be commercially sensible for the parties to have agreed. The problems are more difficult here, though. In the case of an ambiguity, the court has to resolve it one way or another. In this case, if it is unable to resolve it, then it cannot change the words.

This point cannot be pushed too far. There is some indication in the cases that the **7.52** court will be prepared to choose one of a number of alternative versions of what

---

[80] *Chartbrook v Persimmon Homes* [2009] 1 AC 1101 at [15].
[81] Discussion Paper No. 147 (February 2011) at 48.
[82] [1999] STC 301.
[83] See the second limb of Chadwick LJ's test in *City Alliance v Oxford Forecasting Services* [2001] 1 All ER (Comm) 233 at [13], quoted at para 7.41 above.
[84] [2009] 1 AC 1101 at [25].

the parties might have meant. In *KPMG v Network Rail Infrastructure*,[85] Carnwath LJ said:

> I think it would be wrong to apply too literally Lord Bingham's reference to the need for clarity both as to the omission of words and 'what those relevant words were'.[86] As Lord Millett said,[87] it is sufficient if the court is able to ascertain 'the gist' of what has been omitted. I would go further. Once the court has identified an obvious omission, and has found in admissible background materials an obvious precedent for filling it, it should not be fatal that there may be more than one possible version of the replacement, or more than one explanation of the change.

7.53   It was by reference to this case that Lord Hoffmann said, in *Chartbrook v Persimmon Homes*,[88] that there is no limit to the amount of verbal rearrangement which the court is allowed. Whether such an approach will be adopted more generally is a matter for some doubt. It is suggested that Carnwath LJ went further than most judges are prepared to go. In order for the court to be able to rewrite the contract (for that is what it is doing), it must surely be necessary to establish very clearly what the parties actually intended—even if the precise formulation of that intention might be expressed in a number of different ways.

H. Correcting Clear Drafting Errors

7.54   The courts have always corrected obvious drafting errors or 'typos'.[89] In *Fitzgerald v Masters*,[90] Dixon CJ and Fullagar J in the High Court of Australia said:

> Words may generally be supplied, omitted or corrected, in an instrument, where it is clearly necessary in order to avoid absurdity or inconsistency.

7.55   The principle was expressed in this way by Brightman LJ in *East v Pantiles (Plant Hire)*:[91]

> It is clear on the authorities that a mistake in a written instrument can, in certain limited circumstances, be corrected as a matter of construction without obtaining a decree in an action for rectification. Two conditions must be satisfied: first, there must be a clear mistake on the face of the instrument; secondly, it must be clear what correction ought to be made in order to cure the mistake. If those conditions are satisfied, then the correction is made as a matter of

---

[85] [2007] Bus LR 1336 at [64].

[86] In *The Starsin, Homburg Houtimport v Agrosin* [2004] 1 AC 715 at [23].

[87] Also in *The Starsin, Homburg Houtimport v Agrosin* [2004] 1 AC 715 at [192].

[88] [2009] 1 AC 1101 at [25].

[89] See Lewison, *The Interpretation of Contracts* (6th edn, Sweet & Maxwell, 2015) at 9.01 and 9.02; McMeel, *The Construction of Contracts* (2nd edn, Oxford University Press, 2011) at 17.02–17.11.

[90] (1956) 95 CLR 420 at 426–7.

[91] [1982] 2 EGLR 111 at 112.

construction ... In *Snell's Principles of Equity* [92] the principle of rectification by construction is said to apply only to obvious clerical blunders or grammatical mistakes. I agree with that approach. Perhaps it might be summarised by saying that the principle applies where a reader with sufficient experience of the sort of document in issue would inevitably say to himself, 'Of course X is a mistake for Y'.

In *Chartbrook v Persimmon Homes*,[93] Lord Hoffmann approved this statement, but **7.56** added that the mistake does not need to appear on the face of the instrument. The background and context must always be taken into consideration.[94]

There are a number of examples in the books of courts correcting obvious errors of **7.57** this type.

Words can be changed because they make no sense in context. So, for instance, in **7.58** *Littman v Aspen Oil (Broking)*,[95] the word 'Landlord' in a lease was read as 'Tenant' because to do otherwise would have made a nonsense of the clause. And in *Wilson v Wilson*,[96] in a separation deed, the words 'John W.H. Wilson' were replaced by 'Mary W.H. Wilson' because the clause would not otherwise have made sense.

Anyone who has drafted a contract will know how easy it is for a 'not' to be omitted **7.59** by accident, or to creep in by mistake. In *Glen's Trustees v Lancashire and Yorkshire Accident Insurance Company*,[97] an insurance policy was interpreted as if the word 'not' had been deleted because it was clearly a grammatical error. Similarly, in *Fitzgerald v Masters* (see para 7.39), a document was expressed to embody a set of standard form conditions 'so far as they are inconsistent' with the document. The court read 'inconsistent' as 'consistent' because of the absurdity of reading it any other way.

That other bane of a draftsman's life—cross-references to other clauses—can also be **7.60** amended if the cross-reference is clearly a mistake.[98]

In some cases, the subject matter of the contract, or even the names of the parties, **7.61** may be misdescribed. If they are obvious errors, the court can correct them as a matter of interpretation. In *Reardon Smith Line v Yngvar Hansen-Tangen*,[99] the vessel was misdescribed in a shipbuilding contract and the court corrected the obvious error. In *Nittan (UK) v Solent Steel Fabrications*,[100] the name of a party to an insurance policy was corrected because it was a misnomer—an obvious mistake.

---

[92] 27th edn, 611.
[93] [2009] 1 AC 1101 at [22]–[25].
[94] See Principle 4.
[95] [2006] 2 P&CR 2.
[96] (1854) LR 5 HLC 40.
[97] (1906) 14 SLT 168.
[98] *Booker Industries v Wilson Parking* (1982) 149 CLR 600 at 603.
[99] [1976] 1 WLR 989.
[100] [1981] 1 Lloyd's Rep 633.

7.62   The more difficult question is how far this principle now extends. That requires a discussion of the types of case in which it has been used.

I. Going Beyond Correcting Clear Drafting Errors

7.63   The ability of the courts to give an unnatural meaning to the words used in a contract is not limited to particular types of clause. But the cases do illustrate certain trends, and there can be little doubt that the courts are more wary of certain types of clause than others. Examples of the approach of the courts will be discussed in relation to six types of case:

(1) fraud;
(2) taking advantage of one's own breach of contract;
(3) exclusion and limitation clauses;
(4) liability for negligence;
(5) guarantees;
(6) termination for minor breach.

There will then be a discussion of those cases which defy categorization. They include some of the most important recent cases.

J. Fraud

7.64   As Lord Denning once said, fraud unravels everything.[101] As a matter of public policy, it is not possible for a person to contract out of liability for his own fraud in inducing the making of a contract.[102] It is not yet clear whether this rule of law extends to the fraud of one's agents, but a purported exclusion of liability by an agent will not extend to fraud unless it is specifically referred to in the clause. General words of exclusion, which on their face would cover fraud, will not do so. Express reference to fraud is required.[103] As Lord Hoffmann said in *HIH Casualty and General Insurance v Chase Manhattan Bank*:[104]

> Parties contract with one another in the expectation of honest dealing ... I think that in the absence of words which expressly refer to dishonesty, it goes without saying that underlying the contractual arrangements of the parties there will be a common assumption that the persons involved will behave honestly.

---

[101] *Lazarus Estates v Beasley* [1956] 1 QB 702 at 712.
[102] *HIH Casualty and General Insurance v Chase Manhattan Bank* [2003] 1 CLC 358.
[103] *HIH Casualty and General Insurance v Chase Manhattan Bank* [2003] 1 CLC 358.
[104] [2003] 1 CLC 358 at [68].

K. Taking Advantage of One's Own Breach of Contract

Clear express wording will also be required for a party to be able to obtain a bene- **7.65**
fit from his or her own breach of contract.[105] As Lord Jauncey said in *Alghussein Establishment v Eton College*,[106] there is a 'presumption that it was not the intention of parties that either should be entitled to rely on his own breach in order to obtain a benefit'.

An example of the application of this principle is *Alghussein Establishment v Eton* **7.66**
College itself.[107] An agreement for a lease of land contained an undertaking by the tenant to use its best endeavours to develop the land as a block of flats. The tenant did not do so and, for the purpose of the case, it was assumed that its failure amounted to a repudiation, which would enable the landlord to terminate the agreement. But one clause of the agreement for lease provided that: 'if for any reason due to the wilful default of the tenant the development should remain uncompleted by [a particular date] the lease shall forthwith be completed'. On its face, this suggested that the tenant would be entitled to completion of the lease as a result of its own wilful default. One of the judges in the case referred to the clause as 'half-baked', and the courts had no difficulty in deciding that the parties cannot have intended the tenant to have been entitled to have the lease completed as a result of its own breach of contract.

L. Exclusion and Limitation Clauses

Exclusion clauses were given a hard time by the courts in the twentieth century.[108] **7.67**
For understandable reasons concerned with consumer protection, the courts did their best to strike them down either as offending against a rule of law[109] or by interpreting them out of existence. The necessity to do this in a consumer context was removed by the Unfair Contract Terms Act 1977, and normal service was resumed when the House of Lords gave judgment in *Photo Production v Securicor Transport* in 1980.[110]

In *Photo Production v Securicor Transport*,[111] the House of Lords decided that ex- **7.68**
clusion clauses must be construed strictly against the person relying on them but,

---

[105] See McMeel, Chapter 21; Lewison at 7.10.
[106] [1988] 1 WLR 587 at 595.
[107] [1988] 1 WLR 587.
[108] See Lewison, Chapter 12.
[109] Most notably, the 'fundamental breach' heresy. See Coote, *Contract as Assumption* (Hart, 2010), Chapter 7.
[110] [1980] AC 827.
[111] [1980] AC 827.

subject to that, they were to be construed in the same way as any other clause. As Lord Diplock said:[112] 'it is, in my view, wrong to place a strained construction upon words in an exclusion clause which are clear'.

7.69 Lord Diplock nevertheless said that exclusion clauses 'are to be construed strictly',[113] and this warning is echoed in the later cases, which also express the same concept as a requirement that, if you want to exclude or limit your liability you must do so 'in clear words'.[114] The reason for this is that an exclusion clause either contracts out of an existing liability or, more usually, excludes or limits a liability which would otherwise have been the subject of the contract.[115]

7.70 This is an understandable approach where a party is contracting out of a pre-existing legal liability, but more difficult to understand where the clause excludes or limits a liability which would otherwise have been assumed under the contract. In reality, what the exclusion clause is doing is establishing the extent of the parties' contractual liabilities. It is a very artificial construct to suggest that it excludes a liability which will only exist if the contract is entered into in a different form from that agreed.[116]

7.71 It is nevertheless clear that the courts do require exclusion clauses of both types to be construed strictly. But what does this mean?[117] Is there any difference between a clause which 'clearly' excludes liability, and one which just excludes the liability? When drafting difficult clauses, one is often tempted to add the words: 'and I really mean this' in the expectation that it will not otherwise be taken seriously and in the hope that this might persuade the tribunal to do so.[118] It may be that all that is being done is to say that any ambiguity will be construed against the person relying on the exclusion clause.

7.72 There are suggestions in the cases that the requirement of strict interpretation is applied more stringently to clauses which exclude liability than to those which limit it.[119] The point being made here is the same one which Lord Reid made in *Schuler v Wickman Machine Tool Sales*,[120] which was discussed earlier. The more unreasonable

---

[112] [1980] AC 827 at 851. And see the recent comments of Moore-Bick LJ in *Transocean Drilling v Providence Resources* [2016] 2 Lloyd's Rep 51 at [14] and [21].

[113] [1980] AC 827 at 850.

[114] Lord Bingham's words, in *Dairy Containers v Tasman Orient Line* [2005] 1 WLR 215 at [12].

[115] See Lord Diplock in *Photo Production v Securicor Transport* [1980] AC 827 at 850; and Briggs LJ in *Nobahar-Cookson v Hut Group* [2016] EWCA Civ 128 at [12]–[21].

[116] This point is made with his customary lucidity by Professor Brian Coote in *Contract as Assumption* (Hart, 2010), Chapter 6.

[117] See Lewison at 2.10.

[118] See the comments of Lord Hoffmann in *Mannai Investment Co v Eagle Star Life Assurance Co* [1997] AC 749 at 776.

[119] *Photo Production v Securicor* [1980] AC 827 at 850; *Ailsa Craig Fishing Co v Malvern Fishing Co* [1983] 1 WLR 964. See Lewison at 12.16.

[120] [1974] AC 235 at 251. See para 7.09.

the result, the more unlikely it is that the parties would have intended it and the more necessary it is that they express it clearly.[121]

In spite of these warnings about clarity and strictness of interpretation, the courts **7.73** are undoubtedly prepared to accept that exclusion clauses do what they say.

In *Darlington Futures v Delco Australia*,[122] the High Court of Australia recognized **7.74** that exclusion clauses should be interpreted in accordance with the normal principles of interpretation, and the only gloss they were prepared to place on this was that if the contract was ambiguous, it should be construed *contra proferentem*. In *DHL International v Richmond*,[123] the New Zealand Court of Appeal also applied general principles of contractual interpretation to an exclusion clause, without qualification.

The difference between the approach in England to that in Australia and New **7.75** Zealand is probably more apparent than real. In all three jurisdictions, the basic principle is clear—an exclusion or limitation clause will be interpreted in accordance with the normal principles of contractual interpretation. The requirement in England for a 'strict' interpretation is probably no more than a recognition of the fact that any ambiguities will be interpreted against the person relying on the exclusion. In other words, the *contra proferentem* rule is applied to exclusion clauses.[124]

This was the approach of Lord Bingham in the Privy Council in *Dairy Containers* **7.76** *v Tasman Orient Line*,[125] when he said that a person wishing to limit his liability: 'must do so in clear words; unclear words do not suffice; any ambiguity or lack of clarity must be resolved against that party'.

That the outcomes in all three jurisdictions[126] are likely to be the same can be seen **7.77** by comparing two decisions—that of the House of Lords in *Photo Production v Securicor Transport*[127] and that of the High Court of Australia in *Darlington Futures v Delco Australia*.[128]

In *Photo Production v Securicor Transport*,[129] a security firm contracted with a fac- **7.78** tory owner for the provision of a night patrol service at the factory. When carrying out his tasks, one of the security firm's employees lit a fire, which burned down the factory.

---

[121] This point was made explicitly by Lord Fraser in *Ailsa Craig Fishing Co v Malvern Fishing Co* [1983] 1 WLR 964 at 970.

[122] (1986) 161 CLR 500 at 510.

[123] [1993] 3 NZLR 10 at 17–18.

[124] The *contra proferentem* rule is discussed under Principle 6 at paras 6.43–6.51.

[125] [2005] 1 WLR 215 at [12].

[126] The courts in Canada take a broader view of their power to strike down exclusion clauses: see *Tercon Contractors v R* [2010] 1 RCS 69 at [62] and [122].

[127] [1980] AC 827.

[128] (1986) 161 CLR 500.

[129] [1980] AC 827.

7.79 The contract contained an exclusion clause which said:

> Under no circumstances shall [the security firm] be responsible for any injurious act or default by any employee of [the security firm] unless such act or default could have been foreseen and avoided by the exercise of due diligence on the part of [the security firm] as his employer.

The security firm had exercised due diligence in employing the person concerned.

7.80 The House of Lords held that the exclusion clause was clear, that it covered deliberate acts as well as negligence, and that it relieved the security firm from any liability to the factory owner.

7.81 In *Darlington Futures v Delco Australia*,[130] a contract between a broker and a client for dealings on the commodities futures market contained a clause which said:

> Any liability on the [broker's] part or on the part of its servants or agents for damages for or in respect of any claim arising out of or in connection with the relationship established by this agreement or any conduct under it or any orders or instructions given to [the broker] by the Client ... shall not in any event (and whether or not such liability results from or involves negligence) exceed one hundred dollars.

7.82 The broker carried out dealings which bound the client but which were undertaken without the client's authorization. Applying normal principles of contractual interpretation, the High Court of Australia held that the broker's liability was limited to $100, even though the transaction was unauthorized.

7.83 The purpose of an exclusion clause is to describe the scope of a promise—either by limiting it directly or by limiting the effect of its breach. In principle, therefore, there is no justification for treating an exclusion clause any differently from any other clause in the contract. But it is clear that remnants of the old distrust of exclusion clauses remain in the courts' approach to their interpretation. Perhaps the best approach—which would recognize this hostility, whilst at the same time paying greater regard to the basic principles of contractual interpretation—would be to apply the *contra proferentem* rule to exclusion clauses. There is no logic to doing so, but it would at least limit its application to cases where the clause was ambiguous.

M. Liability for Negligence

7.84 In the past, the courts have applied different techniques to the interpretation of clauses excluding liability for negligence than to the interpretation of other clauses in contracts.[131] And the same is true of clauses by which one party agrees to indemnify another for that other party's negligence.

---

[130] (1986) 161 CLR 500.
[131] See Lewison at 12.06–12.09; McMeel at 21.30–21.56.

The classic statement of the principle to be applied was given by Lord Morton in **7.85** *Canada Steamship Lines v R*:[132]

(1) If the clause contains language which expressly exempts the person in whose favour it is made (hereafter called the 'proferens') from the consequence of the negligence of his own servants, effect must be given to that provision....

(2) If there is no express reference to negligence, the court must consider whether the words used are wide enough, in their ordinary meaning, to cover negligence on the part of the servants of the proferens. If a doubt arises at this point, it must be resolved against the proferens ...

(3) If the words used are wide enough for the above purpose, the court must then consider whether 'the head of damage may be based on some ground other than that of negligence'.[133] The 'other ground' must not be so fanciful or remote that the proferens cannot be supposed to have desired protection against it; but subject to this qualification ... the existence of a possible head of damage other than that of negligence is fatal to the proferens even if the words used are prima facie wide enough to cover negligence on the part of his servants.

In other words, if the words exclude a particular type of liability, but negligence is **7.86** not specifically mentioned, the words will only exclude negligence if that is the only type of liability which could be covered by the words concerned.

In the *Canada Steamship* case, the landlord had leased a freight shed to a tenant. **7.87** Whilst repairing the shed, one of the landlord's employees was using an oxy-acetylene torch and, because of his negligence, a fire broke out which destroyed the shed and its contents. The landlord claimed that it was not liable for the negligence of its employee because a clause in the lease provided that the tenant 'shall not have any claim ... against the [landlord] for ... damage ... of any nature to ... the said shed ... or to any ... things at any time ... being upon ... the said shed'.

Applying the principle set out above, the Privy Council held that this clause did not **7.88** exempt the landlord from liability for the negligence of its employees. Although, on its face, the clause would cover the negligence of the landlord's employees, it did not actually do so because the exemption covered matters other than negligence and therefore negligence was not excluded because it was not specifically mentioned.

The same principle has been applied by the House of Lords to clauses by which **7.89** one party agrees to indemnify the other party for the latter's negligence or for the negligence of its employees.[134]

---

[132] [1952] AC 192 at 208.
[133] The words used by Lord Greene MR in *Alderslade v Hendon Laundry* [1945] KB 189 at 192.
[134] *Smith v South Wales Switchgear* [1978] 1 WLR 165. See Lewison at 12.15.

7.90 This is the same sort of artificial interpretation which, in relation to exclusion clauses, was criticized by the House of Lords in *Photo Production v Securicor*.[135] As Sir Christopher Staughton has said: 'This was to my mind bad law, made by hard cases.'[136] It was nevertheless applied strictly by the Court of Appeal in the 1990s in *E.E. Caledonia v Orbit Valve Co.*[137] In that case, Steyn LJ did say that: 'Ultimately, the third test is not a rigid or mechanical rule. It simply is an aid in the process of construction.'[138] But he nevertheless accepted that negligence is somehow different from other types of liability, by saying that: 'it is prima facie implausible that the parties would wish to release one another from the consequences of the other's negligence and agree to indemnify the other in respect of such consequences'.[139]

7.91 That may have been so on the facts of that particular case, but it cannot be a principle of general application. As Lord Steyn would be the first to recognize, whether or not it is implausible that the parties would wish to contract out of liability for negligence depends on the type of contract concerned viewed against its background facts. It is one thing to exclude liability for negligence if the principal purpose of the contract is for one party to exercise reasonable care and skill in carrying out a particular project. But, in many cases, the potential liability for negligence may be peripheral to the main object of the contract and it may be perfectly understandable that the parties should want to exclude liability of that kind.

7.92 The more recent tendency is to refer to Lord Morton's three tests, but then to apply the normal principles of contractual interpretation to the question of whether or not liability for negligence has been excluded.

7.93 An example of this more recent approach is *HIH Casualty and General Insurance v Chase Manhattan Bank*.[140] One of the questions in this case was whether a provision in an insurance policy that the insured: 'shall have no liability of any nature to the insurers for any information provided by any other parties' was sufficient to exclude liability for the negligent misrepresentation of its agent. The House of Lords held that it was. Although they paid lip service to Lord Morton's three tests, in practice they interpreted the clause in the same way as they would interpret any other clause in the contract.

---

[135] [1980] AC 827.

[136] Staughton, 'Interpretation of (Commercial) Contracts' [1990] Arbitration 326 at 330.

[137] [1994] 1 WLR 1515. This was not an isolated incident. At around the same time, the Court of Appeal adopted the same approach in *The Fiona, Mediterranean Freight Services v BP Oil International* [1994] 2 Lloyd's Rep 506 and in *Shell Chemicals UK v P&O Roadtanks* [1995] 1 Lloyd's Rep 297.

[138] [1994] 1 WLR 1515 at 1522.

[139] [1994] 1 WLR 1515 at 1523.

[140] [2003] 1 CLC 358.

Lord Hoffmann said:[141]   **7.94**

> The question, as it seems to me, is whether the language used by the parties, construed in the context of the whole instrument and against the admissible background, leads to the conclusion that they must have thought it went without saying that the words, although literally wide enough to cover negligence, did not do so. This in turn depends upon the precise language they have used and how inherently improbable it is in all the circumstances that they would have intended to exclude such liability.

Indeed, Lord Hoffmann turned Lord Morton's third test on its head when he said   **7.95**
that:[142]

> [T]here is nothing in the language or context of [the exclusion] to suggest that the parties did not intend [it] to cover negligence. There is no inherent improbability in such an intention.

If this is the right approach, it is not so much that the court has to decide whether the parties really have excluded negligence, but whether they have not.

The Court of Appeal has recently reiterated that Lord Morton's tests 'should not be   **7.96**
applied mechanistically, and ought to be regarded as no more than guidelines'.[143] In doing so, they decided that clear words of exclusion applied not only to negligent actions but also to intentional ones. It was not 'inherently improbable' that they were intended to do so.[144]

It is suggested that, although it is still cited in the cases, Lord Morton's third propo-   **7.97**
sition will gradually lose its potency, and that the courts should approach clauses excluding liability for negligence in the same way as they do any other clauses. If the words concerned are wide enough to cover negligence, they should not ask themselves whether there is any reason why negligence should be excluded, but whether there is any reason why it should not. It is only if they are ambiguous that they should be interpreted *contra proferentem*.

It would nevertheless be a brave draftsman who ignored Lord Morton's tests alto-   **7.98**
gether. It continues to be good practice specifically to refer to negligence if it is intended to exclude liability for it or to claim an indemnity for one's own negligence. Defensive drafting certainly, and possibly unnecessary, but, in the circumstances, an understandable prophylactic.

---

[141] [2003] 1 CLC 358 at [63].
[142] [2003] 1 CLC 358 at [67].
[143] *Mir Steel v Morris* [2013] CP Rep 7 at [35].
[144] [2013] CP Rep 7 at [36].

N. Guarantees

7.99 The hostility which the courts have shown to some types of contractual provision—such as exclusion and limitation clauses—is sometimes applied to particular types of contract as a whole. Perhaps the most striking example is contracts of guarantee. The legislature has imposed particular formal rules for the creation of guarantees,[145] and the courts have always been protective of guarantors. This is doubtless because, in many cases, the guarantor obtains no clear benefit commensurable with the liability which it incurs when giving the guarantee.

7.100 This protective attitude manifests itself in various ways, one of which is that guarantees are frequently said to be construed strictly in favour of the guarantor. In practice, what this doubtless means is that, because most guarantees are drafted by the creditor, any ambiguity will be interpreted *contra proferentem*—against the creditor and in favour of the guarantor.[146]

7.101 The modern approach to guarantees in commercial transactions is, however, to treat them as contracts—like any other—and to interpret them in the light of the background facts and from the point of view of the business people entering into them.[147]

7.102 An example of this approach is *Static Control Components v Egan*.[148] SCC supplied components to TBS on credit, and a director of TBS guaranteed its debts to SCC. Each guarantee was limited in time and, as a result, the guarantor entered into four successive guarantees. The last guarantee was entered into on 2 September and it guaranteed to SCC 'the price of all trade goods that you [SCC] may supply to [TBS]' up to a limit.

7.103 The guarantor argued that the meaning of the guarantee was plain; and that the words 'that you may supply' could only refer to future supplies of goods, rather than to goods already supplied. The Court of Appeal disagreed. It decided that the guarantor was liable for the price of the goods which had been delivered before 2 September. Although the words 'that you may supply' appeared, in isolation, to relate to the future only, those words had to be read against the background facts, which made it clear that the parties intended the guarantor to be liable for all goods supplied by SCC to TBS—whether they were supplied before or after 2 September.

7.104 What is interesting about this case is that the Court of Appeal had no hesitation in increasing the liability of a guarantor beyond that which appeared on the face of the guarantee. Rather than trying to limit the liability of the guarantor, they extended

---

[145] The Statute of Frauds 1677, s 4.
[146] *Eastern Counties Building Society v Russell* [1947] 2 All ER 734.
[147] *Hyundai Shipbuilding & Heavy Industries Co v Pournaras* [1978] 2 Lloyd's Rep 502.
[148] [2004] 2 Lloyd's Rep 429.

it. It does not preclude a court from applying the *contra proferentem* principle in the case of ambiguity, but it certainly suggests that guarantees should be interpreted in the same way as any other commercial contract.

O. Termination for Minor Breach

7.105 Where a long-term contract contains a clause which appears to give one party the ability to terminate the contract as a result of a minor breach by the other party, the court will do its best to read some limitation into the termination provisions. This is illustrated by two cases.

7.106 In *The Antaios*,[149] a three-year time charterparty provided that 'on any breach of this charter party the owners shall be at liberty to withdraw the vessel'. The House of Lords decided that the owners could not withdraw the vessel for any breach, but only for a repudiatory breach. In a much-quoted judgment, Lord Diplock said that:[150]

> If detailed semantic and syntactical analysis of words in a commercial contract is going to lead to a conclusion that flouts business commonsense, it must be made to yield to business commonsense.

7.107 This principle has been applied more recently by the Court of Appeal in *Rice v Great Yarmouth Borough Council*.[151] Mr Rice entered into a four-year contract with the Council to maintain their public parks. The contract contained a clause by which, if the Contractor [Mr Rice]: 'commits a breach of any of its obligations under the Contract ... the Council may ... terminate the Contractor's employment under the Contract by notice in writing having immediate effect'.

7.108 The Court of Appeal decided that this did not give the Council the ability to terminate the contract for a minor breach, but only for a repudiatory breach. Any other interpretation 'flies in the face of commercial common sense'.[152]

7.109 The problem with these decisions is that they deprive the termination clause of any meaning. The innocent party always has the ability to terminate the contract on a repudiatory breach. It does not need the contract to say so. Can the parties really have intended that the only effect of the termination clause in these two contracts was to state the rule which would apply in any event? But there can be no doubt that the courts will do their utmost to read down wide termination provisions in long-term contracts.

---

[149] *Antaios Compania Naviera v Salen Rederierna* [1985] 1 AC 191.
[150] [1985] 1 AC 191 at 201.
[151] [2002] All ER (D) 902.
[152] [2002] All ER (D) 902 at [24].

P. Judicial Distortion of the English Language

7.110 The cases which have been discussed so far are illustrations of certain themes which appear from the cases. The old rules by which exclusion clauses (and, in particular, exclusions of liability for negligence) were read down by the courts now have little part to play in the interpretation process except as examples of the continuing application of the *contra proferentem* rule where the words are ambiguous. There remain certain types of case where the courts regard an outcome as so unlikely to have been agreed by the parties that they require specific wording dealing with the point in issue. This is understandably the case in relation to fraud; but it also applies where a clause apparently gives a party a benefit as a result of its breach of contract or where a long-term contract can be terminated for a minor breach. These are all illustrations of Lord Reid's comment that the more unreasonable the outcome, the less likely it is to have been intended and the more important it is that it is made clear in the contract.

7.111 What is interesting about the more recent cases is that they have opened up the scope of Lord Reid's comment, and have applied it ever more widely in a variety of types of case which do not fit within these categories. This can be illustrated by looking at four recent decisions of the House of Lords which have really established the modern law of contractual interpretation. These are, chronologically:

- *Mannai Investment Co v Eagle Star Life Assurance Co* in 1997;[153]
- *Investors Compensation Scheme v West Bromwich Building Society* in 1998;[154]
- *Bank of Credit and Commerce International v Ali* in 2002;[155]
- *Chartbrook v Persimmon Homes* in 2009.[156]

Mannai

7.112 The first case is *Mannai Investment Co v Eagle Star Life Assurance Co*.[157] A lease contained a break clause, by which the tenant could terminate the lease by serving not less than six months' notice in writing on the landlord or its solicitors to expire 'on the third anniversary of the term commencement date'. The tenants gave six months' notice to determine the lease on 12 January 1995. In fact, the third anniversary of the term commencement date was 13 January 1995.

---

[153] [1997] AC 749.
[154] [1998] 1 WLR 896.
[155] [2002] 1 AC 251.
[156] [2009] 1 AC 1101.
[157] [1997] AC 749.

The landlord argued that the tenant had not properly complied with the terms of **7.113** the lease, and therefore that the termination notice was invalid. The House of Lords, by a majority of three to two, decided that the termination by the tenant was valid even though it had stated the wrong date. The purpose of the notice was to inform the landlord that the tenant had decided to exercise its power to determine the lease in accordance with its terms. The objective meaning of the notice was what a reasonable recipient would understand it to mean, in the light of that purpose. Although the tenant had inserted the wrong date, a reasonable person in the position of the landlord would have understood that the tenant was trying to terminate the lease on the third anniversary, but had made a mistake about what that date was. The tenant had used the wrong words, but it was obvious what it meant. The notice had therefore served its purpose.

Although the tenant only won by three to two in the House of Lords (and by four **7.114** to five overall), this case is analogous with the cases discussed earlier in which there has been an obvious mistake. If you can change 'Landlord' to 'Tenant' or 'John' to 'Mary' because it is obvious what was meant, there is no reason why you cannot change '12 January' to '13 January' for the same reason.

ICS

The next case is *Investors Compensation Scheme v West Bromwich Building Society*.[158] **7.115**

On the advice of financial advisers, investors took out mortgages on their homes **7.116** with building societies and invested the proceeds in bonds, which fell substantially in value. The investors brought claims for compensation against the financial advisers. Because the financial advisers were insolvent, those claims were met by the ICS, which was set up to compensate investors in such cases. The ICS paid each claim and took an assignment of the investor's rights against the financial advisers and against third parties who might be liable. There was excluded from the assignment:

> Any claim (whether sounding in rescission for undue influence or otherwise) that you have or may have against the West Bromwich Building Society in which you claim an abatement of sums which you would otherwise have to repay to that society in respect of sums borrowed by you from that society in connection with the transactions and dealings giving rise to the claim …

The question was whether the ICS was able to make a claim against the building **7.117** society as assignee of the investor's rights, or whether it had been excluded by these words. The judge at first instance decided that only claims relating to rescission had been excluded. The Court of Appeal overruled the judge, and decided that the words were perfectly clear and excluded *any* claim which ICS may have against the building society of the kind referred to in the clause—whether or not it related to

---

[158] [1998] 1 WLR 896.

rescission. By a majority of four to one, the House of Lords overruled the Court of Appeal and decided that the words 'any claim (whether sounding in rescission for undue influence or otherwise)' actually meant 'any claim sounding in rescission (whether for undue influence or otherwise)'.

7.118 The principal judgment was given by Lord Hoffmann. In his view, it was clear that ICS could not have intended to have excluded claims generally against the building society, which was likely to be the most solvent party, and therefore the one most worth pursuing. The words in parenthesis seemed strange—why were claims 'sounding in rescission for undue influence' singled out? There had clearly been a mistake in the drafting, and the court was able to amend it as a matter of interpretation.

7.119 This is still a controversial decision. The assignment document had been produced by the ICS, and it might therefore have been thought that any ambiguity would be construed against it. In fact, the House of Lords did quite the opposite. It decided that:

- the ICS had got the wording wrong;
- a reasonable person in the position of the investor would have realized that it had done so;
- it was obvious what the ICS had meant.

7.120 This case goes much further than *Mannai*. It was obvious in that case not only that the tenant had made a mistake, but what he had actually meant. In *ICS*, it was much more difficult for the court to determine both that there had been a mistake and what was actually intended. The drafting might have been 'slovenly', but that was no reason to do violence to the language.[159] It is undoubtedly one of the high-water marks of Principle 7. The contract was rewritten.

BCCI

7.121 The third case is *Bank of Credit and Commerce International v Ali*.[160] Employees of the bank were made redundant. In consideration of a payment by the bank, the employee:

> agrees to accept the terms set out in the documents attached in full and final settlement of all or any claims whether under statute, common law or in equity of whatsoever nature that exist or may exist … except the applicant's rights under [the bank's] pension scheme.

7.122 The bank went into liquidation as a result of fraudulent activities of its management. The liquidators sought to recover loans made to the employees, and the employees

---

[159] This was the view of Lord Lloyd, who dissented.
[160] [2002] 1 AC 251.

counterclaimed for damages for breach of their employment contracts, as a result of which they alleged they were at a disadvantage on the labour market because of those fraudulent activities. The employees were not aware that they might have such a claim at the time they entered into the settlement agreement and, indeed, at that time no such cause of action was recognized by the law: it was a subsequent development.

By a majority of four to one, the House of Lords decided that the employees' coun-   **7.123** terclaim was not covered by the release. There were two main reasons. The first was that, in the absence of clear language, a court will be slow to infer that a party intends to surrender claims of which he was unaware. This aspect of the judgment was discussed under Principle 5 at paras 5.58–5.65.

The other reason was that the clause cannot have been intended to be read literally   **7.124** because, on the face of it, it would waive claims by the employees to deposits they had made with the bank; and that cannot have been intended. There must, therefore, be some intended limitation on the scope of the clause. It would be possible to limit the clause to claims arising out of the employment relationship, but the court went further and decided that it was limited to claims arising out of the *termination* of the employment relationship. Although the employees' claims arose out of the employment relationship, they did not arise out of its termination, and therefore they were not released.[161]

This is a good example of the perils of drafting too widely. If the clause clearly   **7.125** cannot mean what it says, there must be an implied limitation, and it is up to the court to decide what that limitation is.

Chartbrook

The fourth case is *Chartbrook v Persimmon Homes*.[162] Chartbrook owned a de-   **7.126** velopment site, and entered into an agreement with Persimmon for the development of the site. Persimmon would obtain planning permission, construct the development, and sell the properties on long leases and, from the proceeds, pay Chartbrook an agreed price for the land. The main element of the price was to be established by a simple formula. There was also a provision for the payment of an additional residential payment, and the question in dispute was the amount of that payment.

The additional residential payment was expressed to be '23.4% of the price achieved   **7.127** for each residential unit in excess of the minimum guaranteed residential unit value less the costs and incentives'.

---

[161] [2002] 1 AC 251 at [35].
[162] [2009] 1 AC 1101.

7.128 Chartbrook argued that what this meant was that you took the price achieved, deducted the minimum guaranteed residential unit value and the costs and incentives and then calculated 23.4% of the result.

7.129 Persimmon argued that you deduct the costs and incentives from the realized price to arrive at the net price, then calculate 23.4% of that price, and the additional residential payment is the excess of that figure over the minimum guaranteed residential unit value.

7.130 The first-instance judge, and the majority of the Court of Appeal, decided that Chartbrook's interpretation was the most natural interpretation of the words used, but the House of Lord unanimously found in favour of Persimmon's interpretation.

7.131 The principal judgment was again given by Lord Hoffmann. Building on the discussion in *Investors Compensation Scheme v West Bromwich Building Society*, he concluded that this was an 'exceptional case'[163] in which something must have gone wrong with the language and that 'to interpret the definition ... in accordance with ordinary rules of syntax makes no commercial sense'.[164] He went on to say:[165]

> When the language used in an instrument gives rise to difficulties of construction, the process of interpretation does not require one to formulate some alternative form of words which approximates as closely as possible to that of the parties. It is to decide what a reasonable person would have understood the parties to have meant by using the language which they did. The fact that the court might have to express that meaning in language quite different from that used by the parties ... is no reason for not giving effect to what they appear to have meant.

7.132 In reaching this conclusion, Lord Hoffmann referred with approval to Brightman LJ's judgment in *East v Pantiles (Plant Hire)*[166] that mistakes can be corrected if they are clear on the face of the instrument and it is clear what correction ought to be made in order to cure the mistake. But he qualified Brightman LJ's statement by saying that it was not necessary for the mistake to be made on the face of the document. Since the exercise is part of the task of interpretation, the background and context must always be taken into consideration. And, even more importantly, there is no 'limit to the amount of red ink or verbal rearrangement or correction which the court is allowed'.[167]

7.133 Like the *Investors Compensation Scheme* case, this is an extreme example of the court deciding to rewrite the contract.

---

163 [2009] 1 AC 1101 at [15].
164 [2009] 1 AC 1101 at [16].
165 [2009] 1 AC 1101 at [21].
166 (1981) 263 EG 61, discussed earlier at para 7.54.
167 [2009] 1 AC 1101 at [23]–[25].

The outcome

Of these four seminal cases, *Mannai* can be seen as an example of an obvious error, **7.134** and *BCCI* as an example of a case where a draftsman came to grief by trying to draft too widely. The other two cases—*Investors Compensation Scheme* and *Chartbrook*— are examples of what might be described as the high-water mark of courts rewriting contracts under the guise of interpretation.

They are not the only cases where this has been done. The same approach has been **7.135** followed in other cases. In *Barclays Bank v HHY Luxembourg*,[168] the Court of Appeal interpreted a reference to 'disposal of all of the shares in the capital of an Obligor' as including a disposal of the shares in a subsidiary of the Obligor. In *Aberdeen City Council v Stewart Milne Group*,[169] the Supreme Court interpreted a provision for calculating an earn-out payment on the sale of property as requiring the amount to be calculated on the basis of a sale at market value, rather than at the actual sale price, even though the contract did not provide for it.

A recent example is the decision of Flaux J in *The Alexandros T*.[170] It concerned the **7.136** interpretation of a settlement agreement relating to insurance claims. The agreement was entered into between the assured and the underwriters. The assured agreed to accept a sum of money 'in full and final settlement of all and any claims it may have under [the] Policy against the Underwriters in relation to the loss of [a vessel] … '. The question was whether the agreement also released claims by the assured against the employees and agents of the underwriters.

The assured claimed that it did not release them. The expression 'Underwriters' was **7.137** a defined term which meant certain corporate entities. It did not extend to employees and agents, who were not even parties to the agreement.[171]

Flaux J disagreed. He had no doubt that the reference to 'Underwriters' in the rele- **7.138** vant clause was to be interpreted as encompassing the employees and agents of the underwriters. Anything else would defy business common sense.[172] The intention was that there should be a clean break between the assured and the insurers. Because corporate entities can only act through human agents, it would make no sense for the settlement to have released the insurers themselves but to have left the assured to pursue proceedings against those human agents—who might then have a counterclaim against the insurers. In the result, the employees and agents, who were not parties to the contract, obtained protection under the Contracts (Rights of Third

---

[168] [2010] EWCA Civ 1248.
[169] 2012 SLT 205.
[170] *Starlight Shipping v Allianz Marine and Aviation* [2014] 2 Lloyd's Rep 579.
[171] [2014] 2 Lloyd's Rep 579 at [45].
[172] [2014] 2 Lloyd's Rep 579 at [51].

Parties) Act 1999. This may make good commercial sense, but it is simply not what the contract said.

Q. Resisting the Temptation to Rewrite the Contract

7.139   The cases described in the last section of this chapter show how far the House of Lords has gone in rewriting contracts under the guise of interpretation. But more recently the tendency in the Supreme Court has been to curtail this approach and to place more emphasis on the words which the parties have actually used. There is a reluctance to use 'commercial common sense' to override the natural and ordinary meaning of the words used.

7.140   The most important recent authority is the decision of the Supreme Court in *Arnold v Britton*,[173] which is discussed at paras 7.24–7.28 above. The case involved the interpretation of a clause in a series of leases of holiday chalets on the Gower peninsula. It was intended that the leases should all be granted on similar terms. Clause 3(2) of the leases in question provided for the lessee to pay to the lessor 'a proportionate part of the expenses and outgoings incurred by the lessors in the repair maintenance and renewal ... and the provision of services hereafter set out the yearly sum of £90 and VAT (if any) for the first year of the term hereby granted increasing thereafter by ten pounds per hundred for every subsequent year ... thereof'.

7.141   At the time of the proceedings, the annual service charge for these chalets was over £2,700—the increase resulting from the effect of 10 per cent annual compound interest over many years. Earlier chalets had been leased on terms which provided for a service charge of £90 and VAT increasing by 10 per cent every three years. In these cases, because the amount only compounded every three years, the annual service charge was only £282.

7.142   Because of the great difference between the amounts of service charge payable depending on when the lease was entered into, the lessees under the later leases claimed that the clause did not mean what it appeared to say. They argued that the clause contained two inconsistent provisions—first an obligation to pay 'a proportionate part' of the expenses; and secondly, an obligation to pay a set amount established by a formula. These two concepts were mutually exclusive and, because the natural interpretation of the clause created an absurd result, something must have gone wrong with the drafting. What the parties must have intended was that each tenant would pay a proportionate part of the expenses up to a maximum of the set amount.

---

[173] [2015] AC 1619.

This approach was accepted by Lord Carnwath,[174] and it is entirely consistent with   **7.143**
the approach in cases such as *Investors Compensation Scheme* and *Chartbrook*. But
the majority took a different approach. The clause may not have been entirely free
of infelicities, but its natural and ordinary meaning was clear. The purpose of the
formula was to establish the amount to be paid, and the fact that it produced an odd
result was not a reason for failing to give effect to the words used.[175]

In relation to contractual interpretation, it has been seen that cases are only relevant   **7.144**
for the principles which they propound, rather than their actual decisions—because
those depend on the particular facts of the case in hand. But it is nevertheless useful
to see how the courts have approached cases where it has been unsuccessfully argued
that the words used by the parties cannot mean what they appear to say. *Arnold
v Britton* is discussed above. Six other cases can illustrate the point, three in the
English Court of Appeal, two in the New South Wales Court of Appeal, and one in
the Privy Council:

(1) *East v Pantiles (Plant Hire)*;[176]
(2) *City Alliance v Oxford Forecasting Services*;[177]
(3) *Kooee Communications v Primus Telecommunications*;[178]
(4) *Jireh International v Western Exports Services*;[179]
(5) *Thompson v Goblin Hill Hotels*;[180]
(6) *Sugarman v CJS Investments*.[181]

East v Pantiles (Plant Hire)[182] was decided before *ICS* and *Chartbrook*, but the   **7.145**
statement of the law by Brightman LJ was broadly approved by Lord Hoffmann
in *Chartbrook*, and there is no reason to doubt that the same result would be
achieved today.

A lease provided for the payment of rent 'by equal quarterly instalments in advance   **7.146**
on the 14th day of August the 1st day of November the first day of February and the
first day of May in each year the first payment to be made on the 1st day of August
1972'. The landlord argued that the reference to 14 August was an obvious clerical
error, and that it should have read 1 August. The Court of Appeal refused to alter the
date. There was no reason why the landlord should have chosen to accept the rent in

---

[174] [2015] AC 1619 at [125].
[175] [2015] AC 1619 at [28]–[37] (Lord Neuberger) and [75] (Lord Hodge).
[176] [1982] 2 EGLR 111.
[177] [2001] 1 All ER (Comm) 233.
[178] [2008] NSWCA 5.
[179] [2011] NSWCA 137.
[180] [2011] 1 BCLC 587.
[181] [2015] 1 BCLC 1.
[182] [1982] 2 EGLR 111.

August on the 14th rather than on the 1st, but there was no evidence to suggest that it was a mistake, and that the parties had really intended 1 August.

7.147 In *City Alliance v Oxford Forecasting Services*,[183] a subscription agreement contained an undertaking by the company not to create or issue any share capital or options over share capital, provided that the company: 'may at any time issue ordinary £1 shares to any person at a price per share of not less than £100,000 per share, payable in full on subscription'. It was argued that this proviso must permit the company to grant an option to issue shares in the future on terms that, when issued, the shares would be issued at a price of not less than £100,000 per share payable in full on subscription. The Court of Appeal refused to accept this argument. They said that it was not for the party who relies upon the words actually used to establish that those words effect a sensible commercial purpose. It is for the party challenging the ordinary meaning of the words to show that they produced a result which was so commercially nonsensical that the parties could not have intended it and that what they did intend can be identified with confidence. Neither of those conditions was satisfied.

7.148 In *Kooee Communications v Primus Telecommunications*,[184] Primus agreed to provide telecommunications services in Kooee's name and to pay Kooee a percentage of the revenue it obtained. Some years later, the companies decided to terminate the arrangement on the basis that Kooee would be entitled to collect and retain outstanding debts, in return for a lump sum payment to Primus. The amount of that payment was to be determined by reference to the debts recorded in Primus' books of account less: 'any of those Debts in respect of which Primus has made provision in accordance with its usual bad and doubtful debt policy'.

7.149 On the face of it, this would mean that the amount of the payment from Kooee to Primus would be reduced by the full amount of those debts in respect of which Primus had made a provision, even if the provision was only for part of the debts concerned. Primus argued that must have been a mistake, and that the intention must have been for the amount of the deduction to be the amount of the provision, rather than the amount of the debt. The trial judge accepted this argument, on the basis that Kooee's interpretation presented a 'strong aura of commercial unreality'.[185] But the New South Wales Court of Appeal overruled him. They decided that the terms of the agreement were clear and there was no justification for the court to reformulate them. Basten JA relied on 'the principle that the Court is not able to disregard clear words, nor under the guise of interpreting the contract to re-write it'.[186]

---

[183] [2001] 11 All ER (Comm) 233.
[184] [2008] NSWCA 5.
[185] [2007] NSWSC 91 at [27].
[186] [2008] NSWCA 5 at [38].

In *Jireh International v Western Exports Services*,[187] Western Exports Services (WES) **7.150** was an American company which agreed to assist Jireh, an Australian company, to become the Australian franchisee for an American coffee franchise. The parties entered into an agreement under which WES agreed to assist Jireh to do so. WES would be the exclusive supplier to Jireh and would receive a commission on sales. In addition, clause 3 of the agreement provided that:

> One of the primary goals of negotiations with [the franchisor], is to establish [Jireh], or an associated entity, as a roaster/supplier of [the franchise coffee] … For sales by [Jireh] to [the franchise outlets] … [WES] shall receive a commission of 5% of the ex-factory price of the [coffee].

The question at issue was what clause 3 meant. In practice, sales were made to the fran- **7.151** chise outlets not just by Jireh itself but by associated companies. WES contended that it was entitled to commission under clause 3 for sales made by the associated companies, as well as those made by Jireh. The first-instance judge agreed with WES, but the New South Wales Court of Appeal overruled that judgment and decided that WES was only entitled to commission on sales actually made by Jireh, rather than by its associated com- panies. There was no reason to give the provision anything other than its literal meaning.

MacFarlane JA said:[188] **7.152**

> In my view the provision is unambiguous and there is no basis for departing from its literal meaning. In particular the provision would not have an absurd operation if con- strued literally. I do not agree with the primary judge's apparent conclusion that it is permissible to depart from the literal meaning of an unambiguous provision in order to give it what the Court considers to be 'a commercial and business-like operation'.

In *Thompson v Goblin Hill Hotels*,[189] the articles of association of a hotel development **7.153** company provided that certain costs of maintaining its villas and grounds would be 'borne by each member in proportion to his shareholding in the Company'. Most of the company's shares were held by owners of the villas, but some were held by directors of the company, who did not own villas. The directors argued that the articles could not sensibly require them to pay the expenses *pari passu* with those shareholders who did own villas—they derived no benefit from it. The Privy Council decided that the plain and ordinary meaning of the words could only be displaced if it produced a commercial absurdity, and that had not been established in this case.

The final example is *Sugarman v CJS Investments*.[190] It involved the interpretation **7.154** of the articles of association of the management company of a residential block of

---

[187] [2011] NSWCA 137. Criticized by McLauchlan and Lees in 'Construction Controversy' (2011) 28 JCL 101.
[188] [2011] NSWCA 137 at [7].
[189] [2011] 1 BCLC 587.
[190] [2015] 1 BCLC 1.

flats. There were 104 flats, the majority of which were owned by a limited liability partnership called CJS. Most of the others were owned by individual tenants. Each tenant had one share in the company.

7.155 Article 13 provided that: 'every Member present in person or by Proxy shall have one vote . . . .' CJS argued that this could not mean what it said, and that each tenant should have one vote per share. Otherwise CJS would only be entitled to one vote in respect of all its shares and could routinely be outvoted by the individual tenants.

7.156 The Court of Appeal held that the words meant what they said. Although this interpretation could produce odd results, '[this] is not a case where it can seriously be suggested that a reasonable person seeking to understand the words . . . would react by saying "it cannot mean what it says"'.[191] The result might be unreasonable, uncommercial and unusual, but it was not absurd.[192] 'Whilst one might express a preference for a mechanism which allowed a greater control for those who owned more than one flat, a system based on one member one vote falls well short of commercial absurdity.'[193]

7.157 These cases are nothing more than illustrations of the strong and understandable feeling of many commercial lawyers and judges that it will take a lot to persuade them that the parties have made a mistake in the drafting of a legal document. In many of these cases, it might have been thought that the result was more commercially absurd than it was in *ICS* and *Chartbrook*. They sound a note of warning that there does need to be clear evidence that the parties have made a mistake before this power to change the words can be invoked.

7.158 This approach to the interpretation process is summed up by Lord Grabiner in an article in the Law Quarterly Review in 2012:[194]

> [W]here the wording of a contractual provision (in the context of the contract as a whole) is clear, there is (or should be) limited room for the court to conclude that those words were used by mistake. The courts should not speculate on the commercial common sense behind those words and should not be tempted into constructing an abstract commercial purpose derived from the 'factual matrix' in order to rewrite what is otherwise clear.

R. Conclusion

7.159 Principle 7 is a principle of contractual interpretation, not of rectification. Lord Hoffmann made this clear in *Chartbrook v Persimmon Homes*.[195] But it does look very like a form of summary rectification ('rectification lite').

---

[191] [2015] 1 BCLC 1 at [34].
[192] [2015] 1 BCLC 1 at [49].
[193] [2015] 1 BCLC 1 at [39].
[194] Grabiner, 'The Iterative Process of Contractual Interpretation' (2012) 128 LQR 41 at 41.
[195] [2009] 1 AC 1101 at [23].

As the discussion under Principle 9 will show, if a written contract does not record **7.160** the parties' common intention, it will be rectified in order to reflect that intention. If the court rectifies the contract, the words of the contract are amended to reflect what the parties actually intended. That is not the case when a contract is interpreted in an unnatural way under Principle 7. Here, the words of the contract are not actually amended. Instead, the court reads the words used in a different way from their natural meaning. But the outcome is the same.

It is clearly justifiable to correct obvious errors, such as typos. The real question is **7.161** how much further this principle can be taken. It is easy to state the principle: something must clearly have gone wrong with the language which the parties have used, and it must be clear to a reasonable person what the parties actually intended. As so often, the problem is not with the principle, but with its application to the facts.

This is particularly difficult in relation to interpretation of contracts because there **7.162** will always be a tension between the two schools of thought described at the start of this chapter. Many commercial lawyers will start with the assumption that the parties have set the document in writing with the whole purpose of ensuring that their rights and duties can be found in that document; and that it will take a very strong case indeed to persuade them otherwise. Others will argue that it is necessary to interpret a commercial document in a commercial way, and that one should not stand too firm on the niceties of language if that would defeat the commercial purpose.

This argument will continue as long as there are contracts to be interpreted. **7.163**

Part IV

ADDING WORDS

Principle 8: Words are implied into a contract if the parties must objectively have intended them. This will be the case either if they are so obvious that there was no need to express them, or if they are necessary to make the contract work in a business context.

The purpose of this Part is to establish when words can be added to the contract.   **Pt 4.01**

8

PRINCIPLE 8: IMPLIED TERMS

Principle 8: Words are implied into a contract if the parties must objectively have intended them. This will be the case either if they are so obvious that there was no need to express them, or if they are necessary to make the contract work in a business context.

A. The Principle

The courts imply terms into contracts in order to make them work. When the un- **8.01** expected happens, it is necessary to decide what the parties would have provided for if they had considered the problem.[1]

The implication of terms in a contract is part of the exercise of interpreting the con- **8.02** tract as a whole.[2] The objective—as with any other process of interpretation—is to establish the objective common intention of the parties.[3]

This point was made by Lord Hoffmann in *Attorney General of Belize v Belize* **8.03** *Telecom*:[4]

> The court has no power to improve upon the instrument which it is called upon to construe ... it cannot introduce terms to make it fairer or more reasonable. It is concerned only to discover what the instrument means. However, that meaning is not necessarily or always what the authors or parties to the document would have intended. It is a meaning which the instrument would convey to a reasonable person having all the background knowledge which would reasonably be available to the audience to whom the instrument is addressed ... It is this objective meaning which is conventionally called the intention of the parties ...

---

[1] See Lewison, *The Interpretation of Contracts* (6th edn, Sweet & Maxwell, 2015), Chapter 6; McMeel, *The Construction of Contracts* (2nd edn, Oxford University Press, 2011), Chapters 10 and 11; Hooley, 'Implied Terms After Belize Telecom' (2014) 73 CLJ 315.
[2] See Lewison at 6.03.
[3] This is Principle 1. The objective nature of the enquiry was emphasized by Lord Neuberger in *Marks and Spencer v BNP Paribas* [2016] AC 742 at [21].
[4] [2009] 1 WLR 1988 at [16].

8.04 This suggests that the implication of terms is no different in kind from any other process of interpretation. Certainly, it is often difficult to decide, in any particular case, whether the answer has been achieved by a simple process of interpretation or by the implication of a term. [5] But, as Paul Davies has said:[6] 'Interpretation should be concerned with ascertaining the meaning of words contained in the written agreement, whereas implication acts to supplement that instrument with terms additional to those expressly chosen by the parties.' Conflating the two runs the risk of failing to give sufficient weight to the stringent requirements for the implication of terms.[7]

8.05 The relationship between interpretation and implication was discussed by the Supreme Court in *Marks and Spencer v BNP Paribas*.[8] Although, as Lord Clarke noted, implication is, in a broad sense, part of the process of interpretation,[9] Lord Neuberger commented that the process of implication necessarily follows on from the process of interpretation. It is only once the interpreter has decided what the words mean that he or she can then turn to the question of whether anything should be implied.[10] He said:[11]

> I accept that both (i) construing the words which the parties have used in their contract and (ii) implying terms into the contract, involve determining the scope and meaning of the contract. However, Lord Hoffmann's analysis in *Belize Telecom* could obscure the fact that construing the words used and implying additional words are different processes governed by different rules.

8.06 In the *Belize* case, Lord Hoffmann stated the test for the implication of terms in this way:[12]

> [I]n every case in which it is said that some provision ought to be implied in an instrument, the question for the court is whether such a provision would spell out in express words what the instrument, read against the relevant background, would reasonably be understood to mean.... [T]his question can be reformulated in various ways which a court may find helpful in providing an answer—the implied term must 'go without saying', it must be 'necessary to give business efficacy to the contract' and so on—but these are not ... to be treated as different or additional tests. There is only one question: is that what the instrument, read as a whole against the relevant background, would reasonably be understood to mean?

---

[5] A recent example is *Aberdeen City Council v Stewart Milne Group* [2012] SLT 205.

[6] Davies, 'Recent Developments in the Law of Implied Terms' [2010] LMCLQ 140 at 140.

[7] For a contrary view, see McLauchlan, 'Construction and Implication: in Defence of Belize Telecom' [2014] LMCLQ 203.

[8] [2016] AC 742.

[9] [2016] AC 742 at [76] and [77].

[10] [2016] AC 742 at [27] and [28]. And see *Foo Jong Peng v Phua Kiah Mai* [2012] 4 SLR 1267 at [31] and [36].

[11] [2016] AC 742 at [26].

[12] [2009] 1 WLR 1988 at [21].

As in *Investors Compensation Scheme v West Bromwich Building Society*,[13] Lord **8.07**
Hoffmann does not refer to the parties' intention when he describes the principle.
But it is still generally accepted that it is the determination of the parties' objective
intention which is the ultimate objective of the process which Lord Hoffmann describes. See the discussion of Principle 1.

The importance of the *Belize* case is that it shows that the implication of terms **8.08**
is part of the interpretative process. The ultimate question is therefore whether
the parties must objectively have intended the words to be added; and that objective intention is established by looking at the contract as a whole and the
background facts.

But Lord Hoffmann went further than this. He said that there is just one test of **8.09**
implication:[14] 'is that what the instrument, read as a whole against the relevant
background, would reasonably be understood to mean?'

The problem with this formulation is that, although it sets out what needs to be **8.10**
achieved, it does not give any assistance in deciding how to do it.[15] Lord Hoffmann
may well have thought that no other assistance was required. But, as he indicates,
there are other ways in which the question can be reformulated which courts have
found helpful. In particular, the two formulations that an implied term must 'go
without saying' or that it must be 'necessary to give business efficacy to the contract'
are well established in the law. Are they still relevant?

The answer to that question is: yes. Although Lord Hoffmann cautioned against the **8.11**
'dangers in treating these alternative formulations of the question as if they had a life
of their own',[16] he did accept that the court might find them helpful in providing
an answer.[17] Indeed, when the Court of Appeal had to consider the *Belize* case in
Mediterranean Salvage & Towage v Seamar Trading & Commerce,[18] the court emphasized the importance of establishing that the proposed implied term is not merely
reasonable, but that it is necessary to make the contract work.

In *Foo Jong Peng v Phua Kiah Mai*,[19] Andrew Phang Boon Leong JA (giving the **8.12**
judgment of the Singapore Court of Appeal) said that the problem with the *Belize
Telecom* approach is that it: 'does not, in and of itself, tell us *how* a particular term
ought—or ought not—to be implied'. Tests are needed; and they are supplied by

---

[13] [1998] 1 WLR 896.
[14] [2009] 1 WLR 1988 at [21].
[15] The problems with the approach are clearly articulated by Paul Davies, 'Recent Developments
in the Law of Implied Terms' [2010] LMCLQ 140.
[16] [2009] 1 WLR 1988 at [22].
[17] [2009] 1 WLR 1988 at [21].
[18] [2009] 1 CLC 909 at [15].
[19] [2012] 4 SLR 1267 at [36]. Emphasis in the original.

the two formulations described above, which he describes as the 'officious bystander' and 'business efficacy' tests,[20] which are discussed in section D of this chapter.

8.13 The same approach was taken by the United Kingdom Supreme Court in *Marks and Spencer v BNP Paribas*.[21] In that case, Lord Neuberger said:[22]

> It is necessary to emphasise that there has been no dilution of the requirements which have to be satisfied before a term will be implied, because it is apparent that *Belize Telecom* has been interpreted by both academic lawyers and judges as having changed the law.

8.14 Perhaps the best way of describing the relationship between interpretation and implication is that implication is one part of the overall process of interpretation. Their common purpose is to establish the objective common intention of the parties. This is primarily done by reading the words which the parties have used in the context of the relevant background facts. Occasionally it is necessary to add words to those which the parties have used. But this can only be done in very limited circumstances, in accordance with the requirements discussed later in this chapter. In particular, a term can only be implied if it is so obvious that there was no need to express it or if it is necessary to make the contract work in a business context.

B. Distinguishing Express Terms

8.15 Implication of terms is concerned with filling gaps—adding words that are not there. It needs to be distinguished from another type of 'implication'—determining the necessary effect of the express words of the contract. For instance, if a contract says that: 'the benefit of this contract can be assigned with the consent of X', it is a necessary implication that the benefit of the contract cannot be assigned without the consent of X. The express term is written in a positive form ('it can be done if X consents') but it is a necessary implication from the words actually used that it is also intended to encompass the negative ('it cannot be done unless X consents'). The interpreter here is not adding a term; he or she is giving effect to the words actually used.[23]

C. Terms Are Rarely Implied

8.16 The implication of terms should be a rare occurrence.[24] As Lord Hoffmann said in *Attorney General of Belize v Belize Telecom*:[25]

---

[20] [2012] 4 SLR 1267 at [33].
[21] [2016] AC 742.
[22] [2016] AC 742 at [24].
[23] *Borys v Canadian Pacific Railway Co* [1953] AC 217.
[24] See Lewison at 6.04.
[25] [2009] 1 WLR 1988 at [17].

The question of implication arises when the instrument does not expressly provide for what is to happen when some event occurs. The most usual inference in such a case is that nothing is to happen. If the parties had intended something to happen, the instrument would have said so. Otherwise, the express provisions of the instrument are to continue to operate undisturbed. If the event has caused loss to one or other of the parties, the loss lies where it falls.

Parties to a contract try to agree everything, but it is not uncommon that they deliberately fail to reach agreement on something which they think is unlikely to happen, in the hope that it does not. If that event does happen, there is no room for implying a term. As Mason J said in the High Court of Australia in *Codelfa Construction v State Rail Authority of New South Wales*:[26]   **8.17**

> For obvious reasons the courts are slow to imply a term. In many cases, what the parties have actually agreed upon represents the totality of their willingness to agree; each may be prepared to take his chance in relation to an eventuality for which no provision is made.

The implication of terms is therefore the exception, rather than the rule. The reason for this was explained by Sir Thomas Bingham MR in *Philips Electronique v British Sky Broadcasting*:[27]   **8.18**

> The courts' usual role in contractual interpretation is, by resolving ambiguities or reconciling apparent inconsistencies, to attribute the true meaning to the language in which the parties themselves have expressed their contract. The implication of contract terms involves a different and altogether more ambitious undertaking: the interpolation of terms to deal with matters for which, *ex hypothesi*, the parties themselves have made no provision. It is because the implication of terms is so potentially intrusive that the law imposes strict constraints on the exercise of this extraordinary power.

D. The Tests for Implication of Terms

There have traditionally been two tests which have been used to imply terms. One is that it is 'necessary to give business efficacy to the contract'. The other is that 'it is so obvious, that it goes without saying'.[28]   **8.19**

The first test was described by Bowen LJ in *The Moorcock*:[29]   **8.20**

> [T]he law is raising an implication from the presumed intention of the parties with the object of giving to the transaction such efficacy as both parties must have intended that at all events it should have. In business transactions ... what

---

[26] (1981–1982) 149 CLR 337 at 346.
[27] [1995] EMLR 472 at 481.
[28] See Lewison at 6.08 and 6.09.
[29] (1889) 14 PD 64 at 68.

the law desires to effect by the implication is to give such business efficacy to the transaction as must have been intended at all events by both parties who are business men.

8.21 Bowen LJ did not specifically refer to necessity, but his judgment has been taken to establish the following test: is the implication of a term necessary to give business efficacy to the contract?[30] In other words, is it necessary to make the contract work in a business context?[31] It is not necessary to show that the contract simply cannot work on any basis without the implication of the term. What is required is to show that the contract will not work in any sensible business manner without the implication of the term.[32]

8.22 The other common test for the implication of terms was described by MacKinnon LJ in *Shirlaw v Southern Foundries*:[33]

Prima facie that which in any contract is left to be implied and need not be expressed is something so obvious that it goes without saying; so that, if, while the parties were making their bargain, an officious bystander were to suggest some express provision for it in their agreement, they would testily suppress him with a common 'Oh, of course!'

8.23 MacKinnon LJ saw this as an elaboration of Bowen LJ's test of implication in *The Moorcock*. The test which has been developed from *The Moorcock* is an objective one—what needs to be done to make the contract work? The test in *Shirlaw v Southern Foundries* draws inspiration from the parties themselves, and what they would have said. But it is concerned not with the subjective intentions of the parties, but with their objective intentions.[34]

8.24 Scrutton LJ combines the two tests in his description of the test in *Reigate v Union Manufacturing Company*:[35]

A term can only be implied if it is necessary in the business sense to give efficacy to the contract; that is, if it is such a term that it can confidently be said that if at the time the contract was being negotiated someone had said to the parties, 'What will happen in such a case', they would both have replied, 'Of course, so and so will happen; we did not trouble to say that; it is too clear'.

---

[30] See, for instance, Lord Simon's description of it in the Privy Council in *BP Refinery (Westernport) v Shire of Hastings* (1977) 16 ALR 363 at 376, discussed at para 8.29 below.
[31] See the observations of Steyn J in *Associated Japanese Bank v Credit du Nord* [1989] 1 WLR 255 at 263.
[32] See Lord Hoffmann's comments in *Attorney General of Belize v Belize Telecom* [2009] 1 WLR 1988 at [22]–[23].
[33] [1939] 2 KB 206 at 227.
[34] See Lord Hoffmann's comments in *Attorney General of Belize v Belize Telecom* [2009] 1 WLR 1988 at [25].
[35] [1918] 1 KB 592 at 605. Showing remarkable foresight, bearing in mind that MacKinnon LJ did not give his judgment for another twenty years.

These two tests are sometimes seen as cumulative,[36] sometimes as alternatives.[37]   **8.25**
In *Marks and Spencer v BNP Paribas*,[38] Lord Neuberger described the tests as
alternatives, in the sense that only one of them needs to be satisfied, although in
practice he suspected that it would be a rare case where only one would be satisfied. It is suggested that they are probably best seen as different ways of saying the
same thing.[39]

The requirement that the term is necessary to give business efficacy to the con-   **8.26**
tract underlines two important points. One is the requirement of necessity,
rather than just reasonableness. The other is the focus on the contract in a business context. The contract may work perfectly well in the sense that both parties
can perform their express obligations, but the consequences would contradict
what a reasonable person would understand the contract to mean. As Lord
Neuberger said in *Marks and Spencer v BNP Paribas*,[40] necessity for business
efficacy involves a value judgement. The test is not one of 'absolute' necessity.
A term will be implied if, without it, the contract would lack commercial or
practical coherence.

The other test, that the implied term must 'go without saying', illustrates the point   **8.27**
that the court is ultimately concerned with what the parties intended. But it must
not be seen as a requirement to establish the subjective intentions of the parties. The
question is how a reasonable person would see their common intention, and it is
vital to formulate the question with care.[41]

In summary, the implication of terms is part of the process of interpretation. The   **8.28**
ultimate question is therefore to establish what the parties must objectively have
intended—in other words, what the document, read as a whole against the relevant
background, would reasonably be understood to mean. The court will carry out this
exercise by asking itself two questions:

(1) Is the implied term so obvious that there is no need to express it?
(2) Is the implied term necessary to make the contract work in a business context?

---

[36] *BP Refinery (Westernport) v The Shire of Hastings* (1997) 16 ALR 363 at 376 (Lord Simon giving
the opinion of the Privy Council); *Codelfa Construction v State Rail Authority of New South Wales*
(1981–1982) 149 CLR 337 at 355 (Mason J in the High Court of Australia).

[37] For example, see Steyn J in *Associated Japanese Bank v Credit du Nord* [1989] 1 WLR 255 at 263
and in *Mosvolds Rederi v Food Corporation of India* [1986] 2 Lloyd's Rep 68 at 70–1; and Bingham
LJ in *The Manifest Lipkowy, Markan Shipping (London) v Polish Steamship Co* [1989] 2 Lloyd's Rep
138 at 143.

[38] [2016] AC 742 at [21].

[39] This is the approach of Lord Hoffmann in *Attorney General of Belize v Belize Telecom* [2009] 1
WLR 1988 at [21]–[22].

[40] [2016] AC 742 at [21].

[41] *Marks and Spencer v BNP Paribas* [2016] AC 742 at [21] (Lord Neuberger).

E. Other Potential Requirements

8.29   In *BP Refinery (Westernport) v Shire of Hastings*,[42] Lord Simon in the Privy Council laid down five conditions for the implication of terms:

> [F]or a term to be implied, the following conditions (which may overlap) must be satisfied: (1) it must be reasonable and equitable; (2) it must be necessary to give business efficacy to the contract so that no term will be implied if the contract is effective without it; (3) it must be so obvious that 'it goes without saying'; (4) it must be capable of clear expression; (5) it must not contradict any express term of the contract.

8.30   In the *Belize* case,[43] Lord Hoffmann re=garded this list:

> not as a series of independent tests which must each be surmounted, but rather as a collection of different ways in which judges have tried to express the central idea that the proposed implied term must spell out what the contract actually means, or in which they have explained why they did not think that it did so.

8.31   Conditions (2) and (3) have already been discussed. As we have seen, they are really alternative ways of asking the same question, rather than cumulative requirements.

8.32   The other three conditions are obvious. They themselves 'go without saying'. A court will not want to imply a term if it is not reasonable and equitable,[44] and will not be able to do so if it is not capable of clear expression. The requirement that an implied term must not contradict an express term is also obvious. How can the parties objectively have intended something which contradicts what the contract actually says?

8.33   The requirement that an express term must not contradict an implied term is nevertheless important because, in practice, it is often the reason why terms cannot be implied.[45] An example is *Lynch v Thorne*.[46] A builder agreed to sell a partially erected house to a purchaser, and to complete it in accordance with detailed specifications, including nine-inch brick walls. When it was built, it transpired that the walls did not keep out the driving rain. The buyer claimed that he had relied on the builder's skill, and that there was an implied term that the house should be fit for human habitation. The Court of Appeal decided that no such term could be implied because it would be inconsistent with the express term concerning the width of the walls.

---

[42] (1977) 16 ALR 363 at 376.
[43] *Attorney General of Belize v Belize Telecom* [2009] 1 WLR 1988 at [27].
[44] In *Marks and Spencer v BNP Paribas* [2016] AC 742 at [21], Lord Neuberger thought they added little to the test.
[45] See Lewison at 6.11.
[46] [1956] 1 WLR 303.

F. What Needs to be Established?

The implication of a term requires certainty about two matters: **8.34**

(1) that a term should be implied;
(2) what that implied term should say.[47]

This two-fold test is similar to that required to give words an unnatural meaning **8.35** under Principle 7; and, as with that test, it is the second requirement—certainty as to what the implied term should say—which frequently creates a problem in practice. The parties may well have skated over a problem which they hoped was unlikely to occur, in the hope that it would not.[48]

The first requirement—that it is clear that a term should be implied—also needs **8.36** to be treated with great caution. The starting point is that nothing is to be implied[49] and, as Sir Thomas Bingham MR said in *Philips Electronique v British Sky Broadcasting*:[50] 'the court comes to the task of implication with the benefit of hindsight, and it is tempting for the court then to fashion a term which will reflect the merits of the situation as they then appear. Tempting, but wrong.' The implication exercise must be carried out by reference to the date of the contract.

The presumption that nothing should be implied[51] is particularly strong where the **8.37** contract is lengthy and carefully drafted.[52] As Mason J said in the High Court of Australia in *Codelfa Construction v State Rail Authority of New South Wales*:[53] 'The more detailed and comprehensive the contract the less ground there is for supposing that the parties have failed to address their minds to the question at issue.' And if a clause deals with a particular matter and is silent about an aspect of that matter, it is difficult to imply a term which goes beyond what has been expressed.[54]

That is not to say that terms cannot be implied even into quite elaborate commer- **8.38** cial contracts. They can. An example is *Associated Japanese Bank v Credit du Nord*.[55] In that case, a person had sold machines to a bank, which then leased them back to him, and his obligations under the lease were guaranteed by another bank. It

---

[47] See, for instance, the approach of Ormrod LJ in *Shell UK v Lostock Garage* [1976] 1 WLR 1187 at 1200–1.
[48] See the remarks of Sir Thomas Bingham MR in *Philips Electronique v British Sky Broadcasting* [1995] EMLR 472 at 482.
[49] *Attorney General of Belize v Belize Telecom* [2009] 1 WLR 1988 at [17].
[50] [1995] EMLR 472 at 482.
[51] *Luxor (Eastbourne) v Cooper* [1941] AC 108 at 137.
[52] *Phllips Electronique v British Sky Broadcasting* [1995] EMLR 472 at 481–2.
[53] (1981–1982) 149 CLR 337 at 346.
[54] *Dear v Griffith* [2013] EWCA Civ 89 at [28]–[31].
[55] [1989] 1 WLR 255.

transpired that the machines did not, in fact, exist, and that the lessee had committed a fraud. The lessor sued the guarantor under the terms of its guarantee. Steyn J held that the guarantor was not liable on various grounds, one of which was that the existence of the machines was an implied condition precedent to the guarantor's liability. This was not expressed in the guarantee because it was so obvious that it went without saying.[56] Even quite elaborately drafted commercial documentation can fail to deal with issues which are so fundamental that no thought is given to them. The existence of the machines was such an issue.

G. Examples

8.39 In common with other types of interpretation, it is necessary to be wary about examples of cases where terms have, or have not, been implied. Each case depends on an interpretation of the contract as a whole in the context of the background facts, and a case is only a precedent to the extent that it establishes the basic principles. With that warning, it is nevertheless useful to see how courts have approached the exercise in practice. In this section, we will look at six cases—two where a term was implied and four where it was not.

8.40 It is perhaps best to start with the cases where a term was not implied—the decisions of the Court of Appeal in *The Manifest Lipkowy*[57] and *Mid Essex Hospital Services NHS Trust v Compass Group*,[58] the decision of the High Court of Australia in *Codelfa Construction v State Rail Authority of New South Wales*,[59] and the decision of the Supreme Court in *Marks and Spencer v BNP Paribas*.[60]

8.41 In *The Manifest Lipkowy*,[61] a shipbroker negotiated the sale of a vessel from its owners to a potential buyer. A sale and purchase contract was entered into, which provided for future delivery of the vessel, and gave the buyer an option to cancel if the vessel was not ready for delivery by a particular date. The vessel was not ready in time and the buyer cancelled the contract. The shipbroker then brought a claim against the owners, claiming damages for breach of an implied term of his contract with the owners that the owners would not by breach of the sale purchase agreement deprive the shipbrokers of their opportunity to earn commission.

8.42 The Court of Appeal refused to imply a term. It was not necessary to make the contract work.

---

[56] [1989] 1 WLR 255 at 263.
[57] *Marcan Shipping v Polish Steamship Co* [1989] 2 Lloyd's Rep 138.
[58] [2013] EWCA Civ 200.
[59] (1981–1982) 149 CLR 337.
[60] [2016] AC 742.
[61] *Marcan Shipping v Polish Steamship Co* [1989] 2 Lloyd's Rep 138.

In *Mid Essex Hospital Services NHS Trust v Compass Group*,[62] a company had entered **8.43** into a seven-year contract with an NHS trust to provide catering and cleaning services in two hospitals. The contract contained formulae to test the performance of the company under the contract, and it gave the trust the power to make deductions from its payments to the company in the light of the figures provided by the formulae. At first instance, Cranston J held that the trust's power to make deductions was subject to an implied term that it would not act in an arbitrary, capricious, or irrational manner.

The Court of Appeal (Jackson, Lewison, and Beatson LJJ) disagreed. They con- **8.44** sidered that the clause contained precise rules for determining what deductions were due. That exercise was a matter of calculation, and did not involve a discretion. Once the correct figures had been established, the trust then had a discretion. It could make deductions or not at a level that it chose. There was no necessity to imply a term that it would not exercise this power in a particular way. The discretion simply permitted the trust to decide whether or not to exercise an absolute contractual right. There was therefore no justification for implying a term.

In *Codelfa Construction v State Rail Authority of New South Wales*,[63] a construction **8.45** company contracted with a railway authority to perform excavations for the construction of an underground railway. The company was required to complete the work within a fixed period. Because of the noise and vibrations from the work, third parties obtained injunctions to prevent the work being carried out during certain periods. The intention had been that the work should be carried out continuously, and the injunction had prevented this from happening. The authority had told the company that such an injunction could not be obtained. The company claimed an indemnity for its additional costs.

The High Court of Australia refused to imply a term into the contract. The par- **8.46** ties had assumed that no injunction would be granted, and had therefore failed to explore what they might do if it was. Negotiations might have yielded any one of a number of alternative provisions, each being regarded as a reasonable solution.

In *Marks and Spencer v BNP Paribas*,[64] a lease of commercial premises contained **8.47** a break clause. The tenant could determine the lease by giving the landlord six months' prior written notice to take effect on 24 January 2012. The tenant could only exercise this power if, on the break date, there were no arrears of rent. The tenant also had to pay a premium.

---

[62] [2013] EWCA Civ 260.
[63] (1981–1982) 149 CLR 337.
[64] [2016] AC 742.

8.48 The tenant served a break notice and, shortly before 25 December 2011, paid the next quarter's rent for the period up to and including 25 March 2012. (It had to do this in order to ensure that the break notice was valid.) The lease determined on 24 January 2012. The tenant sued the landlord for a refund of rent for the period from 24 January until 25 March 2012.

8.49 The tenant claimed that there should be a term implied into the lease that, if the tenant exercised its power to terminate the lease, the landlord ought to pay back that proportion of the rent which related to the period after the lease had terminated.

8.50 The Supreme Court refused to imply a term. The principal judgment was given by Lord Neuberger. He recognized the force of the argument that, if no term were implied, the tenant would be unfairly prejudiced and the landlord would obtain a windfall.[65] On the other hand, the lease was a full and detailed document, running to some seventy pages; and, not having provided for a repayment, the parties might be taken not to have intended it.[66] But the key determinant was the legal background against which the lease had been entered into. There was an understanding in the commercial property market that, when paid in advance, rent is not apportionable unless it is expressly provided for; and a term could not be implied which would be inconsistent with that market understanding.[67]

8.51 These four cases illustrate the difficulty which is found in practice in establishing both of the requirements described above—the necessity to imply a provision and certainty as to its terms.

8.52 The two examples of cases in which terms were implied are the decision of the Privy Council in *Attorney General of Belize v Belize Telecom*[68] and that of the House of Lords in *Equitable Life Assurance Society v Hyman.*[69]

8.53 In *Attorney General of Belize v Belize Telecom*,[70] the government of Belize had privatized the telecommunications industry, whilst retaining a degree of control over the company which ran telecommunications services. The articles of association of the company provided for two classes of ordinary shares—B and C; and there was to be one special share, which would be issued to the government and which could only be held by a party authorized by the government.

8.54 There were to be eight directors: two appointed by, and removable by, a majority of the B shareholders; four appointed by, and removable by, a majority of

---

[65] [2016] AC 742 at [33].
[66] [2016] AC 742 at [38]–[40].
[67] [2016] AC 742 at [46] and [50].
[68] [2009] 1 WLR 1998.
[69] [2002] 1 AC 408.
[70] [2009] 1 WLR 1998.

the C shareholders; and two appointed by, and removable by, the holder of the special share.

The articles also provided that, if the holder of the special share owned 37.5 per **8.55** cent of the issued C shares, the special shareholder became entitled to appoint two of the four directors allocated to the C shareholders, and that those directors could only be removed by the special shareholder holding the additional 37.5 per cent of the C shares.

Belize Telecom purchased the special share and 37.5 per cent of the C shares from **8.56** the government. It then appointed two directors in its capacity as a special share-holder holding 37.5 per cent of C shares. Within a year, Belize Telecom found itself in financial difficulties and, although retaining the special share, it ceased to hold 37.5 per cent of the C shares. The articles of association made no provision for the removal of directors appointed by a party acting in its capacity as special shareholder holding 37.5 per cent of the C shares in circumstances where such a party no longer existed.

The question was whether those directors remained directors for life, or whether **8.57** a term could be implied into the articles to the effect that the directors concerned would vacate office once the person who appointed them ceased to hold the share qualification.

The Privy Council held that such a term should be implied. Under the articles, **8.58** board membership was intended to reflect the interests of the participants. Reading the articles as a whole, a term must be implied that, if the person who appointed the directors ceased to be able to do so, then the directors appointed by it should retire. The overriding purpose of the articles was that the membership of the board reflected shareholder interests.

This case is a good example of the principle which Lord Hoffmann expounded **8.59** in that case that implication is part of the process of interpretation of a contract. Reading the articles as a whole, and giving effect to their clear purpose, showed that it was necessary to imply the term.

The final example, and perhaps the most controversial, is *Equitable Life Assurance* **8.60** *Society v Hyman*.[71] The society had issued a policyholder with a policy containing a guaranteed annuity rate. When market rates fell below the guaranteed annuity rate, the society adopted a policy of declaring lower final bonuses to policyholders who chose to take the guaranteed annuity rate. Under the company's articles of associa-tion, the amount of any bonus was within the absolute discretion of the directors of the society, and their decision was to be final and conclusive.

---

[71] [2002] 1 AC 408.

8.61 The House of Lords held that the society was not entitled to do this. In doing so, they decided not only that this was prohibited by the policy, but also that the directors' apparently unlimited discretion as to bonuses which was contained in the articles of association was impliedly limited. The commercial objective of the guaranteed rates was to protect the policyholder against a fall in market annuity rates. The reasonable expectation of the parties must therefore have been that the directors would not exercise their discretion in conflict with those rights. As a result, it was necessary to imply into the articles of association a restriction precluding the directors from declaring bonuses in such a way as to deprive the guarantees of their value.

8.62 This is an extreme case of the implication of terms. On the face of it, a limitation on the powers of the directors under the articles was contrary to the express discretion given to them. But the court decided that their discretion was impliedly limited because the society had issued policies with guaranteed annuity rates. In the *Belize* case,[72] Lord Hoffmann described the *Equitable Life* case as one where the implication of a term was necessary so as not to frustrate the apparent business purpose of the parties. The court was giving effect to the reasonable expectations of the parties by implying the term. This is a very elastic definition of necessity.[73]

H. Terms Implied in Law

8.63 In the context of the interpretation of contracts, we are concerned with terms which are implied, because that is what the parties must objectively have intended. But there are other types of implied terms—often referred to as terms implied in law. These are essentially default rules in particular types of contract, such as contracts for the sale of goods or employment contracts, which govern contracts of that type unless they are expressly excluded.

8.64 The distinction between these two types of implied term was drawn by Lord Denning MR in *Shell UK v Lostock Garage*.[74] He said:

> [T]here are two broad categories of implied terms ... The first category comprehends all those relationships which are of common occurrence. Such as the relationship of seller and buyer, owner and hirer, master and servant, landlord and tenant, carrier by land or by sea, contractor for building works, and so forth. In all those relationships the courts have imposed obligations on one party or the other saying they are 'implied terms'. These obligations are not founded on the intention of the parties, actual or presumed, but on more general considerations ...

---

[72] *Attorney General of Belize v Belize Telecom* [2009] 1 WLR 1988 at [22]–[23].
[73] The decision has been cogently criticized by Lord Grabiner in 'The Iterative Process of Contractual Interpretation' (2012) 128 LQR 41 at 55–8.
[74] [1976] 1 WLR 1187 at 1196–7.

The second category comprehends those cases which are not within the first category. These are cases—not of common occurrence—in which from the particular circumstances a term is to be implied. In these cases the implication is based on intention imputed to the parties from their actual circumstances … such an imputation is only to be made when it is necessary to imply a term to give efficacy to the contract and make it a workable agreement in such manner as the parties would clearly have done if they had applied their mind to the contingency which has arisen. These are the 'officious bystander' types of case …

8.65 Because terms implied in law are essentially default rules for particular types of contract, they have nothing to do with the process of interpretation of contracts and are not discussed here.

8.66 Although the distinction between terms implied in law and those implied in fact is clear, it is not always straightforward to decide which side of the line a particular implied term falls.[75] *Southern Foundries v Shirlaw*[76] is a case in point. Mr Shirlaw was a director of Southern Foundries. He was appointed as managing director of the company for ten years. Three years later, the company was taken over and its articles of association were altered to empower the new holding company to remove any director of the company. The new holding company then removed Mr Shirlaw as a director of the company. Because the company's articles of association provided that a managing director had to be a director, the effect of this was that he ceased to be managing director.

8.67 The question was whether Mr Shirlaw was entitled to damages for wrongful repudiation of his contract of employment. By a majority, the House of Lords decided that he was. Because he could only be the managing director if he was a director, it was an implied term of the agreement between Mr Shirlaw and the company that the company would not remove him from his position as a director during the period for which he was appointed as managing director.

8.68 The decision was to some extent based on a well-known judgment of Cockburn CJ in *Stirling v Maitland*[77] that:

If a party enters into an arrangement which can only take effect by the continuance of a certain existing state of circumstances, there is an implied engagement on his part that he shall do nothing of his own motion to put an end to that state of circumstances, under which alone the arrangement can be operative.

8.69 In this case, the company had put it out of its power to continue the employment of Mr Shirlaw as managing director; and it was therefore liable for breach of contract.

---

[75] See Lewison at 6.01.
[76] [1940] AC 701.
[77] (1864) 5 B&S 840 at 852.

8.70 This can be seen as involving the implication of a term into the contract which is necessary to give it business efficacy. Alternatively, it can be seen as involving the application of a general rule of contract law. In the words of Lord Atkin:[78]

> Personally I should not so much base the law on an implied term, as on a positive rule of the law of contract that conduct of either promisor or promisee which can be said to amount to himself 'of his own motion' bringing about the impossibility of performance is in itself a breach. If A promises to marry B and before performance of that contract marries C, A is not sued for breach of an implied contract not to marry anyone else, but for breach of his contract to marry B.

[78] [1940] AC 701 at 717.

PART V

CHANGING WORDS

Principle 9: If a written contract does not record the parties' common intention at the time it was entered into, it will be amended to reflect that intention.

Principle 10: If the parties to a contract have dealt with each other on the basis of a common understanding about the meaning or effect of the contract, that interpretation will bind them if it would be unjust to go back on it.

The purpose of this Part is to establish when the words of a contract can be changed. **Pt 5.01** This can be done as a result of two legal doctrines—rectification and estoppel by convention.

9

PRINCIPLE 9: RECTIFICATION

Principle 9: If a written contract does not record the parties' common intention at the time it was entered into, it will be amended to reflect that intention.

A. Types of Rectification

Rectification always seemed so simple. If a document did not reflect what the parties had agreed, then it was amended.[1] For a long time, there was little new authority on rectification because the principles seemed so clear. And then, in 2009, the House of Lords gave judgment in *Chartbrook v Persimmon Homes*,[2] and all of a sudden we realized that we had not really understood rectification at all.[3] **9.01**

The result is that the law is in a state of flux. The extent to which the approach in *Chartbrook* will be followed is still not entirely clear in England, and whether it will be followed at all in jurisdictions such as Australia and New Zealand has yet to be decided. **9.02**

There is a further complication. Rectification is also available in a different type of case—where one party has made a mistake about the contract and it would be unfair of the other party to rely on the contract terms. **9.03**

The discussion of this Principle is mainly concerned with the circumstances in which a contract will be rectified because it does not reflect the common intention of the parties. Although the court is rectifying (in other words amending) the words of the contract, rather than interpreting them, it is performing the basic function of interpretation—to establish the common intention of the parties. And there is a **9.04**

---

[1] See McMeel, *The Construction of Contracts* (2nd edn, Oxford University Press, 2011), Chapter 17; Hodge, *Rectification* (2nd edn, Sweet & Maxwell, 2016).

[2] [2009] 1 AC 1101.

[3] For an intriguing insight into *Chartbrook* by counsel for one of the parties, see Christopher Nugee, '*Rectification after Chartbrook v Persimmon*: Where Are We Now?' (2012) 26 Trust Law International 76.

clear link with Principle 7, which allows words to be given an unnatural meaning if the parties cannot have intended them to have their natural meaning.

9.05   At the end of the chapter, there will be a brief discussion of the circumstances in which a contract can be rectified where one party is mistaken and it would be unfair for the other party to rely on the contract terms. Here, rectification is performing a very different purpose, which has little to do with interpretation.

9.06   The first type of mistake will be described as common intention rectification, the second as unilateral mistake rectification.

B. Common Intention Rectification

9.07   At a very basic level, the principle of common intention rectification is clear. If a written contract does not record the parties' common intention at the time it was entered into, it will be amended to reflect that intention. The key question is whether that intention is determined subjectively or objectively. This, in turn, is determined by establishing why the courts rectify contracts. And here, the approach tends to divide down common law/equity lines. Those with a common law approach take one view; those looking at it in equitable terms take the other.

9.08   Rectification is an equitable remedy, and so it is hardly surprising that one approach is to look at the requirements for rectification in the light of general equity jurisprudence. Equity acts on the conscience, and the underlying question is therefore whether it would be unconscionable for one party to refuse to allow the contract to be altered in the way in which the other party wants. It would be unconscionable to do so if both parties had reached a common subjective intention which was not reflected in the document. But it would not necessarily be unconscionable to do so where the document did not reflect the objective common understanding of the parties.

9.09   At common law, the question is ultimately one of the objective intention of the parties. The guiding principle of contractual interpretation is to establish the objective intention of the parties, and all that rectification is doing is giving effect to that. If the document does not reflect the objective common intention of the parties, then it is wrong and needs to be changed, regardless of what the parties subjectively thought.

9.10   Because rectification is an equitable remedy, the natural starting point is to look at the subjective intention of the parties—not their individual intentions, but their common intention. But the problem with this approach is that it sits very uneasily with the basic principle of objective interpretation of contracts. It would mean that a written contract is subject to a different regime from an oral contract. The meaning of both depends on the objective intention of the parties, but a written document could be amended to reflect their subjective common intention, rather than their objective common intention.

C. The Requirements

There are normally said to be four requirements of common intention rectification: **9.11**

(1) The parties reached a common intention.
(2) It was objectively manifested.
(3) It continued at the time the written contract was entered into.
(4) The written agreement does not reflect that intention.

If these requirements are satisfied, the written agreement will be amended to reflect the intention. As we will see, the first two requirements may just be different ways of saying the same thing.

These requirements are described in two cases in the Court of Appeal—the judg- **9.12**
ment of Slade LJ in *The Nai Genova*[4] and that of Peter Gibson LJ in *Swainland Builders v Freehold Properties*.[5]

In *The Nai Genova*, Slade LJ said:[6] **9.13**

First, there must be a common intention in regard to the particular provisions of the agreement in question, together with some outward expression of accord. Secondly, this common intention must continue up to the time of execution of the instrument. Thirdly, there must be clear evidence that the instrument as executed does not accurately represent the true agreement of the parties at the time of its execution. Fourthly, it must be shown that the instrument, if recti-fied as claimed, would accurately represent the true agreement of the parties at that time …

In *Swainland Builders v Freehold Properties*, Peter Gibson LJ expressed the require- **9.14**
ments in this way:[7]

The party seeking rectification must show that:
(1) the parties had a common continuing intention, whether or not amounting to an agreement, in respect of a particular matter in the instrument to be rectified;
(2) there was an outward expression of accord;
(3) the intention continued at the time of the execution of the instrument sought to be rectified;
(4) by mistake, the instrument did not reflect that common intention.

---

[4] *Agip v Navigazione Alta Italia* [1984] 2 Lloyd's Rep 353 at 359.
[5] [2002] 2 EGLR 71 at 74.
[6] [1983] 2 Lloyd's Rep 353 at 359.
[7] [2002] 2 EGLR 71 at 74.

This formulation was cited with approval by Lord Hoffmann in *Chartbrook v Persimmon Homes*.[8]

9.15 The fourth requirement is obvious, but the first three need to be elaborated on.

9.16 Like any equitable remedy, rectification is discretionary, and so it may be refused, or granted on terms.[9] There are also specific protections for third parties, which are discussed in paras 9.92–9.97 below.

D. Common Intention at the Time of the Contract

9.17 The parties must have reached a common intention, and that intention must continue up to the time the written contract is entered into.

9.18 Rectification is commonly thought of as a way of amending a written contract in order to bring it into line with what the parties actually agreed. This is correct, but that agreement does not need to take the form of a legally binding contract. What is required is that, at the time the document was entered into, the parties had a common intention about a matter which was to form part of that contract.

9.19 This point was made by Simonds J in *Crane v Hegeman-Harris Co*:[10]

> [I]n order that this court may exercise its jurisdiction to rectify a written instrument, it is not necessary to find a concluded and binding contract between the parties antecedent to the agreement which it is sought to rectify. . . . [I]t is sufficient to find a common continuing intention in regard to a particular provision or aspect of the agreement. If one finds that, in regard to a particular point, the parties were in agreement up to the moment when they executed their formal instrument, and the formal instrument does not conform with that common agreement, then this court has jurisdiction to rectify, although it may be that there was, until the formal instrument was executed, no concluded and binding contract between the parties.

9.20 This raises the question as to the nature of the common intention which has to be proved—is it subjective or objective?

E. The Subjective View

9.21 One view is that the purpose of rectification is to mitigate the harshness of the principle that the law is concerned with the objective intention of the parties, rather than their subjective intention. This is, of course, the classical approach to the way

---

[8] [2009] 1 AC 1101 at [48].
[9] *Marley v Rawlings* [2015] AC 129 at [40] (Lord Neuberger).
[10] [1939] 1 All ER 622 at 664.

in which equity impinges upon the common law. It is expressed very clearly by Lord Wright in *The Commissioners of Inland Revenue v Rafael*:[11]

> [T]he principle of the common law has been to adopt an objective standard of construction and to exclude general evidence of actual intention of the parties; the reason for this has been that otherwise all certainty would be taken from the words in which the parties have recorded their agreement ... If in some cases hardship or injustice may be effected by this rule of law, such hardship or injustice can generally be obviated by the power in equity to reform the contract, in proper cases and on proper evidence that there has been a real intention and a real mistake in expressing that intention: these matters may be established, as they generally are, by extrinsic evidence. The Court will thus reform or rewrite the clauses in order to give effect to the real intention. But that is not construction, but rectification.

According to Lord Wright, rectification is therefore concerned with the parties' sub- **9.22** jective intention. In *Joscelyne v Nissen*,[12] the Court of Appeal qualified this approach by saying that 'some outward expression of accord is required' for rectification. This was criticized by Leonard Bromley QC in an article in the Law Quarterly Review in 1971.[13] He argued that what rectification requires in the case of a contract is the establishment of the common subjective intention of the parties, and that outward expression of accord is not a requirement of rectification, but simply goes to the proof of the subjective common intention.

One view of rectification is therefore that it requires—and only requires—that the **9.23** document does not reflect the common subjective intention of the parties. But this is not generally accepted, even by those who favour a subjective interpretation of rectification. The cases indicate that an outward manifestation of that intention is required.[14]

This was the view taken by Campbell JA in the New South Wales Court of Appeal **9.24** in *Ryledar v Euphoric* after a detailed discussion of the cases and articles.[15] Campbell JA distinguished between the types of intention relevant to the formation and interpretation of contracts, and that required for rectification. Although the former type of intention is objective, the latter is subjective—the actual intention of the parties. As Mason J had said in *Codelfa Construction v State Rail Authority of New South Wales*:[16] 'Rectification ensures that the contract gives effect to the parties' actual intention.'

---

[11] [1935] AC 96 at 143.
[12] [1970] 2 QB 86 at 98.
[13] Bromley, 'Rectification in Equity' (1971) 87 LQR 532.
[14] *Joscelyne v Nissen* [1970] 2 QB 86 at 98 (Buckley LJ), *The Nai Genova, Agip v Navigazione Alta Italia* [1984] 2 Lloyd's Rep 353 at 359 (Slade LJ) and *Swainland Builders v Freehold Properties* [2002] 2 EGLR 71 at 74 (Peter Gibson LJ).
[15] (2007) 69 NSWLR 603 at [257]–[316].
[16] (1981–1982) 149 CLR 337 at 346.

9.25   But, unlike Leonard Bromley QC, Campbell JA took the view that there must be some outward expression of that intention. This was because the purpose of rectification was to prevent unconscionable conduct:[17]

> If two negotiating parties each had a particular intention about the agreement they would enter, and their intentions were identical, but that intention was disclosed by neither of them, and they later entered a document that did not accord with that intention, what would be the injustice or unconscientiousness in either of them enforcing the document according to its terms?

9.26   It is suggested that the position in New Zealand is similar. The leading case is *Westland Savings Bank v Hancock*[18] in 1987. Tipping J in the High Court said that a single corresponding intention must exist in the minds of both parties and this must be objectively apparent from what was said and done. This has consistently been followed by the courts in New Zealand.[19]

F. The Objective View

9.27   The other view is that what is required is that the document does not reflect the objective common intention of the parties. This view is most clearly expressed by Denning LJ in *Frederick E. Rose v William H. Pim Jnr & Co*:[20]

> Rectification is concerned with contracts and documents, not with intentions. In order to get rectification it is necessary to show that the parties were in complete agreement on the terms of their contract, but by an error wrote them down wrongly; and in this regard, in order to ascertain the terms of their contract, you do not look into the inner minds of the parties—into their intentions—any more than you do in the formation of any other contract. You look at their outward acts, that is, at what they said or wrote to one another in coming to their agreement, and then compare it with the document which they have signed. If you can predicate with certainty what their contract was, and that it is, by a common mistake, wrongly expressed in the document, then you rectify the document; but nothing less will suffice.

9.28   This approach was taken up by Marcus Smith in an article in the Law Quarterly Review in 2007.[21] He put forward two related propositions. The first was that one party's subjective intentions are irrelevant if the other party is not aware of them. The second was that the requirement for a common intention is not a distinct

---

[17]   (2007) 69 NSWLR 603 at [315].

[18]   [1987] 2 NZLR 21 at 30.

[19]   See, for instance, the decision of the New Zealand Court of Appeal in *Robb v James* [2014] NZCA 42 at [21] and [22]. For a different reading of the cases, see McLauchlan, 'The Many Versions of Rectification for Common Mistake' in Degeling, Edelman, and Goudkamp (eds), *Contract in Commercial Law* (Thomson Reuters, 2016).

[20]   [1953] 2 QB 450 at 461.

[21]   Smith, 'Rectification of Contracts for Common Mistake, *Joscelyne v Nissen*, and Subjective States of Mind' (2007) 123 LQR 116.

requirement from the need for an outward manifestation of that intention. As a result, what is actually required is to establish the common objective intention of the parties.

The first of these propositions is consistent with the view of Campbell JA in the **9.29** *Ryledar* case, and with the concept that what is required is subjective common intention—albeit with some outward manifestation. But the second proposition is inconsistent with Campbell JA's approach. It is applying the purely objective approach of Lord Denning.

G. Where Are We Now?

In England, it is the objective approach which has won the day, as a result of the **9.30** decision of the House of Lords in *Chartbrook v Persimmon Homes*[22]—although the ramifications of that case have yet to be fully worked out, as can be seen from the decision of the Court of Appeal in *Daventry District Council v Daventry & District Housing*.[23]

Chartbrook v Persimmon Homes[24] is one of the key cases on interpretation of con- **9.31** tracts, and is discussed under Principles 4 and 7 (see particularly paras 7.125–7.132). The case was decided as a matter of interpretation of the contract, but the House of Lords did consider the question of rectification in some detail. Although its judgment on the rectification issue was strictly *obiter*, it was a considered judgment given after full discussion and is therefore likely to be followed in the future, as it was by the Court of Appeal in the *Daventry* case.[25]

By exchange of letters, the parties had agreed the basis for the calculation of an 'ad- **9.32** ditional residential payment', and those provisions were then drafted into the written contract. Persimmon argued that rectification was not possible because the document as drafted represented their understanding of the exchange of letters. The House of Lords would nevertheless have ordered rectification if it had been necessary. What was important was not the subjective intentions of the parties, but their objective intentions as set out in the exchange of letters. If the written contract did not accurately reflect how a reasonable person would read the exchange of letters, then it should be rectified in order to reflect that objective agreement.

Lord Hoffmann said that the case was argued at trial on the assumption that recti- **9.33** fication required both parties to be mistaken about whether the written agreement

---

[22] [2009] 1 AC 1101.
[23] [2012] 1 WLR 1333.
[24] [2009] 1 AC 1101.
[25] [2012] 1 WLR 1333.

reflected what they believed their prior consensus to have been. This was incorrect. He approved the submission of counsel for Persimmon that:[26]

> Rectification required a mistake about whether the written instrument correctly reflected the prior consensus, not whether it accorded with what the party in question believed that consensus to have been. In accordance with the general approach of English law, the terms of the prior consensus were what a reasonable observer would have understood them to be and not what one or even both of the parties believed them to be.

The question is what an objective observer would have thought the intentions of the parties to be.[27]

9.34 This issue had to be considered again by the Court of Appeal in *Daventry District Council v Daventry & District Housing*.[28] A housing authority was negotiating with a company which had been set up as a registered social landlord for the authority to sell its housing stock and transfer its housing department staff to the company. One particular problem in the negotiations concerned what would be done about the deficit on the authority's pension scheme in respect of the staff being transferred to the company. The authority proposed to the company that the company should pay the deficit, with a corresponding reduction in the purchase price, and with the authority being compensated for this in a different way. The company's negotiator told the company that the outcome would be that the authority would pay the deficit, and the proposal was therefore agreed. Negotiations continued, and the contract as signed contained an express clause providing for the payment of the deficit by the authority. The authority then tried to get the contract rectified on the basis that it did not represent the earlier agreement.

9.35 At first instance, Vos J refused to rectify the contract on the basis that the amended wording in the written contract was an intentional variation of the earlier agreement, and therefore that the earlier common intention of the parties had not continued up to the time of the contract being signed. By a majority, the Court of Appeal overruled this decision and granted rectification. It would seem that the majority took the view that the parties had agreed that the company should pay the deficit, and that a reasonable person would not consider that what subsequently happened signalled a departure from that agreement.[29] So, at the time the contract was executed, the parties intended that the company should pay the deficit, but the document provided for the authority to do so. It would therefore be rectified.

---

[26] [2009] 1 AC 1101 at [57].
[27] [2009] 1 AC 1101 at [60].
[28] [2012] 1 WLR 1333.
[29] Because a new clause was inserted into the contract specifically to cover the point, this is difficult to accept. See Davies, 'Rectification Versus Interpretation' (2016) 75 CLJ 62 at 77.

The difference of view between, on the one hand, Vos J at first instance and **9.36**
Etherton LJ (who dissented in the Court of Appeal), and on the other Lord
Neuberger and Toulson LJ, was largely on the facts. Although Lord Neuberger
and Toulson LJ reached the same decision on the facts, Lord Neuberger expressly
agreed with the legal analysis of Etherton LJ which, in some respects, differed
from that of Toulson LJ. It is therefore Etherton LJ's legal analysis which, it is suggested, is currently binding, at least to Court of Appeal level.

Etherton LJ[30] accepted that, although the decision on rectification in *Chartbrook* **9.37**
was not strictly binding, it should be followed. He said:[31]

> Lord Hoffmann's clarification [of Peter Gibson LJ's summary of the requirements for
> rectification in the *Swainland Builders*[32] case] was that the required 'common contin-
> uing intention' is not a mere subjective belief but rather what an objective observer
> would have thought the intention to be ... In other words the requirements of 'an
> outward expression of accord' and 'common continuing intention' are not separate
> conditions, but two sides of the same coin since an uncommunicated inward inten-
> tion is irrelevant. I suggest that Peter Gibson LJ's statement of the requirements for
> rectification for mutual mistake can be rephrased as: (1) the parties had a common
> continuing intention, whether or not amounting to an agreement, in respect of a
> particular matter in the instrument to be rectified; (2) which existed at the time of
> execution of the instrument sought to be rectified; (3) such common continuing
> intention to be established objectively, that is to say by reference to what an objective
> observer would have thought the intentions of the parties to be; and (4) by mistake
> the instrument did not reflect that common intention.

Toulson LJ, although in the majority in the result, took a rather different view of **9.38**
the law from the other judges in the Court of Appeal. He was concerned about the
correctness of the principle of the decision in the *Chartbrook* case. He said:[33]

> I have difficulty in accepting it as a general principle that a mistake by both parties
> as to whether a written contract conformed with a prior non-binding agreement,
> objectively construed, gives rise to a claim for rectification.

This seems to be a common concern of judges in rectification cases. In *Tartsinis v* **9.39**
Navona Management Company[34] in 2015, Leggatt J considered that the purpose of
rectification was to avoid the injustice that would otherwise be caused when the
objective principle of interpretation leads to a result which fails to reflect the parties'
real intention.[35] He was bound by *Chartbrook*, but clearly did not like it. He said:[36]

---

[30] [2012] 1 WLR 1333 at [78]–[90].
[31] [2012] 1 WLR 1333 at [80].
[32] [2002] 2 EGLR 71 at [33].
[33] [2012] 1 WLR 1333 at [176].
[34] [2015] EWHC 57 (Comm).
[35] [2015] EWHC 57 (Comm) at [92].
[36] [2015] EWHC 57 (Comm) at [90].

It is one thing to say that a contract should not be rectified just because both parties privately intend it to bear a meaning different from its meaning objectively ascertained. It is quite another thing, however, to say that a contract should be rectified to conform to what a reasonable observer would have understood the parties previously to have agreed, irrespective of the parties' own understanding.

9.40 This concern was reflected by Cooke J in 2016 in *LSREF III Wight v Millvalley*.[37] In both cases, the judges rectified the contract concerned but, in each case the rectification reflected what they considered to be the parties' actual subjective common intention as well as their objective common intention.

9.41 It is hard to overestimate the passions which have been aroused by the decision in *Chartbrook*.[38] There has been an unprecedented number of extra-judicial comments by members of the judiciary. Lord Toulson found it surprising that rectification should be available when the parties have not actually agreed something different from what the written contract said.[39] Similarly, Sir Nicholas Patten was puzzled why Chartbrook was held to be bound by the objective effect of a prior accord which had no legal effect, when Chartbrook itself believed that accord to have the same meaning and effect as the contract it eventually signed.[40]

9.42 Not all judges take this approach. Perhaps unsurprisingly, Lord Hoffmann has justified the objective approach.[41] So has Sir Terence Etherton[42] who considers that there are strong policy objections to giving contractual force to the uncommunicated subjective beliefs and intentions of the parties.

9.43 As a matter of precedent, the position in England is that an objective common intention is required. How other common law jurisdictions will react to this approach is not yet clear, but it is likely in Australia and New Zealand a more subjective approach will prevail. Since *Chartbrook* was decided, the New Zealand Court of Appeal has continued to require subjective common intention, albeit objectively manifested.[43] Even in England, it is unlikely that *Chartbrook* will be the last word. The issue will eventually need to be re-examined in the Supreme Court.

---

[37] [2016] EWHC 466 (Comm) at [70].

[38] The various views are explained and analysed by David McLauchlan in 'The Many Versions of Rectification for Common Mistake' in Degeling, Edelman, and Goudkamp (eds), *Contract in Commercial Law* (Thomson Reuters, 2016).

[39] Toulson, 'Does Rectification Require Rectifying?' (TECBAR Annual Lecture, 31 October 2013).

[40] Patten, 'Does the Law Need to be Rectified?' (The Chancery Bar Association 2013 Annual Lecture, 29 April 2013). And see, Davies 'Rectification Versus Interpretation' (2016) 75 CLJ 62 for a strong justification of the subjective approach.

[41] Hoffmann, 'Rectification and Other Mistakes' (Lecture to the Commercial Bar Association, 3 November 2015); and see the judgment of Lord Hoffmann NPJ in the Hong Kong Court of Final Appeal in *Kowloon Development Finance v Pendex Industries* [2013] HKCFA 35 at [19]–[24].

[42] Etherton, 'Contract Formation and the Fog of Rectification' (2015) 68 CLP 367.

[43] *Robb v James* [2014] NZCA 42 at [21] and [22].

H. Objective or Subjective: the Pros and Cons

The issues involved can be clarified by a series of examples. A and B agree on the **9.44** terms of their contract, and they are then put into writing and signed. How might the writing not reflect what was agreed? There are a number of possibilities, three of which will be discussed.

Example 1

A and B agree on the terms of their contract, and they are then put into writ- **9.45** ing. The document reflects the parties' subjective common understanding of the agreement, but not their objective common intention. Should the writing be rectified?

- The common law approach is that the writing does not reflect the objective common intention of the parties, and therefore must be rectified. That is necessary to give effect to the underlying principle of objectivity in contract law.
- The equitable approach would be to say that if A now wants to give effect to the objective intention, but B does not, B's conscience is not affected because the document simply reflects what the parties had subjectively agreed. So the writing cannot be rectified.

Both approaches are possible, and each has something to recommend it.

Example 2

A and B agree on the terms of their contract, and they are then put into writing. **9.46** The document reflects the parties' objective common intention, but does not reflect their subjective common understanding of the agreement.

- The common law approach would be to say that there is no right to rectify here because the contract reflects the objective common intention of the parties.
- The equitable approach would be to allow rectification because the written document does not reflect what the parties have subjectively agreed—at least if there has been some outward manifestation of that subjective agreement. And if A asks for the document to be amended to reflect that agreement, it would be unconscionable for B to refuse consent.

Here, it is suggested that the equitable position creates a curious result. If the contract had not been put into writing, it would have been the objective common intention of the parties which would have determined what the contract meant. But if the contract is then put into writing, should it be possible for one of the parties to go back to the parties' subjective common intention?

Example 3

9.47 A and B agree on the terms of their contract, and they are then put into writing. The document does not reflect either the common objective intention of the parties, or their common subjective intention.

Here, it is clear that rectification is available. The contract does not comply with either the objective or the subjective common intention of the parties.

Discussion

9.48 If the parties have reached a common intention, both subjectively and objectively, and the contract does not reflect that, then it should be rectified. That is clear.

9.49 What is less clear is whether the contract should be rectified where the objective common intention differs from the subjective common intention. The first approach would be to deny rectification in either case. The second would be to allow it where the writing does not reflect the objective common intention. The third would be to allow it where the writing does not reflect the subjective common intention. There are pros and cons of all three approaches. At present, the law in England would allow rectification only where the document does not reflect the objective common intention of the parties. But the law is in a state of flux, and it is by no means clear that it will remain in its current form. And the indications from Australia and New Zealand are that subjectivity is likely to have a greater part to play than in England.

9.50 One possibility would be to decide that rectification should only be available if the objective and subjective common intentions are the same, and they are not reflected in the document (in other words, Example 3). The argument here would be that to allow rectification in Example 2 would result in the parties' contract saying something different if it is put in writing than if it is not; and to allow rectification in Example 1 would allow one party to change the document even though it reflects what they actually agreed.

9.51 Another possibility would be to allow rectification in any case in which the document does not reflect the objective consensus—in other words in Example 1 as well as in Example 3. Only by doing this, is the objective basis of contract law given effect.

9.52 In practice, there may be very little difference between these two approaches. It is generally recognized that, in the case of a contract, proof of subjective intention is really only practicable by looking at what has passed between the parties. So even if the document does not reflect the parties' subjective intention, rectification will only be available to the extent that it has been externally manifested. This was the position in England before *Chartbrook*,[44] and it is the position in Australia following *Ryledar*.[45]

---

[44] *Chartbrook v Persimmon Homes* [2009] 1 AC 1101. The relevant cases are: *Joscelyne v Nissen* [1970] 2 QB 86 at 98 (Buckley LJ), *The Nai Genova, Agip v Navigazione Alta Italia* [1984] 2 Lloyd's Rep 353 at 359 (Slade LJ), and *Swainland Builders v Freehold Properties* [2002] 2 EGLR 71 at 74 (Peter Gibson LJ).
[45] *Ryledar v Euphoric* [2007] 69 NSWLR 603 at [257]–[316].

In this context, there is a distinction between the rectification of a contract and the **9.53** rectification of a unilateral instrument such as a voluntary settlement. In the case of a voluntary settlement, what is required for rectification is that the subjective intention of the settlor is not reflected in the settlement document. As Sir Terence Etherton said in *Day v Day*:[46]

> What is relevant in such a case is the subjective intention of the settlor. It is not a legal requirement for rectification of a voluntary settlement that there is any outward expression or objective communication of the settlor's intention equivalent to the need to show an outward expression of accord for rectification of a contract for mutual mistake ...

The reason is that a common intention is irrelevant to a voluntary settlement. **9.54** There is only one relevant person; and so what matters is the intention of the settlor.[47]

But in the case of a contract, what the court is required to do is to establish the **9.55** parties' *common* intention. An intention is not really held in common merely because of the coincidence that each party subjectively and independently believes the same thing. It is only held in common if there has been a meeting of minds, and that is only possible through external manifestation of their individual subjective intentions.[48] So, by its nature, a common intention must be established objectively—by reference to what has passed between the parties.

It is therefore suggested that there is very little difference between requiring the **9.56** claimant to establish the objective common intention of the parties, and requiring him or her to establish a subjective common intention which has been externally manifested. In both cases, what needs to be established is the *appearance* of consensus, based on what has passed between the parties. In theory, the subjective approach also requires that there is an actual meeting of minds; but, since this can only be proved by what has passed between the parties, it is not at all clear that in practice this requirement adds anything material to the requirement of objective consensus.

I. A Possible Solution

How might this problem be resolved in practice? It is suggested that the starting **9.57** point is to distinguish between two different ways in which common intention

---

[46] [2013] EWCA Civ 280 at [22].

[47] *Day v Day* [2013] EWCA Civ 280 at [21].

[48] There are also strong policy objections to the use of subjective intentions, which are discussed by Sir Terence Etherton in 'Contract Formation and the Fog of Rectification' (2015) 68 CLP 367.

rectification is used—a distinction which has been pointed out by a number of writers, but most notably by James Ruddell.[49]

9.58   There are two types of case in which a written contract will be rectified because there has been a common mistake:

- The first type of case involves rectifying a document. If a document does not reflect the contract which it is intended to record, the document will be changed to reflect the contract.
- The second type of case involves rectifying a contract. If a contract does not reflect what was agreed, the contract will be changed to reflect what was agreed.

Rectifying a document

9.59   The first type of case arises where the parties have entered into a binding unwritten contract which is then put into writing. Here, the document will be rectified if, by mistake, it does not reflect the terms of the contract.

9.60   At common law, once the parties had signed the document, that was generally the end of the matter. But equity would intervene to rectify the document. It would do so in order to enforce the contract. The parties had made a contract. They intended to record it in writing. By mistake, they failed to do so accurately. The court gave effect to the contract by amending the document. It is analogous to specific performance.

9.61   What is rectified is the document, not the contract. In order to rectify a document on this basis, it must be established that:

- the parties entered into an unwritten contract;
- that contract was then put in writing; and
- by mistake the terms of the document do not reflect the terms of the contract.

9.62   The purpose of rectification in this type of case is to ensure that the document accords with the terms of the contract. The terms of a contract are objectively ascertained. The question is: what would a reasonable person in the position of the parties understand the terms of the contract to have been? The subjective intentions of the parties—even their subjective common intention—are irrelevant because what the court is doing is establishing the terms of the contract and then seeing if the document states them accurately. In this type of case, therefore, the test must be objective.

9.63   In some markets, contracts are still made orally and then put into writing. An example is contracts which are made by dealers over the telephone and then put into

---

[49]   Ruddell, 'Common Intention and Rectification for Common Mistake' [2015] LMCLQ 48.

writing on the basis of standard form contracts. For contracts of this kind, a document can be rectified if it does not accord with the terms of the contract, objectively ascertained.

Rectifying a contract

However, where lawyers are involved, it is rare for a contract to be made before the written contract is signed. In a corporate or financial transaction, for instance, where drafts of a contract move back and forth between the parties' lawyers, it is uncommon for the parties to intend to be bound until they have signed a written contract. In a case of this kind, it follows that the document cannot be rectified to reflect the contract. The contract is only made when it is signed, and there is therefore no prior contract, the terms of which can be inconsistent with the document.   **9.64**

This would in practice have restricted the availability of rectification considerably.[50] But, in the twentieth century, the courts decided that rectification is available even if there was no prior contract.[51] If the parties had reached agreement on a term of the contract and that agreement continued up to the time the contract was signed, then the contract will be rectified if it does not reflect that agreement.   **9.65**

In order to rectify a contract on this basis, it must be established that: **9.66**

- the parties entered into a written contract;
- at the time they did so, they had agreed that the contract would contain a particular term; and
- by mistake, the written contract does not reflect that agreement.

This is a major extension of the doctrine of rectification. The court is not rectifying a document on the basis that it does not accord with the contract it is meant to record. It is rectifying a contract because it does not accord with what the parties had agreed.[52]   **9.67**

Why should equity intervene in such a case? Why should a non-binding agreement override a binding written contract?   **9.68**

It is often said that the document should be rectified because it is against conscience for a party to attempt to enforce the document when he or she knows that it does   **9.69**

---

[50] See the comments of Sir W M James V-C in *MacKenzie v Coulson* (1869) LR 8 Eq 368 at 375.
[51] Clauson J in *Shipley UDC v Bradford Corporation* [1936] Ch 375; Simonds J in *Crane v Hegeman-Harris Co* [1939] 1 All ER 622 at 644; and the Court of Appeal in *Joscelyne v Nissen* [1970] 2 QB 86.
[52] *Davey v Baker* [2016] NZCA 313 at [37] (New Zealand Court of Appeal).

not reflect what was agreed.[53] But it is suggested that the real reason that equity intervenes is because the writing does not reflect the agreement. The reference to 'conscience' adds nothing to the analysis.[54]

9.70 Equity intervenes to rectify the contract because the contract does not reflect what the parties had actually agreed. That is not a self-evident truth, but it is a reasonable position to adopt. The law enforces bargains and, if it is clear that the written contract does not reflect the bargain, then the bargain should prevail.[55]

9.71 The more recent cases on rectification for common mistake tend to use the expression 'common intention' rather than 'agreement'.[56] Indeed in the *Swainland Builders* case,[57] Peter Gibson LJ said that the parties must have 'a common continuing intention, whether or not amounting to an agreement'. But it is suggested that, when he used the word 'agreement' here, what he meant was a binding contract. He was reflecting the extension of the doctrine of rectification to cases where there was no preceding contract. Indeed, in *Joscelyne v Nissen*,[58] the Court of Appeal clearly used the expressions 'common intention' and 'agreement' as synonyms.

9.72 The question, then, is what we mean by 'common intention' or 'agreement' in this context. There are at least three[59] possible approaches:

- to rectify the contract only if it does not accord both with the objective common intention of the parties and also with their subjective common intention;
- to rectify the contract if it does not accord with the parties' objective common intention; and
- to rectify the contract if it does not accord with the parties' subjective common intention.

9.73 The third possibility can be disposed of quickly. None of the cases warrant rectification without at least some objective manifestation of subjective intention. Indeed,

---

[53] See Francis Dawson in 'Interpretation and Rectification of Written Agreements in the Commercial Court' (2015) 131 LQR 344 at 347, and Leggatt J in *Tartsinis v Navona Management Company* [2015] EWHC 57 (Comm) at [87]–[99].

[54] It is the general justification for equity's involvement, not the test for intervention in any particular type of case.

[55] See the decision of Palmer J in the High Court of New Zealand in *Clode v Sullivan* [2016] NZHC 1561 at [118]: rectification allows a court to give effect to the 'true bargain'.

[56] *The Nai Genova, Agip v Navigazione Alta Italia* [1984] 1 Lloyd's Rep 353 at 359; *Swainland Builders v Freehold Properties* [2002] 2 EGLR 71 at 74.

[57] [2002] 2 EGLR 71 at 74.

[58] [1970] 2 QB 86 at 98.

[59] There is a fourth possibility—to rectify the contract if it does not accord either with the objective common intention of the parties or with their subjective common intention. This is the approach of David McLauchlan in 'Refining Rectification' (2014) 130 LQR 83, but it provides a very expansive approach to rectification for which there is, as yet, little judicial support.

an intention can only be held in common if each party has communicated its intention to the other. A party can individually intend something, but it is only by communicating it to the other party and reaching an apparent consensus that both parties can have a common intention about it. Only then can they be said to have reached agreement.

That leaves two options—to allow rectification only where there is a congruence **9.74** of objective and subjective common intention, or to rectify where there is an objective common intention. In England, the law at the moment is that objective common intention is sufficient, but there is plenty of judicial and extra-judicial support for the alternative, and it is clear that *Chartbrook* is not the last word on this important issue.

The strongest argument in favour of requiring both objective and subjective **9.75** common intention is that to rectify the document on the basis only of objective intention gives precedence to an informal earlier agreement over a later formal one. There is therefore much to be said for the view that, in this type of case, rectification should only be available where the parties have reached both actual agreement and the appearance of agreement.

But it does not necessarily follow that rectification will therefore be refused where— **9.76** as in *Chartbrook* itself—one party convinces the judge that he did not subjectively agree to what had apparently been agreed. A simple assertion by one party—even if believed by the judge—that he did not understand what was apparently agreed should have no bearing on the outcome. Agreement can only be reached by the parties communicating with each other. If it is clear in correspondence that one party does not agree with a particular outcome, then there can be no agreement. But, if the party keeps his disagreement bottled up within himself, then it cannot be of any relevance to the outcome.

In short, in common law jurisdictions, agreement is by its very nature established **9.77** objectively. Assume that the parties enter into a written contract and one party then alleges that it fails to record an agreed term. If the parties agree that they did agree it, then they will rectify the agreement consensually.[60] If one party denies that he has agreed it and brings forward communications between the parties to prove it, then the other party cannot objectively have thought the point was agreed; and rectification will be refused. But if one party says that in his own mind he did not agree it, that is irrelevant to any question of *common* intention; rectification will be available if he appeared to have agreed.

---

[60] This happens all the time in practice.

9.78 In practice, therefore, it is suggested that there is no real distinction between requiring objective common intention and requiring both objective and subjective common intention. When we are contracting, we cannot look into each other's minds. All we can do is to look at what has passed between us. Individual subjective intentions can only be held in common once they have been communicated and appear to be agreed.

9.79 For these reasons, it is suggested that the approach in *Chartbrook*[61] has much to recommend it. It is a clear test and it is consistent with basic principles of contract law. Rectification—like interpretation—should be concerned with the objective common intention of the parties.

J. The Nature of the Mistake

9.80 This leads on to a related question. What is the nature of the common mistake which has to be established in order to obtain rectification?

9.81 In principle, what needs to be established in order to rectify the contract is that there has been a mistake in translating the parties' common intentions to the page. It should not be enough that they had a common misunderstanding about the effect of the words in the contract.[62] What is required is a common mistake about the words used—they intended to say *x* and the contract says *y*.

9.82 Take *Rose v Pim*[63] as an example. The parties agreed to sell and buy horsebeans. They may both have thought that horsebeans were feveroles, but they agreed on horsebeans and that is what the contract said. There was no mistake as to the terms of the contract, only a mistake as to their underlying assumptions. As David McLauchlan has said, the key question is to decide what was the term which the parties agreed.[64]

9.83 In *Pukallus v Cameron*,[65] the parties were agreed on the identity of property to be transferred, but shared a common mistake about what the property contained. The High Court of Australia decided that the mistake was insufficient to enable the contract to be rectified. The written contract described what the parties intended to transfer, even though they were mistaken as to what it contained.

---

[61] *Chartbrook v Persimmon Homes* [2009] 1 AC 1101.
[62] *Frederick E. Rose v William H. Pim Jnr* [1953] 2 QB 450.
[63] [1953] 2 QB 450.
[64] McLauchlan, 'The Many Versions of Rectification for Common Mistake' in Degeling, Edelman, and Goudkamp (eds), *Contract in Commercial Law* (Thomson Reuters, 2016).
[65] (1982) 180 CLR 447.

The position was described by the New Zealand Court of Appeal in these terms:[66] **9.84**

> It is suggested that a mistake in the interpretation of an instrument or in the legal consequences of entering into an instrument is regarded as insufficient to ground rectification; rectification is a remedy to ensure the instrument contains the provisions which the parties intended it to contain, and not those which it would have contained had the parties been better informed.

But there have been cases in which the courts have rectified a contract which, al- **9.85** though it expressed what the parties had agreed, did not give effect to what they had intended. In *Re Butlin's Settlement Trusts*[67] Brightman J said that:

> rectification is available not only in a case where particular words have been added, omitted or wrongly written as the result of careless copying or the like. It is also available where the words of the document were purposely used but it was mistakenly considered that they bore a different meaning from their correct meaning as a matter of true construction. In such a case … the court will rectify the wording of the document so that it expresses the true intention …

An example is *Jervis v Howle & Talke Colliery Company*.[68] The consideration for the **9.86** grant of a lease was expressed to be a royalty of three pence per ton 'free of tax'. This reflected the oral agreement of the parties, but they had misunderstood the effect of the tax legislation, which required the payer to deduct tax. Clauson J held that the parties had intended that the payee would get three pence per ton and should not have to bear any of the tax on it. He accordingly rectified the contract so that it had that effect, even though the words actually written in the contract were what the parties had agreed.

This approach is difficult to reconcile with the underlying principle that rectifica- **9.87** tion is concerned with the objective intention of the parties. It runs counter to the approach in *Chartbrook*.[69] It remains to be seen whether, in the future, the courts will rectify a contract which expresses in words what the parties intended, but does not reflect what they thought the effect of that intention would be.[70]

K. A Continuing Intention

It is a requirement of rectification that the common intention of the parties contin- **9.88** ued at the time of the execution of the instrument which is sought to be rectified.[71]

---

[66] *Davey v Baker* [2016] NZCA 313 at [40].
[67] [1976] 1 Ch 251 at 260. It was cited with approval by the Court of Appeal in *Day v Day* [2013] EWCA Civ 280 at [21].
[68] [1937] 1 Ch 67.
[69] *Chartbrook v Persimmon Homes* [2009] 1 AC 1101.
[70] In an appropriate case, estoppel by convention might be available. See Principle 10.
[71] This is Peter Gibson LJ's third requirement of rectification in *Swainland Builders v Freehold Properties* [2002] 2 EGLR 71 at 74. See earlier at para 9.14.

The importance of this requirement can be seen from the *Daventry* case,[72] where one of the key issues was whether the drafting of a different approach to the payment of the deficit was to be regarded as a mistake or simply as a change of position. Two judges went one way, two the other. That illustrates very clearly the factual difficulties involved in cases of this type.

9.89 If a different provision is contained in the signed document from that which had previously been agreed, the most likely explanation is that the deal has changed.[73] But that will not always be the case since, otherwise, no claim for rectification could ever be brought. It must be possible for one party successfully to argue that the amendment was a mistake. But the courts have always made it clear that the burden of proof is a high one. Faced with a document which he has signed, a party needs to provide compelling evidence that it does not reflect what had been agreed.

L. Available Materials

9.90 It has been seen under Principle 4 that, when a court is interpreting a written contract, certain materials are excluded from the background facts. In particular, evidence of prior negotiations is not generally admissible for the purpose of interpreting the contract.

9.91 In contrast, prior negotiations are available in an action for rectification.[74] This is necessary because it will be from the negotiations that evidence will be available that the parties reached a common understanding on something which was not then properly reflected in the written document. But, as has been seen, what the court is seeking to find is the objective intention of the parties, and therefore subjective declarations of intent are as irrelevant to a claim for rectification as they are in the process of interpretation.

M. Third Party Rights

9.92 The similarities between rectification and what might be described as 'creative interpretation' have been discussed under Principle 7. There is a strong body of opinion that the courts should only be able to rewrite the contract as a matter of interpretation where there is a clear typographical error, and that other cases of mistake should be left to rectification.

---

[72] *Daventry District Council v Daventry & District Housing* [2012] 1 WLR 1333.
[73] This was the case in *Liberty Mercian v Cuddy Civil Engineering* [2013] EWHC 2688 (TCC) at [123]–[126].
[74] *Chartbrook v Persimmon Homes* [2009] 1 AC 1101.

There are two main reasons why it is considered that it is better to proceed by way **9.93** of rectification than interpretation. One is that rectification requires clear proof of the continuing common intention of the parties at the time the contract was entered into, and that this is a good discipline. The other is that creative interpretation could adversely affect third parties, and that this would not happen if rectification were to be ordered.

Why does rectification not adversely affect third parties? Take the case of a contract, **9.94** the benefit of which has been assigned. The starting point is that the assignee takes the benefit of the contract subject to equities, whether the assignment is statutory[75] or equitable.[76] Rights of set-off,[77] and the right to rescind a contract[78] are equities, and the assignee therefore takes subject to them. It is not clear whether a power to rectify a contract is an equity which can bind third parties.[79] If not, it is a personal right, which will not affect an assignee.

But even if a power to rectify a contract is an equity, it will not affect a person who **9.95** acquires a proprietary interest in the contract (even if only an equitable interest) in good faith and without notice.[80] An assignee or chargee of a contract right obtains a proprietary interest in the benefit of the contract,[81] and will therefore take free of the equity if he or she takes the interest in good faith and without notice of the facts giving rise to the power to rectify.[82]

In any event, rectification is a discretionary remedy and would not be granted if it **9.96** would prejudice a third party who had acted innocently and provided consideration.[83]

For these reasons it is suggested that rectification is not possible if it would adversely **9.97** affect the rights of an innocent third party.

N. Unilateral Mistake Rectification

Rectification for unilateral mistake is very different from common intention rectifi- **9.98** cation. All the latter is doing is to bring the writing into line with what was agreed.

---

[75] Law of Property Act 1925, s 136(1).
[76] *Coles v Jones & Coles* (1715) 2 Vern 692.
[77] *Government of Newfoundland v Newfoundland Railway Co* (1888) LR 13 App Cas 199.
[78] *Re Eastgate* [1905] 1 KB 465.
[79] *Smith v Jones* [1954] 1 WLR 1089 at 1091 suggests not.
[80] *Latec Investments v Hotel Terrigal* (1965) 113 CLR 265.
[81] *Fitzroy v Cave* [1905] 2 KB 364 at 372.
[82] *Bell v Cundall* (1750) Amb 101; *Garrard v Frankel* (1862) 30 Beav 445; *Thames Guaranty v Campbell* [1985] QB 210 at 240. This was the view of Briggs J at first instance in *Chartbrook v Persimmon Homes* [2007] 2 P&CR 9 at [37]. It was criticized by Alan Berg in 'Richard III in New Zealand' (2008) 124 LQR 6 at 12 but, for the reasons stated above, it is suggested that Briggs J was correct.
[83] *Marley v Rawlings* [2015] AC 129 at [40]; *Davey v Baker* [2016] NZCA 313 at [39] (New Zealand Court of Appeal).

Unilateral mistake rectification, on the other hand, is not concerned with giving effect to the agreement of the parties but, rather, with varying it because one party is mistaken about what the contract says and it would be unfair for the other party to rely on the agreement.[84]

9.99   The underlying philosophy is this: if A and B enter into a written contract and A makes a mistake about what the contract contains, it will be amended to reflect what A had thought if it would be unconscionable for B to rely on what the contract actually says.

9.100   The current case law indicates that it would be unconscionable for B to rely on the mistake if, at the time the contract was entered into, he or she either knew of A's mistake or suspected the mistake, but nevertheless encouraged A to enter into the contract without rectifying it.

9.101   The first type of case was described by Pennycuick J in *A Roberts & Co v Leicestershire County Council*[85] in these terms:

> [A] party is entitled to rectification of a contract upon proof that he believed a particular term to be included in the contract, and that the other party concluded the contract with the omission or a variation of that term in the knowledge that the first party believed the term to be included … The principle is stated in *Snell on Equity*, 25th Ed. (1960), p.569, as follows: 'By what appears to be a species of equitable estoppel, if one party to a transaction knows that the instrument contains a mistake in his favour but does nothing to correct it, he (and those claiming under him) will be precluded from resisting rectification on the ground that the mistake is unilateral and not common.'

9.102   In *Thomas Bates & Son v Wyndham's (Lingerie)*,[86] Buckley LJ added a further requirement that:

> the conduct of the defendant must be such as to make it inequitable that he should be allowed to object to the rectification of the document.

9.103   Buckley LJ expressed the principle in this way:[87]

> For this doctrine … to apply I think it must be shown: first, that one party A erroneously believed that the document sought to be rectified contained a particular term or provision, or possibly did not contain a particular term or provision which, mistakenly, it did contain; secondly, that the other party B was aware of the omission

---

[84] For contrasting discussions of the conceptual justification for unilateral mistake rectification, see 'Burrows, Construction and Rectification', Chapter 5 in Burrows & Peel (eds), *Contract Terms* (Oxford University Press, 2007), and McLauchlan, 'The "Drastic" Remedy of Rectification for Unilateral Mistake' (2008) 124 LQR 608.

[85] [1961] 1 Ch 555 at 570.

[86] [1981] 1 WLR 505 at 515.

[87] [1981] 1 WLR 505 at 515–16.

or the inclusion and that it was due to a mistake on the part of A; thirdly, that B has omitted to draw the mistake to the notice of A. And I think there must be a fourth element involved, namely, that the mistake must be one calculated to benefit B. If these requirements are satisfied, the court may regard it as inequitable to allow B to resist rectification to give effect to A's intention on the ground that the mistake was not, at the time of execution of the document, a mutual mistake.

In the second type of case, although the defendant is not aware of the claimant's mistake, he or she suspects it, and encourages the claimant to enter into the contract without it being rectified.   **9.104**

The principle was described by Stuart-Smith LJ in *Commission for the New Towns v*   **9.105**
Cooper (Great Britain):[88]

> I would hold that where A intends B to be mistaken as to the construction of the agreement, so conducts himself that he diverts B's attention from discovering the mistake by making false and misleading statements, and B in fact makes the very mistake that A intends, then notwithstanding that A does not actually know, but merely suspects, that B is mistaken, and it cannot be shown that the mistake was induced by any misrepresentation, rectification may be granted.

In this case, one of the parties had deliberately raised a smokescreen in the negotia-   **9.106**
tions in a way which the court regarded as dishonest.

In brief, rectification will be available where one party makes a mistake about what   **9.107**
the contract contains and, at the time the contract is entered into, the other party either knows of the mistake or otherwise acts dishonestly in relation to it.

---

[88] [1995] Ch 259 at 280.

10

PRINCIPLE 10: ESTOPPEL BY CONVENTION

Principle 10: If the parties to a contract have dealt with each other on the basis of a common understanding about the meaning or effect of the contract, that interpretation will bind them if it would be unjust to go back on it.

A. Estoppel

Only a lawyer could have invented estoppel. The idea behind an estoppel is that a **10.01** person will be prevented ('estopped') from denying the truth of something for which he is responsible. If I have made you think that something is the case, then I may be prevented from denying it.

The law of estoppel has many facets, not all of which are easy to reconcile. In spite of a **10.02** long history, it is still developing, and it is this mercurial nature which makes it difficult to be definitive about the circumstances in which it applies. For that reason, any discussion of estoppel needs to be tentative.

This is particularly true of estoppel by convention. It is a relatively minor branch of **10.03** estoppel and, although it is often discussed, there are few cases in which estoppel by convention has successfully been applied.

Most estoppels derive from a representation made by one person to another. Estoppel **10.04** by convention is, however, different. Its purpose is to ensure that, where parties share a common understanding about the meaning or effect of a contractual provision, they are bound by that common understanding—even if it is incorrect—if it would be unjust to go back on it.

B. The Authorities

10.05 The High Court of Australia described estoppel by convention in these terms in *Con-Stan Industries of Australia v Norwich Winterthur Insurance (Australia):*[1]

> Estoppel by convention is a form of estoppel founded not on a representation of fact made by a representor and acted on by a representee to his detriment, but on the conduct of relations between the parties on the basis of an agreed or assumed state of facts, which both will be estopped from denying.

10.06 Lord Steyn elaborated on this description in the House of Lords in *Republic of India v India Steamship Co:*[2]

> It is settled that an estoppel by convention may arise where parties to a transaction act on an assumed state of facts or law, the assumption being either shared by them both or made by one and acquiesced in by the other. The effect of an estoppel by convention is to preclude a party from denying the assumed facts or law if it would be unjust to allow him to go back on the assumption … It is not enough that each of the two parties acts on an assumption not communicated to the other. But … a concluded agreement is not a requirement for an estoppel by convention.

10.07 The two leading English cases on estoppel by convention are both decisions of the Court of Appeal—*Amalgamated Investment & Property Co v Texas Commerce International Bank* in 1981[3] and *The Vistafjord* in 1988.[4] In both cases, the court relied upon the following description of estoppel by convention in Spencer Bower and Turner on *Estoppel by Representation:*[5]

> This form of estoppel is founded, not on a representation of fact made by a representor and believed by a representee, but on an agreed statement of facts the truth of which has been assumed, by the convention of the parties, as the basis of a transaction into which they are about to enter. When the parties have acted in their transaction upon the agreed assumption that a given state of facts is to be accepted between them as true, then as regards that transaction each will be estopped against the other from questioning the truth of a statement of facts so assumed.

10.08 The genesis of estoppel by convention is therefore the idea that parties should not be able to resile from a statement of the facts on which they have based their contract—for instance, in the recitals to the contract.[6] This statement in Spencer Bower and Turner was approved by Eveleigh and Brandon LJJ in the *Amalgamated Investment*

---

[1] (1985–1986) 160 CLR 226 at 244.

[2] [1998] AC 878 at 913.

[3] [1982] 1 QB 84.

[4] *Norwegian American Cruises v Paul Mundy* [1988] 2 Lloyd's Rep 343.

[5] 3rd edition at p. 157.

[6] See the comments of Tipping J in the New Zealand Court of Appeal in *National Westminster Finance NZ v National Bank of NZ* [1996] 1 NZLR 548 at 550.

case[7] and by Bingham LJ in the *Vistafjord* case.[8] But it is not a complete statement of the law. As Peter Gibson J said in *Hammel-Smith v Pyecroft* and *Jetsave*,[9] estoppel by convention is available in other circumstances. Peter Gibson J qualified the statement in Spencer Bower and Turner in three important respects:

(1) First, the agreed assumption need not be of fact, but may be of law—e.g. an assumption as to the legal effect of a document.
(2) Second, the common assumption does not need to be made at the time the parties are about to enter into the transaction concerned. It can be made subsequently—i.e. after the contract has been entered into.
(3) Third, even if the parties have acted on a common mistaken assumption, it does not follow that the estoppel will follow as a matter of course. An estoppel will only be granted if it would be unjust for one of the parties to go back on the common assumption.

Whilst denying an intention to define estoppel by convention, Peter Gibson J did say that it would arise where:[10] **10.09**

(1) parties have established by their construction of their agreement or their apprehension of its legal effect a conventional basis,
(2) on that basis they have regulated their subsequent dealings, to which I would add,
(3) it would be unjust or unconscionable if one of the parties resiled from that convention.

His judgment was endorsed by Bingham LJ in the *Vistafjord* case.[11]

A further elaboration of the principles was given by Tipping J, who gave the judgment of the New Zealand Court of Appeal in *National Westminster Finance NZ v National Bank of NZ*:[12] **10.10**

> The authorities show that for an estoppel by convention to arise the following points must be established by the party claiming the benefit of the estoppel (the proponent):
> (1) The parties have proceeded on the basis of an underlying assumption of fact, law, or both, of sufficient certainty to be enforceable (the assumption).
> (2) Each party has, to the knowledge of the other, expressly or by implication accepted the assumption as being true for the purposes of the transaction.
> (3) Such acceptance was intended to affect their legal relations in the sense that it was intended to govern the legal position between them.

---

[7] [1982] 1 QB 84 at 126 and 130.

[8] [1988] 2 Lloyd's Rep 343 at 349.

[9] Unreported: 5 February 1987; cited with approval by Bingham LJ in the *Vistafjord, Norwegian American Cruises v Paul Mundy* [1988] 2 Lloyd's Rep 343 at 351–2.

[10] Quoted by Bingham LJ in the *Vistafjord* case, *Norwegian American Cruises v Paul Mundy* [1988] 2 Lloyd's Rep 343 at 352.

[11] *Norwegian American Cruises v Paul Mundy* [1988] 2 Lloyd's Rep 343 at 352.

[12] [1996] 1 NZLR 548 at 550.

    (4) The proponent was entitled to act and has, as the other party knew or intended, acted in reliance upon the assumption being regarded as true and binding.

    (5) The proponent would suffer detriment if the other party were allowed to resile or depart from the assumption.

    (6) In all the circumstances it would be unconscionable to allow the other party to resile or depart from the assumption.

10.11 Although expressed in different terms, these judgments all proceed on a common footing that what is required is that the parties have acted on a common assumption as to the effect of the contract and that it would be unjust to go back on that. This basic idea underpinning estoppel by convention was encapsulated by Lord Denning MR in the *Amalgamated Investment* case in the following terms:[13]

> When the parties to a transaction proceed on the basis of an underlying assumption— either of fact or of law—whether due to misrepresentation or mistake makes no difference—on which they have conducted the dealings between them—neither of them will be allowed to go back on that assumption when it would be unfair or unjust to allow him to do so. If one of them does seek to go back on it, the courts will give the other such remedy as the equity of the case demands.

C. The Principles

10.12 The principles of estoppel by convention are based on a relatively small number of cases and, like other aspects of estoppel, are subject to change, or at least refinement, as new cases come along. It is nevertheless important to try to describe the key principles.

10.13 It is suggested that there are four requirements of an estoppel by convention:

    (1) the parties have entered into a contract;

    (2) the contract means x;

    (3) the parties have dealt with each other on the assumption it means y, or has the effect of y;

    (4) it would be unjust to go back on that assumption.

10.14 The first two requirements are relatively straightforward, but the last two need some elaboration.

10.15 Although the contract means x, the parties have dealt with each other on the assumption that it means y, or has the effect of y. Three points need to be made here.

10.16 The first is that what needs to be established is that the parties had a common (i.e. shared) understanding of what they thought the contract meant. As with

---

[13] *Amalgamated Investment & Property Co v Texas Commerce International Bank* [1982] 1 QB 84 at 122.

rectification, it is not sufficient that the parties thought the same thing independently. There needs to be clear objective evidence of that shared understanding. As Lord Steyn said in *Republic of India v India Steamship Co*:[14] 'It is not enough that each of the two parties acts on an assumption not communicated to the other.'

Second, it is important to distinguish estoppel by convention from rectification. **10.17** A party can bring a claim for rectification if the words in the contract do not reflect the common intention of the parties at the time it was entered into. Estoppel by convention is different. It applies where the parties intended the words which they have written, but were mistaken as to their meaning or effect.

Third, the shared understanding of what the contract means can exist at the time of **10.18** the contract, but can also be established by evidence of subsequent conduct. Indeed, that is the normal case.[15] All relevant background materials are available in a claim for estoppel by convention, including prior negotiations and subsequent conduct.[16]

The final requirement of an estoppel by convention is that it would be unjust for **10.19** one party to go back on the common assumption of what the contract means. This requirement is expressed in various ways—it must be 'unfair', 'unjust', or 'unconscionable'. In this context, it is suggested that there is no real distinction between any of these expressions. The court must be satisfied that it would not be right for one party to go back on the shared misunderstanding.

D. Examples

The cases in which a claim for estoppel by convention have succeeded are rare,[17] but **10.20** two cases illustrate the issues involved—*Amalgamated Investment & Property Co v Texas Commerce International Bank*[18] and *The Vistafjord*.[19]

The *Amalgamated Investment* case

The *Amalgamated Investment* case[20] involved a dispute about a guarantee given by a **10.21** parent company to a bank. It was initially intended that a subsidiary of the parent

---

[14] [1998] AC 878 at 913.
[15] *Amalgamated Investment & Property Co v Texas Commerce International Bank* [1982] 1 QB 84; *The Vistafjord, Norwegian American Cruises v Paul Mundy* [1988] 2 Lloyd's Rep 343.
[16] *Chartbrook v Persimmon Homes* [2009] 1 AC 1101.
[17] For a recent example, see the decision of the New South Wales Court of Appeal in *Caringbah Investments v Caringbah Business and Sports Club* [2016] NSWCA 165. There is a great deal of (rather inconclusive) Australian case law. See J D McKenna, 'Estoppel by Convention and the Sanctity of Contract' (a paper presented to the Current Legal Issues Seminar series, Queensland, May 2009).
[18] [1982] 1 QB 84.
[19] *Norwegian American Cruises v Paul Mundy* [1988] 2 Lloyd's Rep 343.
[20] [1982] 1 QB 84.

company would borrow money from the bank, to be secured by a mortgage over property owned by the subsidiary and also by a guarantee from the parent company. The parent company accordingly executed a guarantee by which it guaranteed to pay to the bank on demand 'all moneys which now are or shall at any time or times hereafter be due or owing or payable to [the bank] on any account whatsoever by [the subsidiary]'.

10.22 There was then a change of plan. For exchange control purposes, it was decided that the loan should be made to an associated company, Portsoken, rather than to the subsidiary and that it would then be on-lent by Portsoken to the subsidiary. As a result, the bank made a loan to Portsoken, rather than to the subsidiary. But the guarantee was not altered to take account of the changed circumstances.

10.23 The group got into financial difficulties. The mortgaged property was sold, but there was still a shortfall owing in respect of the loan to Portsoken. The bank therefore applied a credit balance owing by the parent company in discharge of the shortfall. This was done on the basis that the parent company was liable for the shortfall under its guarantee. The parent company then went into liquidation, and the liquidators argued that the parent company was not liable under the guarantee in respect of the loan made to Portsoken, and therefore that the bank should not have set off the credit balance. Their point was that the guarantee was of the obligations of the subsidiary, not of Portsoken.

10.24 This raised two questions:

(1) Could the guarantee be interpreted to apply to the loan to Portsoken, and, if not
(2) was the parent company estopped by convention from contending that it did not?

10.25 The first question was one of interpretation. On the face of it, the guarantee was expressed to cover money owing to the bank by the subsidiary—not by Portsoken. At first instance, Robert Goff J accepted that the guarantee could not be interpreted to extend to the loan made to Portsoken. But the Court of Appeal disagreed. They decided that, as a matter of interpretation, the guarantee extended to the loan made by the bank to Portsoken, even though it did not actually say so. In doing so, they relied on Principles 4 and 7. The parties must objectively have intended the guarantee to cover the transaction which had actually occurred, rather than one which had not. The reference to all money payable by the subsidiary could only have referred to the facility which the bank actually advanced—i.e. the one to Portsoken. Although, in isolation, the words appeared only to cover a loan made to the subsidiary, when viewed in the context of the background facts, it was clear that they must have been intended to cover the facility made to Portsoken.

There was therefore strictly no reason to consider estoppel by convention, but the **10.26** issue was considered in detail by the court and its approach has been followed in subsequent cases.

At first instance, Robert Goff J found in favour of the bank on the basis of an es- **10.27** toppel by convention. The Court of Appeal would have done the same had they found it necessary to do so. Eveleigh and Brandon LJJ both relied on the passage from Spencer Bower and Turner on *Estoppel by Representation* described at para 10.07. The negotiations and transactions between the parties—both at the time of the transaction and subsequently—showed that both parties had believed that the guarantee did cover the facility as it was actually made, and that the conduct of the parent company influenced the bank in its belief. The parties assumed the truth of a certain state of affairs and the transaction took place on the basis of that assumption.

The Vistafjord

The issue in *The Vistafjord*[21] was whether shipowners had to pay their agents a com- **10.28** mission on a particular transaction.

The shipowners had agreed to pay their agents a commission on certain ticket sales. **10.29** They subsequently entered into a transaction by which the shipowners entered into a time charter of a vessel for a particular purpose. The arrangement was heavily negotiated between the owners, the agent, and the charterer and, in order to complete the transaction, it was arranged that the agent would take a sub-charter for a particular period as part of the arrangements.

The representatives of the owners and the agents who negotiated the arrangements **10.30** believed that the agents would get a commission on the charterparty. They assumed that it was covered by their previous agreement, and each appreciated that the other was making the same assumption.

The question in dispute was whether the commission was actually payable. The **10.31** court decided that, as a matter of interpretation of the contract, it did not cover the charterparty. But they nevertheless held that the agent was entitled to the commission as a result of an estoppel by convention. The parties had proceeded on the shared assumption that the commission would be payable, and it would not be fair to allow one of the parties to repudiate that assumption.

---

[21] *Norwegian American Cruises v Paul Mundy* [1988] 2 Lloyd's Rep 343.

EPILOGUE

A. Drafting Contracts

It would not be fitting to leave the subject of contractual interpretation without **Ep.01** considering its effect on drafting. Reading contracts is the obverse of writing them, and anyone drafting contracts must be mindful of the way in which they are interpreted. What clues do the principles of contractual interpretation give us to the way in which we should draft contracts? And, more generally, what is good drafting?

The only rule of drafting is that there are no rules. As the Prologue makes clear, **Ep.02** interpretation of contracts is an art, not a science; and the same is true of drafting. One person's deathless prose is another's legal jargon. To some, simple drafting is a form of brutalism.[1]

It is nevertheless possible to lay down certain general principles of good drafting, **Ep.03** and this is what this Epilogue tries to do. Each of the principles of contractual interpretation is considered with a view to deciding how it affects the way in which contracts are written and the extent to which it can be contracted out of. In the light of this, there is then a brief discussion of principles of drafting in a broader context.

B. Using the Interpretation Principles when Drafting

Principle 1

The purpose of contractual interpretation is to establish the objective common in- **Ep.04** tention of the parties. In principle, therefore, it must be possible for the parties to decide for themselves how they want their contract to be interpreted and to make this clear to those who will interpret it. The clearest external manifestation of what the parties intend is for them to say what they intend in the contract. If the parties decide in the contract how they want it to be interpreted, it is no business of the courts to tell them that they do not mean what they have said.[2] What can be

---

[1] I speak here from personal experience.
[2] Adapting the comment of Longmore LJ on entire agreement clauses in *North Eastern Properties v Coleman* [2010] 2 EGLR 161 at [82].

clearer evidence of the parties' objective intention than what they have said in their contract?

Ep.05   There is little clear case-law authority for the proposition that the parties are able to decide how their contract can be interpreted. Like many self-evident propositions, it is rarely necessary to express it. But the Scottish Law Commission did refer to this issue in its Discussion Paper on Interpretation of Contract, issued in February 2011.[3] It is also discussed in detail in Chapter 5 of Catherine Mitchell's book, *Interpretation of Contracts*.[4] There seems to be little dissent from the proposition that the parties can decide how their contract can be interpreted. As Catherine Mitchell comments:[5]

> [I]f contract law is to remain a facilitative and supportive institution for the parties, the courts must remain mindful of the fact that in the end, commercial parties should have as much control over interpretative method as they do over other terms of the contract.

Principle 2

Ep.06   Where the contract is in writing, it is the writing which is the primary source of the parties' objective intention.

Ep.07   Commercial parties need to know what the terms of their contract are. And the demise of the parol evidence rule has made it even more important that they regulate that in their contract. Hence the ubiquity of entire agreement clauses in commercial contracts. The purpose of an entire agreement clause is to establish what it is which constitutes the contract. In practice, it is likely to go further and provide that any pre-contractual statements do not give rise to non-contractual liability, for instance in equity or in tort. As the discussion of Principle 2 makes clear, there is no doubt that a properly drafted clause of this type will do what it says.[6] That is what the parties have agreed.

Ep.08   Entire agreement clauses come in various shapes and sizes but, in essence, they are concerned to ensure two things:

(1) that the entire agreement between the parties is set out in one contract (or in a series of contracts, which constitute the transaction documents), and that any prior agreement or arrangement has been superseded and is therefore of no effect;

---

[3] Scottish Law Commission, Discussion Paper No. 147 at 7.23–7.25.
[4] Mitchell, *Interpretation of Contracts* (Routledge Cavendish, 2007), Chapter 5.
[5] Mitchell at 148.
[6] Subject to any relevant statutory constraints on evading liability for misrepresentation, for instance under section 3 of the Misrepresentation Act 1967.

(2) that the parties agree that they are not relying on any statement (whether or not in writing) made before the contract, except to the extent that it is expressly set out in the contract.

The first part of the clause describes what the contract is and therefore the limits of the contractual liability of the parties. The second part excludes any potential extra-contractual liability for misrepresentation (for instance, to rescind in equity or to claim damages in tort or by statute). **Ep.09**

If properly drafted, there is no doubt that an entire agreement clause can describe what the contract is. If it is sufficiently clear,[7] it can also exclude liability for mis-representation[8] subject to any relevant statutory provisions.[9] What it cannot do is to provide for what happens once a contract has been entered into. Whatever the contract may say about this, it is capable of being varied by agreement. The parties are always free to change their mind in the future.[10] **Ep.10**

Principle 3

The principle that contracts are read as a whole encourages the draftsman to provide a proper structure for the contract. As anyone who has drafted a long contract will know, the problems frequently come not within individual clauses but in trying to make the clauses fit together as a whole. How does one clause, in one part of the contract, affect another, in a different part? How does an undertaking by one party to do something specific affect a more general undertaking which, on the face of it, encompasses the more specific undertaking? And where there are mutual undertakings, to what extent is the performance by one party conditional on performance by the other? **Ep.11**

The only way to deal with these problems is to have a clear understanding at the outset of drafting as to the structure of the contract and how the various parts fit together. In practice, of course, that is easier said than done, and it would be a bold draftsman who would be confident that all the inconsistencies had been ironed out. But, nevertheless, time spent at the outset planning the structure of the contract is rarely wasted. And, where there is more than one contract, the structuring needs to ensure that they fit together as seamlessly as possible. **Ep.12**

It has been seen in the discussion of Principle 3 that, where possible, courts try to give effect to each part of the contract. This can often create problems in practice **Ep.13**

---

[7] *AXA Sun Life v Campbell Martin* [2011] EWCA Civ 133 at [94] (Rix LJ).
[8] *Peekay Intermark v Australia and New Zealand Banking Group* [2006] 1 CLC 582 at [56]–[57] and *Springwell Navigation v J P Morgan Chase* [2010] 2 CLC 705 at [143]–[171].
[9] Such as the Unfair Contract Terms Act 1977 or section 3 of the Misrepresentation Act 1967.
[10] *Globe Motors v TRW Lucas* [2016] EWCA Civ 396 and *MWB Business Exchange Centres v Rock Advertising* [2016] EWCA Civ 553.

where the draftsman has covered the same point more than once. The courts are aware of this problem, but it is nevertheless better to avoid overlap where possible. Brevity and simplicity are required, rather than length and complication.

Principle 4

Ep.14 Contracts are read in the context of their background facts. One of the problems with this principle is the increasing tendency of the courts to consider that more and more background information should be available in the interpretation process. This is understandable in principle if the background information is relevant to establishing the objective intention of the parties, but many commercial lawyers recognize that it can create practical problems by reducing certainty, increasing the time and cost where there is a dispute, and potentially adversely affecting third parties. As has been seen in the discussion of Principle 4, it is not entirely clear at the moment how these problems will be resolved. All the more reason, then, for the parties to make the decision themselves and record it in the contract.

Ep.15 It is not common in practice for the parties to regulate the scope of background material available to interpret their contract. But, for the reasons discussed in relation to Principle 1 above, there is no reason why they should not do so. The advantage of doing so is that it can settle in advance the question of what background information is available—at a time when the law on this point is in a state of flux.

Ep.16 Commercial contracts commonly contain interpretation clauses, which deal with relatively minor issues such as the use of singulars and plurals and the status of amendments to documents. But the parties could go further, and establish the matters which can be taken into account in interpreting the contract. For instance, the contract could provide that its terms will be interpreted only in the light of:

- the other provisions of the contract;
- the other transaction documents (if there are any);
- certain specific permitted background facts to the extent that they were reasonably available to persons in the position of the parties to the contract at the time the contract was entered into.

Ep.17 This issue has been discussed by Catherine Mitchell:[11]

> If we accept that commercial parties can choose their contracting partners and their obligations, why shouldn't the parties also choose the interpretative theory that will be applied to their contract? Or, in other words, why shouldn't the contract tell the court not to look at the context? Contracts frequently do include 'interpretation'

---

[11] Catherine Mitchell, 'Entire Agreement Clauses: Contracting Out of Contextualism' (2006) 22 JCL 222 at 236–7. And see Mitchell, *Interpretation of Contracts*, Chapter 5.

clauses and there is no more objective statement of the parties' intentions than the terms they commit to writing.

The parties could then decide which background facts should be relevant—such as **Ep.18** the identity of the parties, the nature of the transaction, and the market in which the transaction was entered into. If the courts continue to extend the scope of relevant background facts under the general law, it would be no surprise to see the parties taking the law into their own hands and regulating it themselves. An approach to the drafting of such a clause is set out at the end of the Epilogue. It contains a suggested outline structure, which can be adapted to reflect the nature of the contract concerned. It is essentially concerned to do two things:

(1) to require the words used in the contract to be given their ordinary meaning;
(2) to limit the amount of background information which can be used in the interpretation process.

Principle 5

Principle 5 emphasizes that the courts generally give effect to what the contract says. **Ep.19** Words are nearly always given their ordinary meaning in their context. That therefore gives the draftsman a substantial amount of freedom to express what the parties intend in the expectation that the court will give effect to it.

Although styles of drafting differ widely, it would be hard to disagree that drafting **Ep.20** should be as simple and clear as possible. There is no reason why a contract cannot be drafted in straightforward, ordinary language, rather than what is sometimes known as 'legalese'. Experience would suggest that the former is the more likely to produce clarity and certainty. As many a law student will attest, it is much easier to understand a judgment of Lord Denning than of many of his contemporaries. And the reason for that is the clarity and simplicity of his writing. It is not possible to translate that directly into contractual drafting. Creating legal obligations is an endeavour of a different kind from describing them, and so the drafting of a legal agreement involves different skills from the writing of a judgment or of a letter of advice. But that is not to deny that they have certain fundamental features in common, and that clarity and simplicity are important tools for both.

Few contracts can be written without the use of definitions. They serve a useful pur- **Ep.21** pose by enabling the draftsman to use a word or phrase to express a more complex thought. But definitions need to be used with discretion. They should only be used where necessary. They should be as short as possible. And they should not be used to express an operative part of the document. It is also helpful to try to ensure that the word used to describe the concept captures the basic idea of the defined term. It is possible to define a stripy animal with a long neck as an elephant, but it is not particularly helpful for the reader. Something else to be avoided if possible (and it is not always possible), is definitions which cross-refer to each other, so that to understand what one means requires an analysis of a number of others.

Ep.22   The extent to which the canons of construction should still be used is a matter of debate, but the discussion of Principle 5 shows that some are still used in practice. There is no reason why the parties should not contract out of the use of the *eiusdem generis* rule or the *contra preferentem* rule, for instance, or indeed out of the use of canons of construction more generally. But the best way to evade the *eiusdem generis* rule is to avoid lists altogether or, if they must be used, to use them as illustrations of a general principle.

Principle 6

Ep.23   Ambiguous words are given the meaning the parties are most likely objectively to have intended. We all strive to avoid ambiguity, but we do not always succeed. Again, although there is little consensus on styles of drafting, it is hard to disagree with the idea that the words used should be as clear as possible. If particular words are ambiguous, the overall structure of the contract can often assist in clarifying what they mean.

Principle 7

Ep.24   Very occasionally, the courts rewrite contracts—or at least clauses. They may do so less frequently in common law jurisdictions than in civil law ones, but it does happen. If you want to prevent them from doing this, can you do so?

Ep.25   As has been seen in the discussion of Principle 7, the reason why courts do rewrite clauses of contracts is because they regard them as being so unreasonable that the parties cannot possibly have intended them. The answer, for the draftsman, is simple. Do not make your contracts so unreasonable that a court is likely to believe that the parties cannot have intended what has been said. As one of my former partners said about a clause which had just been drafted (admittedly by himself): 'It probably won't work: it's too clever by half.'

Ep.26   It is a mistake when drafting contracts to try to be too clever. You may think that you are winning a famous victory for your client by imposing yet more obligations on the other side and reducing yet further the scope of your own client's commitment, but if you carry it too far, a court is likely to say that it is so unreasonable that the parties cannot have intended it. And they will then rewrite it. It is true that there is no general duty of good faith in English law. It is true that parties do not have a general obligation to exercise their contractual rights reasonably. But there can be little doubt, in the light of Principle 7, that the courts will interfere in cases of egregious unreasonableness.

Ep.27   The best approach, therefore, is not to draft so unreasonably that the court will be minded to find a way round the drafting. If you want to impose a very wide obligation on the other side, put yourself in the position of a judge reading the obligation and consider whether it might, on the face of it, apply where it might not be expected to do so. *Bank of Credit and Commerce International v Ali*[12] is a good example. There, the release purported to exclude 'all or any claims … of whatsoever nature that exist or may exist' by the employee against the employer. On the face of it, this applied to all claims, whether or not they arose out of the employment relationship. Can that really have been intended? The House of Lords thought not. And it was therefore able to rewrite the clause so that it only applied to claims arising out of the *termination* of the employment contract. If the contract had expressly limited the release to claims arising out of the employment relationship, the court would not have been able to rewrite the contract in a more limited way.

In addition to the general injunction not to draft so unreasonably that the court will try to find a way round it, the draftsman needs to be aware that the courts do try, with particular vigour, to avoid giving effect to clauses which they regard as being particularly unfair. In this category are clauses which allow a party to terminate a contract for a minor breach by the other, or which exclude or limit liability. **Ep.28**

It is generally unwise to provide that a party to a contract can terminate it as a result of *any* breach of the contract by the other party. The response of a court to such a provision is that the parties cannot have intended that a very minor breach should allow the other party to terminate. They will then read it down—possibly by implying a term that the breach concerned must be repudiatory. This, of course, defeats the whole purpose of the clause, since the innocent party can terminate in any event for a repudiatory breach. **Ep.29**

In practice, it is better to draft a termination clause in a way in which the court is unlikely to want to find a way round. This can be done by limiting the ability to terminate to 'material' breaches, and then defining clearly what they are. In addition, the clause can establish a process by which the party in breach is given a period of time to rectify the breach before the contract can be terminated. What is appropriate depends, of course, on the contract concerned. The key point is that the end result should not be so unreasonable that the court will try to find a way round it. **Ep.30**

The approach of the courts to exclusion and limitation clauses is much less hostile than it used to be. In principle, such a clause ought to be interpreted in the same way as any other, except that any ambiguity will be construed against the person relying on it. The moral is to make such a clause as clear as possible. In practice, if the liability of a party for a deliberate or negligent breach is to be excluded, it is better expressly to say so. **Ep.31**

---

[12] [2002] 1 AC 251.

Ep.32 The other way in which the parties can deal with the problem of the courts rewriting contracts is by prohibiting it in the contract. If interpretation is ultimately a matter of establishing the objective intention of the parties, it must be open to the parties to decide how they want their words to be interpreted. In principle, therefore, the parties must be able to include a clause in the contract to the effect that, when interpreting it, the words will be given their ordinary meaning in the context of the transaction documents and of those background facts which are permitted to be used for this purpose. That still gives a substantial amount of flexibility in the interpretation process.[13] But it should limit some of the more egregious examples of rewriting contracts.

Ep.33 There will doubtless need to be exceptions—for instance, where there is an obvious typographical error and it is clear what was intended. But, subject to those exceptions, the parties would have made it clear that they mean what they say and that the court has no licence to rewrite the contract. This would be the equivalent of adding the words 'and I really mean it' to each contentious clause.

Ep.34 An approach to drafting such a clause is set out at the end of the Epilogue.

Principle 8

Ep.35 Words are implied into a contract if the parties must objectively have intended them. It is, of course, the wish of every draftsman to avoid the necessity for implication of terms but it is almost impossible in practice to achieve this. However elaborate the document, a circumstance can occur which will not have been considered, and where a term might therefore be implied. And because of this, there is no point in trying to provide for it in the contract. By definition, it will be the event that you had not anticipated which will cause the problem.

Ep.36 In practice, all that can be done is to try to ensure that the document is as complete as it practically can be.

Principle 9

Ep.37 Rectification is available if a written contract does not record the parties' common intention at the time it was entered into. It seems generally to be accepted that this is not something which can be contracted out of, even if the parties wanted to do so. Since, by definition, the parties do not know of the problem at the time the contract is entered into, and because it can happen to either party, the likelihood is that they will not want to forego the possibility of rectifying the contract if it can be established that the contract does not properly record the agreement reached between them.

---

[13] As *The Aragon* demonstrates—*Segovia Compagnia Naviera v R Pagnan & Fratelli* [1977] 1 Lloyd's Rep 343, discussed in Chapter 5, at paras 5.11 and 5.12.

Principle 10

Estoppel by convention will be available if the parties have dealt with each other on the basis of a particular interpretation of the contract and it would be unjust for the parties to go back on that. The parties might well want to avoid the possibility of this happening but, in practice, it is impossible to do so. If there is an estoppel by convention, it will normally arise as a result of matters which take place after the contract has been entered into, and it is therefore difficult to see how the contract itself can prevent this. **Ep.38**

C. Principles of Drafting

In the light of this review of the way in which the principles of contractual interpretation impinge upon drafting, are there any general principles of drafting which can be established? **Ep.39**

Since drafting, like contractual interpretation, is an art rather than a science, it is only possible to state principles at a high level of generality and, in reality, they do little more than state the obvious. But then sometimes the obvious is worth stating. **Ep.40**

The aim of drafting should be to produce a document which is as clear and as brief as possible. **Ep.41**

There can be little doubt that the contract should be as clear as possible—in other words, plain, simple, straightforward, understandable, direct, and to the point; and without confusion, complication, or doubt. There is little controversial there. The suggestion that it needs to be as clear *as possible* reflects the fact that, in giving effect to complicated arrangements, clarity is an aspiration which cannot always be achieved. **Ep.42**

It is also suggested that the document should be as brief as possible—consistent with the nature of the contractual arrangements being documented. This is perhaps more controversial. If clarity requires a lengthy document, then so be it. The suggestion is not that documents should be short, but that they should be as short as possible in the light of what needs to be achieved. This reflects the fact that legal documents, unlike novels, are not read for pleasure; and it seems reasonable to assume that business people would like their contracts to be as short as they sensibly can be. **Ep.43**

In order to achieve a document which is as clear and brief as possible, the draftsman needs to consider three things: **Ep.44**

(1) the structure of the transaction;
(2) the layout of the document;
(3) the words to be used in the document.

Ep.45 As far as structure is concerned, the contract needs to be planned logically, and the individual clauses need to fit with each other. This requires planning in advance before drafting.

Ep.46 In practice, the layout of a document can be almost as important as the words used. The purpose of any document is to tell a story—in this case as clearly and briefly as possible. Anyone who has had to read a document which consists of pages of text without indentations and with no indication that the sentence will ever end (and many legal documents are like that) will need no instruction in the importance of spaces in documents. It will never be a pleasure to read a legal document, but the role of the draftsman must surely be to make it as little of a penance as possible. This is helped by:

- the use of spaces;
- short sentences;
- short paragraphs;
- the use of parts in long documents;
- the clever use of headings.

These all go to making the document easier to read.

Ep.47 As far as the words are concerned, there is no requirement to use 'legalese' and every incentive to use ordinary, understandable words to make points which the reader will understand. The draftsman should put himself or herself in the position of the persons who will read the contract—the parties, transferees, and the court—and ask how they will understand it.

Ep.48 One of the problems which the courts have to deal with in relation to drafting is the use of lists. The problem with lists is that the draftsman normally ends up by using a general sweeping concept in case he or she has missed something. But, as can be seen from the discussion of Principle 5, this invites the court to read the general words *eiusdem generis*, and thereby defeats the object of the exercise. Far better to use general, all-encompassing words to express the concept which needs to be covered, and then, if necessary, to use lists as examples of the general concept. In that way, the court cannot read down the general words. The use of general words also enables the draftsman to cut down the number of words used, which is itself an advantage.

Ep.49 On a more substantive note, the draftsman should always have in mind the reasonableness of what he or she is producing. As has been seen in the discussion of Principle 7, the more unreasonable the drafting, the more the court will try to unravel it.

These principles are set out in tabular form in the next section of the book, Principles **Ep.50** of Drafting, and they are followed by a draft interpretation clause.

If one wanted to express the basic principles of drafting in just two simple concepts, **Ep.51** I would suggest that drafting should be:

- as clear and brief as possible;
- not so unreasonable that the court will try to get round it.

PRINCIPLES OF DRAFTING

Aim: drafting should be:

- as clear and brief as possible;
- not so unreasonable that the court will try to get round it.

Clarity involves:

Structure:

Plan in advance.

Layout:

Tell a story.

Put contents in a logical order.

Divide into parts where necessary.

Use headings where necessary (but not too many).

Use short paragraphs—a new one for each point.

Use short sentences.

Use spaces.

Use definitions carefully:

- keep them to a minimum;
- keep them short;
- make sure the word you use captures the concept;
- do not put the substance (i.e. the operative part) in the definitions.

Words:

Use as few words as necessary.

Use ordinary/understandable words.

Use general words, and avoid lists where possible.

AN INTERPRETATION CLAUSE

The purpose of this clause is to limit the ability of the tribunal interpreting it to:

- *rely on too many background facts;*
- *rewrite the contract.*

Whether, and if so the extent to which, it is appropriate depends on the circumstances. Its intention is to provoke discussion of how such a clause might be drafted.

Interpretation

1.1 The following provisions explain how this agreement will be interpreted.

1.2 The words and expressions used in this agreement will be given their ordinary meaning in the context of:

(a) the Transaction Documents as a whole; and

(b) the Permitted Background Facts,

unless there is an obvious typographical error and it is clear what was intended.

1.3 The Transaction means [*describe the transaction*].

1.4 The Transaction Documents means this agreement and [*others*].

1.5 The Permitted Background Facts means the following facts to the extent that they were reasonably available to the parties at the time this agreement was entered into:

(a) the identity of the parties;

(b) the nature and purpose of the Transaction;

(c) the market in which the Transaction was entered into;

(d) [*others*].

INDEX